# African Ecological Ethics and Spirituality for Cosmic Flourishing

†

# STUDIES IN WORLD CATHOLICISM

*Michael L. Budde and William T. Cavanaugh, Series Editors*
*Karen M. Kraft, Managing Editor*

### Other Titles in This Series

*Beyond the Borders of Baptism: Catholicity, Allegiances, and Lived Identities.*
Edited by Michael L. Budde. Vol. 1, 2016. ISBN 9781498204736

*New World Pope: Pope Francis and the Future of the Church.*
Edited by Michael L. Budde. Vol. 2, 2017. ISBN 9781498283717

*Scattered and Gathered: Catholics in Diaspora.*
Edited by Michael L. Budde. Vol. 3, 2017. ISBN 9781532607097.

*A Living Tradition: Catholic Social Doctrine and Holy See Diplomacy.*
A. Alexander Stummvoll. Vol. 4, 2018. ISBN 9781532605116.

*Fragile World: Ecology and the Church.* Edited by William T. Cavanaugh.
Vol. 5, 2018. ISBN 9781498283403.

*Love, Joy, and Sex: African Conversation on Pope Francis's Amoris Laetitia and the Gospel of Family in a Divided World.* Edited by Stan Chu Ilo.
Vol. 6, 2017. ISBN 9781532618956.

*The Church and Indigenous Peoples in the Americas: In Between Reconciliation and Decolonization.* Edited by Michel Andraos.
Vol. 7, 2019. ISBN 9781532631115.

*Pentecostalism, Catholicism, and the Spirit in the World.*
Edited by Stan Chu Ilo. Vol. 8, 2019. ISBN 9781532650352.

*Gathered in My Name: Ecumenism in the World Church.*
Edited by William T. Cavanaugh. Vol. 9, 2020. ISBN 9781532685583.

*For God and My Country: Catholic Leadership in Modern Uganda.* J. J. Carney. Vol. 10, 2020. ISBN 9781532682520.

### Forthcoming Titles in This Series

*Daughters of Wisdom: Women and Leadership in the Church.*
Edited by Ahida Pilarski Calderón.

# African Ecological Ethics and Spirituality for Cosmic Flourishing

An African Commentary on *Laudato Si'*

EDITED BY
*Stan Chu Ilo*

FOREWORD BY
*Agbonkhianmeghe E. Orobator, SJ*

CONTRIBUTORS

*Anne Arabome, SSS*
*Stan Chu Ilo*
*Touissant Murhula Kafarhire, SJ*
*Emmanuel Katongole*

*Peter Knox, SJ*
*Evelyn Namakula Birabwa Mayanja*
*Odomaro Mubangizi, SJ*
*Kinikonda Okemasisi*

 CASCADE Books • Eugene, Oregon

AFRICAN ECOLOGICAL ETHICS AND SPIRITUALITY FOR COSMIC FLOURISHING
An African Commentary on *Laudato Si'*

Studies in World Catholicism 11

Copyright © 2022 Wipf and Stock Publishers. All rights reserved. Except for brief quotations in critical publications or reviews, no part of this book may be reproduced in any manner without prior written permission from the publisher. Write: Permissions, Wipf and Stock Publishers, 199 W. 8th Ave., Suite 3, Eugene, OR 97401.

Cascade Books
An Imprint of Wipf and Stock Publishers
199 W. 8th Ave., Suite 3
Eugene, OR 97401

www.wipfandstock.com

PAPERBACK ISBN: 978-1-6667-3871-1
HARDCOVER ISBN: 978-1-6667-9976-7
EBOOK ISBN: 978-1-6667-9977-4

## *Cataloguing-in-Publication data:*

Names: Ilo, Stan Chu, editor. | Orobator, A. E. (Agbonkhianmeghe E.), foreword.

Title: African ecological ethics and spirituality for cosmic flourishing : an African commentary on *Laudato Si'* / edited by Stan Chu Ilo ; foreword by Agbonkhianmeghe E. Orobator.

Description: Eugene, OR : Cascade Books, 2022 | Series: Studies in World Catholicism 11 | Includes bibliographical references and index.

Identifiers: ISBN 978-1-6667-3871-1 (paperback) | ISBN 978-1-6667-9976-7 (hardcover) | ISBN 978-1-6667-9977-4 (ebook)

Subjects: LCSH: Environmental ethics-Africa. | Francis, Pope, 1936– Laudato Si'. | Environmental protection—Religious aspects—Catholic Church. | Human ecology—Religious aspects—Catholic.

Classification: BX1795.H82 A37 2022 (paperback) | BX1795.H82 A37 (ebook)

VERSION NUMBER 061322

# Contents

*Contributors* | vii

Foreword by Agbonkhianmeghe E. Orobator, SJ | xi

Introduction by Stan Chu Ilo | 1

1: United by the Same Concern: An African Womanist's Plea | 12
ANNE ARABOME, SSS

2: Our Common Home:
An African Cry of the Earth, Our Home | 21
PETER KNOX, SJ

3: The Gospel of New Creation:
An African Ecotheological Ethics for Human
and Cosmic Flourishing | 38
STAN CHU ILO

4: The Human Roots of the Ecological Crisis:
An African Ecotheology of Peace on Earth | 64
EVELYN NAMAKULA BIRABWA MAYANJA

5: Integral Ecology:
An African Ecotheology of *Ubuntu*, Participation,
and Our Common Sharing in the Bond of Life | 82
ODOMARO MUBANGIZI, SJ

6: Lines of Approach and Action:
An African Ecotheology of Justice, Praxis, and Social
Transformation | 106
TOUSSAINT MURHULA KAFARHIRE, SJ

7: Ecological Education and Spirituality:
An African Ecological Ethics and Spirituality | 126
KINIKONDA OKEMASISI

8: Enacting *Laudato Si'* in Africa | 142
EMMANUEL KATONGOLE

*Bibliography* | 149
*Index* | 163

# Contributors

**Anne Arabome, SSS**, is a member of the Sisters of Social Service in Los Angeles, California. Presently, she is the associate director of the Faber Center for Ignatian Spirituality at Marquette University in Milwaukee, Wisconsin. She holds a Doctor of Ministry (DMin) from Catholic Theological Union in Chicago, Illinois, and a PhD from the University of Roehampton, London, UK.

**Stan Chu Ilo** is a research professor of world Christianity and African studies at the Center for World Catholicism and Intercultural Theology at DePaul University in Chicago. He is an honorary professor of religion and theology at Durham University in England, the 2017 recipient of the Afro-Global Excellence Award for Global Impact, and the coordinator of the Pan-African Theology and Pastoral Network. He serves as a member of the board of editors of *Concilium: International Journal of Theology*. Some of his most recent books include *Church and Development in Africa* (Pickwick, 2014); *Wealth, Health, and Hope in African Christian Religion* (Lexington, 2017); *A Poor and Merciful Church* (Orbis, 2018); *Someone Beautiful to God* (Paulist, 2020); *365 Days Walk with God: African Biblical Reflection for a Good Christian Life* (Paulines Africa, 2021). He also coedited the three-volume work *Faith in Action in Africa*, published by Wipf and Stock, and is the editor of *The Handbook of Catholicism in Africa* (Orbis, 2022).

**Toussaint Murhula Kafarhire, SJ**, is Jesuit priest from the Democratic Republic of Congo. He currently teaches political science and International Relations at Université Loyola du Congo (ULC) in Kinshasa, the Democratic Republic of Congo. His research interest focuses on social justice, democracy and peace, conflicts and political violence, and religion in Africa. He is a certified Executive Coach and a published poet. His recent publications include "Briser les chaines et les representations mentales," in *Reseau Elikya Magazine* (Mai 2021), 29–32; "Mgr. Christophe Munzihirwa: Un leadership qui inspire," in *Reseau Elikya Magazine* (Mars 2021), 17–22; "Afterword: Reflecting on The Pan-African Congress on Theology, Society, and Pastoral life" and "The Jesuit in Africa: Mission, Ministry, and Moments of Grace in Advancing Catholic Intellectual and Social Traditions in Africa," respectively in *Faith in Action* (Vol. I and Vol. III), edited by Stan Chu Ilo Nora K. Nonterah Idara Otu, MSP (Abuja: Paulines Publications Africa, [2020], 432–42 and 61–87); "Trajectory Analysis of the Last Thirty Years of the Democratic Experiment in the DRC: A Survey," in *Democracy in Mosaic Societies* (Nairobi: EARH, 2019); "Homelessness and Sustainable Development Goal 11: A Neoliberal Paradox?," in *Street Homelessness and Catholic Theological Ethics*, edited by James F. Keenan, SJ, and Mark McGreevy, 120–28 (New York: Orbis, 2019), among many others.

**Emmanuel Katongole** is a Catholic priest, ordained for the Archdiocese of Kampala, Uganda. He currently serves as professor of theology and peace studies in the Keough School, University of Notre Dame. Before joining the Notre Dame faculty, he served as associate professor of theology and world Christianity at Duke University and as founding codirector of the Duke Center for Reconciliation. He is the author of several books, including *Reconciling All Things* with Chris Rice (InterVarsity, 2008); *The Sacrifice of Africa: A Political Theology for Africa* (Eerdmans, 2010); *Born from Lament: The Theology and Politics of Hope in Africa* (Eerdmans, 2017); and *The Journey of Reconciliation: Groaning for New Creation in Africa* (Orbis, 2017).

**Peter Knox, SJ**, is a South African Jesuit who has always had an interest in natural history and conservation and is an avid ornithologist and scuba diver. Since 2013, he has taught systematic theology at the Jesuit School of Theology at Hekima University College in Nairobi. Since 2014, he has also taught courses on Christian ethics and the environment and has had a new lease of hope since Pope Francis's publication of *Laudato Si'* in 2015.

**Evelyn Namakula Birabwa Mayanja** is assistant professor in the Institute of Interdisciplinary Studies at Carleton University in Ottawa, Canada. She is the recipient of the 2020–21 James N. Rosenau Postdoctoral Fellowship from the International Studies Association, which recognizes excellence in scholarship, outreach, and professional development in academic settings. Her research focuses on the struggle of those marginalized by colonial and neocolonial systems of oppression and natural resources exploitation, mineral resource-based wars/armed conflict, peacekeeping, peacebuilding, and the hype of renewable/green energy versus increasing environmental destruction.

**Odomaro Mubangizi, SJ**, is a Ugandan Jesuit priest who served as the dean of philosophy at the Capuchin Franciscan Institute of Philosophy and Theology in Addis Ababa. He has a new mission as the the Deputy Director and Director of Academic Affairs for the proposed Hekima University of

Eastern Africa Province, Society of Jesus. His research and teaching have covered the following disciplines: social ethics, social and political philosophy, geopolitics, globalization, and the ethics of international relations. He has published chapters in *The Routledge Handbook of African Theology* (2020) edited by Elias Kifon Bongmba; *African Theology, Philosophy, and Religions: Celebrating John Samuel Mbiti's Contribution* (Rowman and Littlefield, 2020) edited by Chammah J. Kaunda et al.; *Reconciliation, Justice, and Peace: The Second African Synod* (Orbis, 2011), edited by A. E. Orobator; and *HIV and AIDS in Africa: Christian Reflection, Public Health, Social Transformation* (Orbis, 2016) edited by Jacquineau Azetsop.

**Kinikonda Okemasisi** is a lecturer and a student mentor at Tangaza University College's School of Education in Nairobi. She has an MA and PhD in educational administration and planning from the Catholic University of Eastern Africa in Nairobi. Her research interest lies in promoting Catholic education in schools. Currently, she is a visiting scholar at St. Mary's University, Twickenham in London where she is writing about the participation of Catholic schools in the care of the environment.

# Foreword

## Agbonkhianmeghe E. Orobator, SJ

Long before the advent of Pope Francis as visionary and prophetic global champion of environmental justice, the late Kenyan Nobel Laureate for Peace, Wangari Muta Maathai, alerted the international community to "the deep ecological wounds visible across the world."[1] Planet Earth, our Mother, she warned, groans under the burden of global warming, pollution of air, water, and land, and the destruction of biodiversity and ecosystems. Maathai was a prophetic voice amidst a cacophony of climate change naysayers, deniers, cynics, and skeptics who, sadly, seem impervious to reason and ethics.

Since the pioneering work of Wangari Maathai, a mounting body of evidence demonstrates that our generation and our civilization teeter on the brink of "a man-made disaster of global scale. Our greatest threat in thousands of years," to quote naturalist Sir David Attenborough.[2] Climate change stands as the defining question of our century. For this reason, the calls to global action are as strident and passionate as the enormity of the situation is grave and consequential. One such call that has resonated across the globe is Pope Francis's encyclical letter, *Laudato Si': On Care for Our Common Home*. In the words of one commentator, *Laudato Si'* "is a love poem to the world. It is a beautiful, heartfelt, and far-reaching plea for action. It speaks straight to our souls and it is rooted in St Francis. . . . It demands a rethink of Catholicism's attitude to the Earth and the creatures who live alongside us."[3]

With prophetic urgency, Pope Francis laments, "Never have we so hurt and mistreated our common home as we have in the last two hundred

---

1. Maathai, *Replenishing the Earth*, 43.
2. United Nations Climate Change, "People's Seat," para. 3.
3. Colwell, "Empty Sky," 4–5.

years."[4] The consequence, he continues, is glaring and incontestable: "The earth, our home, is beginning to look more and more like an immense pile of filth" (*LS* 21). When the pope declares that we are damaging the earth, we do not have to take his word for it. After all, Francis is neither an environmental scientist nor an atmospheric physicist, but his analyses and teachings in *Laudato Si'* are corroborated by countless independent studies, UN and government reports, conclusions from scientific studies, and the profound wisdom of indigenous peoples, as well as agrarian, pastoral, riparian, and coastal communities.

These findings recount the same narrative: that this earth, our common home, labors under the weight of pollution and global warming and can no longer carry its burden—that the phenomenon of climate change "threatens the continuing survival of human societies." There is no gainsaying who is to blame: *we* are the culprits. "Human activities, including industrialization, urbanization, and globalization are all drivers of pollution."[5] In the words of atmospheric scientist Robert Watson, "We are eroding the very foundations of our economies, livelihoods, food security, health, and quality of life worldwide."[6] And in plain language, it means we are hurting the earth and hurting ourselves.

Africa's voice and predicament are pertinent to the conversation about the fate of our common home. Across the continent, there are increasing occurrences of extreme meteorological events. Such calamities expose the skewed logic of climate change, namely that while the poor are the least responsible for global warming and environmental degradation, it is they who disproportionately bear the brunt of its effects. Thus, as we damage our planet, we also blight the lives of poor and vulnerable people and their communities, not least on account of the "intimate relationship between the poor [of this world] and the fragility of the planet" (*LS* 16).

Against the backdrop of this existential threat to life on planet Earth, *Laudato Si'* proposes a prophetic manifesto for our world and appeals passionately to our global conscience about the vital and inseparable nexus between human ecology and environmental ecology, between anthropology and ecology. Pope Francis tells us that planet Earth comprises an integral tapestry of life woven from the collective strands of human life, a biodiversity of flora and fauna, and an ecosystem of natural phenomena. Again and again he reminds us that "[w]e are all related"; "everything in the world is

---

4. Francis, *Laudato Si'*, 53; hereafter cited in-text as *LS*.
5. Das and Horton, "Pollution, Health, and the Planet," 407–8.
6. United Nations Environment Programme (UNEP), "Nature's Dangerous Decline 'Unprecedented,'" para. 2.

connected"; we are dependent on one another; we are a "universal family"; "we are part of nature, included in it and thus in constant interaction with it" (*LS* 16, 42, 89, 91, 92, 117, 120, 138, 141, 142, 240, 139).

I believe that such a vital connection underscores the fundamental solidarity that ought to exist between human beings and our natural environment. The agony of the Earth is the anguish of humanity. For as an African proverb says, "a chicken develops a headache when it sees another chicken inside the cooking pot." In other words, says Francis, "Our relationship with the environment can never be isolated from our relationship with others and with God. Otherwise, it would be nothing more than romantic individualism dressed up in ecological garb, locking us into a stifling immanence" (*LS* 119).

As I see it, the most poignant message of *Laudato Si'* is this notion of "interdependence of forces" between the human person and the cosmos, which allows each to influence and affect the other. Such is the intensity of this vital connection—or, in Francis's terms, "integral ecology" (*LS* 137)—that "one can only save oneself by saving the cosmos." This ecological interdependence is rooted in the principles of the common good, solidarity, and social justice. Hence, Francis declares, "The human environment and the natural environment deteriorate together; we cannot adequately combat environmental degradation unless we attend to causes related to human and social degradation" (*LS* 48).

The wisdom of African religious traditions complements Pope Francis's point that human beings maintain a relationship of solidarity and mutuality with creation, based on the belief in the *livingness of creation*—that is, nothing is life*less* in our natural surroundings. As Laurenti Magesa puts it, "there is inner invisible power in anything at any given moment."[7] I know that Pope Francis shares this belief, because he tells us in *Laudato Si'* that "each creature has its own purpose. None is superfluous. . . . Soil, water, mountains: everything is, as it were, a caress of God" (*LS* 84).

Belief in the livingness of creation also entails a moral duty to protect and care for environmental ecology and human ecology, because in African religious traditions, there is a vital bond between them. As Pope Benedict XVI once said, both are constituted "not only by matter but also by spirit."[8] African religious traditions agree with Christianity in recognizing creation as "the wonderful result of God's creative activity, which we may use

---

7. Magesa, *What Is Not Sacred?*, 27.
8. Benedict, *Caritas in Veritate*, 48, 50.

responsibly to satisfy our legitimate needs, material or otherwise, while respecting the intrinsic balance of creation."⁹

As mentioned, there is a vital connection between human beings and the earth. When we assume our duty to protect and preserve "environmental ecology," we are not doing Mother Earth a favor; rather, we are saving ourselves and our world. We can only save ourselves by saving the earth. Thus, in the spirit of Africa's ethical and philosophical tradition of solidarity and fraternity known as *Ubuntu*, this vital connection empowers individuals and their communities to embrace a horizon of relationships that is infinitely open and mutually enriching for humanity and for our common home. *Ubuntu* is a path of fulfillment of "my relationship with my own self, with others, with God and with the earth" (*LS* 70). The Trinitarian undertones of this belief are unmistakable.

To anyone who perceives and understands that there is no injustice quite so appalling and alarming as that visited on planet Earth by human beings, *Laudato Si'* offers a prophetic proclamation of faith: that this Earth, our Mother, is a gift; it is the outcome of an intentional act by a loving God who is deeply involved and invested in its destiny (*LS* 67, 220). Our moral response to this gift includes a duty of care and a practice of "stewardship" that seeks not to exploit the resources of nature and extract value at all cost but desires primarily to care for and preserve creation. Whether we profess religious faith or not, planet Earth is not the product of an act sequestered in an impenetrable and irretrievable cosmic past. This earth, our common home, represents an enterprise continually being fulfilled, in mutuality and reciprocity. Therefore, according to Francis, for us, today, the focus need not dwell on how the earth came into being but on how "to ensure its fruitfulness for coming generations" (*LS* 67).

The antithesis of the ecological faith professed by Pope Francis is a "globalization of indifference" (*LS* 53) and a "collective selfishness" that only aggravates the crisis. If *Laudato Si'* is right, such indifference and selfishness pose the greatest challenge to any initiative to mitigate and reverse the damage inflicted on our common home. For it is of the nature of indifference to dispense with "that sense of responsibility for our fellow men and women upon which all civil society is founded" (*LS* 25), and it is characteristic of selfishness and greed for "some [people to] consider themselves more human than others, as if they had been born with greater rights" (*LS* 90). Either way, Pope Francis's teaching is clear and decisive: if we capitulate to indifference and selfishness, we become what he calls culpable "silent witnesses to terrible [ecological] injustices" (*LS* 36).

---

9. Benedict, *Caritas in Veritate*, 48.

Yet there is some hopeful news. *Laudato Si'* testifies to the truth that, individually and collectively, we are not bound inexorably to a practice of ecological violence. We can chart a different course; we can embark on a path of care, healing, and protection of Mother Earth. Protecting, caring for, and healing the earth is primarily about protecting, caring for, and healing humanity, because how we treat Mother Earth is a reliable measure of how we treat ourselves. In the context of the present ecological crisis, the commitment to healing the earth must now shift the narrative from threat of destruction to the promise of survival and action towards the flourishing of the biosphere.

The ecological crisis of our times does not leave us bereft of ideas and initiatives. *Laudato Si'* reassures us that we can all do something. We can all make a difference. As Wangari Maathai once said, "It's the little things citizens do. That's what will make the difference. My little thing is planting trees."[10] We are all part of the unfolding drama of climate change, and Pope Francis encourages us to become protagonists of "small everyday things"[11] and "little everyday gestures" (*LS* 231), practitioners of "simple daily gestures" (*LS* 230), and "small gestures of mutual care" (*LS* 231). In the same vein, teenage climate activist Greta Thunberg complements the message of *Laudato Si'* with her simple yet inspiring mantra: "no one is too small to make a difference."[12]

Perhaps, then, for those who explicitly self-identify as Catholic educators, or simply as educators, the global ecological crisis doubles as "an educational challenge" (*LS* 209) to rethink the shape of education in the age of climate change. *Laudato Si'* outlines pedagogical models of "ecological education," or "environmental education," consisting of wide-ranging goals. What is the profile of this ecological education?

First, ecological education prioritizes "ecological equilibrium [that strives to establish] harmony within ourselves, with others, with nature and other living creatures, and with God" (*LS* 210). Second, ecological education teaches "ecological citizenship" and cultivates "sound virtues" that enable people "to make a selfless ecological commitment" in their local communities (211). Third, ecological education empowers people to overcome the paradigm of unbridled consumerism and promotes "a new way of thinking about human beings, life, society and our relationship with nature" (*LS* 215). Finally, ecological education helps people learn "to see and appreciate beauty [and] . . . learn to reject self-interested pragmatism" (*LS* 215).

10. Project Learning Tree, "Words to Live by," para. 1.
11. Francis, *Gaudete et Exsultate*, 143.
12. Thunberg, *No One Is Too Small*.

For this ecological education to transform our present crisis, a new kind of educator is needed. In the words of Pope Francis, what is needed are "educators capable of developing an ethics of ecology, and helping people, through effective pedagogy, to grow in solidarity, responsibility, and compassionate care" (LS 210).

*Laudato Si'* summons educators in the Catholic tradition to become creators of a new pedagogy of ecology—one that nurtures and inculcates "ecological virtues" (LS 88) in those whom we teach. Let us interrogate ourselves: How many students leave our educational establishments converted and transformed as stewards of environmental integrity? To what extent do our educational establishments enhance knowledge and awareness of the present global crisis and deepen commitment to ethical responsibility and duty to care for and protect our common home? How many of our educational institutions teach, not only in words but more especially and intentionally in practice, the critical significance of environmental responsibility? In how many of our educational institutions do we teach our students according to the prayer of *Laudato Si'*, "to discover the worth of each thing, to be filled with awe and contemplation, to recognize that we are profoundly united with every creature as we journey towards [God's] infinite light?" (LS 247).

Such are the prophetic interrogations addressed to us by Pope Francis for our collective examination of conscience. Like Greta Thunberg, "What kind of world," asks Pope Francis, "do we want to leave to those who come after us, to children who are now growing up?" (LS 160). "Young people demand change" (LS 13). This interrogation about the future of our children contains a moral imperative to protect and care for our common home.

*Laudato Si'* calls us to be educators of a whole new world of women, men, and children imbued with a renewed attitude to our common home, to one another, and to the creatures who live alongside us. According to the ecological gospel of *Laudato Si'*, "an integral ecology [founded upon] a serene harmony with creation (LS 255)" invites us to replace "the logic of violence, exploitation, and selfishness" (LS 230) and "a tyrannical anthropocentrism unconcerned for other creatures" (LS 70) with a genuine ecology of gratitude—"the gratitude we ought to feel for what the earth gives us."[13]

Ecological gratitude is akin to gratitude for what a mother gives a child. An African proverb says that "a child can never (re)pay for its mother's milk." Ecological gratitude manifests as respect and reverence, empathy and solidarity, mutuality and reciprocity, generosity and compassion towards Mother Earth and towards one another.

---

13. Maathai, *Replenishing the Earth*, 10; see LS 85, 213, 220, and 227.

As ancient forests continue to fall around us, and plastic bags and bottles clog the bellies of whales and dolphins; as irreplaceable animal and plant species disappear from the face of our planet; as carbon emissions raise global temperatures, melt glaciers, damage coral reefs, and raise sea levels; as lethal effluents kill our lakes and rivers; and as marginalized communities lose their livelihoods, and the cry of the earth and cry of the poor grow agonizingly weaker and fainter, *Laudato Si'* invites us to respond with hope and courage; and, like Saint Francis of Assisi, to see with eyes of faith that "our common home is like a sister with whom we share our life and a beautiful mother who opens her arms to embrace us" (*LS* 1).

In our time, our sister, Mother Earth, thirsts for new life and yearns to hear anew the Franciscan *Canticle of the Creatures*: "Praise be to you, my Lord, through our Sister, Mother Earth, who sustains and governs us, and who produces various fruit with colored flowers and herbs" (*LS* 1). Let us echo the prayer of Pope Francis: that we may "be 'protectors' of creation, protectors of God's plan inscribed in nature, protectors of one another and of the environment."[14]

Amen!

---

14. Francis, "Inaugural Homily," para. 8.

# Introduction

## Stan Chu Ilo

In May 2020, a very close friend of mine who coordinates the initiatives for the defense of children, and promotes policies and programs for the prevention of child abuse and neglect for a UN agency in northern Nigeria, woke me up early in the morning with a sad phone call. He was broken, because he had spent the previous night on the streets rescuing more than 200 children between the ages of five and ten who had been abandoned on the streets of Kaduna, one of the largest cities in northern Nigeria. In his sadness, he said to me, "What kind of society will allow her most vulnerable ones who should be the *first call* on society's resources to suffer this way?"

Many of these children, he said, were malnourished; some had visible signs of physical and sexual abuse, and most of them were emotionally distressed and were infected with, and afflicted by, many diseases, including the dreaded COVID-19. In Nigeria, these children are referred to in the local Hausa language as *almajiri*, which is derived from the Arabic word *al-Muhajirun*, or "emigrant." Having been "given away" to Islamic teachers (called *malams*) very early in their lives, most of these children no longer know their family roots or village of origin.

These *malams*, who are usually poor, teach the kids, who pay the *malams* for their education through the money they receive from begging along the major streets and highways. In return, the *malams* provide them with food and lodging, often in squalid and unhealthy conditions. Following the outbreak of COVID-19 in Kano and Kaduna, and the closure of this form of home-based schooling, and also driven by the fear that some of these children could be infected through their contact on the streets with people, most of the *malams* shut their doors on these kids, who ended up homeless on the streets.

According to the BBC, the Kaduna State government (which later banned this practice) had sent social workers to pick up these children from the streets and "repatriate" them to their states of origin. As a result of this forced "repatriation" of these children, northern Nigeria witnessed the largest mass movement of minors in living memory in West Africa, with as many as 30,000 of these minors being moved to different states in an effort to locate their families. It is those kids who did not know their roots, who were left on the streets or herded into unhealthy settlements, who were being rescued by UNICEF and other local and international agencies. The pitiable condition of these children, which my friend observed that May morning, broke his heart. It also broke mine. Africa's children continue to bear the brunt of diseases and pandemics like COVID-19; they also bear the brunt of failed governments and failing social and health safety nets.[1]

What future are we building for our children and young people? At the personal level, the thoughts about the future of children like these *almajiri* was what gripped my attention as I wrote this text. As one reads through the texts of the contributors to this volume, one would immediately see that they are informed by the same common concerns for our children and our common future. Greta Thunberg, the Swedish climate child activist who led millions of children on a "climate strike" in September 2019, made the challenge facing humanity so stark, especially for the children, when she said in her address to the United Nations:

> You say you love your children above all else, and yet you are stealing their future in front of their very eyes. Until you start focusing on what needs to be done rather than what is politically possible, there is no hope. We cannot solve a crisis without treating it as a crisis. We need to keep the fossil fuels in the ground, and we need to focus on equity. And if solutions within the system are so impossible to find, maybe we should change the system itself.[2]

*Laudato Si'* offers a very comprehensive analysis of the crisis we face and also practical solutions for ecological conversion, mitigation, and adaptation to climate change and the ecological crisis of our times. *Laudato Si'* has been well-received globally, and this volume puts it in conversation with African ecospirituality, environmental ethics, and narratives of the condition for human and cosmic flourishing through the contributions of some of the leading African scholars and leaders whose scholarship, advocacy, and ministries touch on the themes, issues, and practical steps that Pope Francis proposes in this important document.

---

1. UNICEF, "Children Adjust to Life."
2. Mesey, "Greta Thunberg's Speech," para. 9.

## Why an African Commentary on *Laudato Si'*?

The plan for this special African commentary on *Laudato Si'* emerged at the Pan-African Catholic Congress in December 2020. This Congress was convoked as part of the conclusion of the fiftieth anniversary of the founding of the Symposium of the Episcopal Conferences of Africa and Madagascar (SECAM) and the twenty-fifth anniversary of the First African Synod. At this Congress, African theologians, pastoral agents, and leaders in diverse fields affirmed their commitment for a new heaven and a new earth with these words:

> Indeed, unless our theology, institutional structures, and pastoral practices are translated into tools of liberation and the flourishing of life for Africans, the growth of the Church will only be in number. The kingdom of God does not grow simply in number. Rather, it grows in love, faith, and hope. This growth transforms communities, cultures, and traditions. We acknowledge that sometimes our theology has been far removed from our contexts and has not helped to deepen the faith of our people and the transformation of society. Going forward, this theology must necessarily be inclusive of all voices in its formulation, presentation, and application.[3]

However, one topic that was not given enough time during the Congress was ecology. Even though there were two sessions on ecology and another that celebrated the gift of the earth, most of the participants in the Pan-African Catholic Theology and Pastoral Network felt that we needed to devote a full-length volume to *Laudato Si'*. The goal was to put together a book that clearly sets out the meaning and message of *Laudato Si'*, while developing in conversation with it the theoretical and conceptual frameworks for understanding African ecotheology, Africa ecoethics, Africa ecospirituality, and African notions and praxis for human and cosmic flourishing. At the Congress, COVID-19 came up only in our prayers for our Chinese brothers and sisters in Wuhan. Little did we know that the world would be upended by what soon became the most serious and devastating pandemic that humanity has faced in our lifetime.

We were already putting the framework and structure for this volume into place when the Vatican's dicastery launched the fifth anniversary celebration of the publication of *Laudato Si'* as well as the celebration of the Year of *Laudato Si'* from May 24, 2020—May 24, 2021. The announcement of this celebration was received with so much joy by African theologians

---

3. "Statement of the Pan-African Catholic Congress," 1:11.

and leaders, because the anniversary gave greater attention to some of the important developments in the African theology of creation, ecological ethics, and earth-friendly and earth-keeping practices which contributors to this volume write of with so much depth and precision.

The fifth anniversary of the publication of *Laudato Si'* highlighted three important developments which informed this volume's publication. First, *Laudato Si'* is a prophetic document about our common future. The pandemic of COVID-19 emphasizes why churches and humanity need to take seriously the message of *Laudato Si'*. Here in particular is the affirmation of our common destiny and the need for global solidarity in meeting the common threats that we face in any part of the world. As Pope Francis writes in *Laudato Si'*, all things are deeply interconnected and interdependent: "everything is closely interrelated, and today's problems call for a vision capable of taking into account every aspect of the global crisis."[4]

It is obvious that there are limits to our human-designed systems, structures, and institutions. COVID-19 has revealed the false sense of security on which the world has been built. We humans have lived as if we were the center of the universe. Our world operates on a dysfunctional value system which glories in all forms of iniquitous hierarchies of power, hardened walls of indifference, and isolationist national and cultural practices and stratagems. Through the flaccid paralysis that it has left in its wake, COVID-19 has laid bare our collective vulnerabilities. Indeed, this pandemic is a mirror into the brokenness and woundedness of our world, which was already bleeding as a result of climate change. Rather than frightening us, this situation should motivate us to embrace the vulnerabilities and sufferings in the world today and the fragility of the earth with humility, courage, and hope.

Second, *Laudato Si'* can provide us with "the moral and spiritual compass for the journey to create a more caring, fraternal, peaceful and sustainable world. We have, in fact, a unique opportunity to transform the present groaning and travail into the birth pangs of a new way of living together, bonded together in love, compassion, and solidarity, and a more harmonious relationship with the natural world, our common home."[5]

Third, the contributors to this volume wish to offer the universal church an African voice on ecology and how to live the message of *Laudato Si'* in both Africa and the rest of the world. This is a response to Pope Francis's invitation when he said, "All of us can cooperate as instruments of God for the care of creation, each according to his or her own culture,

---

4. Francis, *Laudato Si'*, 137 (hereafter cited in-text as *LS*).
5. "*Laudato Si'* Anniversary Year Plan," para. 1.

experience, involvements, and talents" (*LS* 14). This volume offers Africa's gifts, talents, experience, and practical approaches for understanding the crisis we face, as well as the wisdom of our traditions and practices in conversation with Catholic social teaching on ecology as contained in this impactful encyclical.

The 2014 IPCC regional report for Africa, *Climate Change: Impacts, Adaptation and Vulnerability*, points to frightening statistics and trends in Africa today which validate Pope Francis's assertion about the exploitation of Africa. Worth noting from the IPCC report are the following facts:

(i) Decadal analyses of temperatures strongly point to evidence of warming over land regions across Africa over the last fifty to a hundred years.

(ii) Variation in rainfall in Africa due to a reduction in precipitation is leading to unpredictable rain patterns which adversely affects farming and worsens the sad food security and human security in Africa.

(iii) Climate change will create water scarcity in Africa since water resources are subjected to high hydro-climatic variability over space and time and will have negative impact on the continent's economic development.

(iv) Climate change is affecting African ecosystems with substantial impact on life forms in the oceans, forests, rivers, and other areas.

(v) Agricultural production will also be severely affected, especially some of Africa's stable crops like cereal, other high-value crops, and livestock, among others.

(vi) Climate change in Africa will also increase the burden of a range of climate-relevant health outcomes and will exacerbate existing health vulnerabilities in Africa.

(vii) There are other multistressor contexts with regard to desert encroachment, flooding, erosion, and urbanization which have negatively affected human livelihood, ecosystem health, and natural vegetation, leading to changing migratory patterns for animals and humans and the spread of diseases and social and economic stress, violence, and war.[6]

The challenges posed to Africa by some of these threats to sustainable livelihood and human and cosmic flourishing are worsened by the fact that the continent lacks the capacity to mitigate and adapt to the threats of

---

6. Niang et al., "Africa," 1203–5.

climate change and global warming. Conference of the Parties 26 (COP26), in 2021, failed to address these lingering concerns of Africa, nor have African religious and political leaders come up with any clear, consistent, and unified approach for an African-wide commitment to combating the devastating impact of climate change on Africa. However, there lies in the heart of Africa some rich ecological wisdom and traditions which need to be recovered and appropriated by Africans in order to begin—in small ways—to protect, preserve, and guard the rich human, cultural, and natural wealth of the continent. This wisdom is not only a gift for Africa but also a rich resource for developing a global ecological ethics for abundant life. This is the wisdom which this volume's authors write of in the chapters that follow.

The essays have been structured in such a way that each contributor brings his or her original thoughts to the text, while at the same time maintaining in all the chapters a consistently unique African mode of discourse and methodology. The essays achieve three goals, each in its unique way, within a synthetic structural collage. First, the authors have engaged each chapter by telling the stories of ecological crisis in the world in general, and in Africa in particular. Second, they engage the teachings of *Laudato Si'* in a thematic manner, drawing out the intelligibilities in the text through an African reading and deploying the full range of what Jacob Olupona calls "indigenous hermeneutics" in representing the themes through African ecoethics and the narrative of creation and abundant life.[7] The focus on indigenous hermeneutics is also a deliberate attempt to contest the regnant false order of knowledge and history mediated through Western notions of modernity and the kind of economies and technologies that kill.[8] It is also an effort to decolonize the current global language, categories, and conceptual framework for addressing the challenges of climate change. Our authors strongly demonstrate the limitations of Western epistemologies and development paradigms in meeting these challenges. This point is well presented by Yirga Gelaw Woldeyes and Tekletsadik Belachew who argue in this way:

> The decolonization of the environment requires a decentering of Eurocentrism, first by acknowledging the violence of slavery and colonialism and second by centering indigenous ways of knowing and acting in relation to the environment. The history of slavery, colonialism and neo-colonialism are inseparable from the destruction of the environment (Ecocide), several indigenous languages (Linguicide), African knowledges

7. Adebanwi et al., "Religion and Indigenous Hermeneutics."
8. Cf. Tornielli and Galeazzi, *This Economy Kills*.

(Epistemicide), and groups of peoples (Ethnocide). The concept of the Anthropocene portrays an abstract human being that claims to represent all people.[9]

Authors in this volume thus privilege narratives and epistemological frameworks for being present with, and in conversation with, nature and an openness to our sharing in nature and our coimbrication in the rhyme and rhythm of creation. The authors use stories to communicate this intricate connection and the painful sundering of this relationship through the many impacts on Africa's vulnerabilities of climate change and environmental degradation. They also write of the resilience of African cultures, peoples, and ecospiritualities as resources for developing practices of ecological conversion, human and cosmic sustainability, and the praxis for strengthening the agencies of Africans in the much-needed quest for wealth, health, and hope for humans, while maintaining ecosystems' health for cosmic harmony and peace.

Anne Arabome's introductory essay sets the stage for the rest of the book by identifying some of the ecological crises facing Africa as she continues to mourn, weep, and bleed, as was the case during Cyclone Idai. She retrieves the wisdom of African ecological spirituality and ethics of motherhood as a hermeneutics of the cry of the earth, the cries of women, and the cry of the poor. Through an intersectional analysis, Arabome develops an African womanist hermeneutics for understanding the seriousness of the ecological crisis facing the world today, the human responsibility in this crisis, and the kinds of ecological practices which could be adopted so that our common home, Mother Earth, can nurture us back to life as we, in reciprocal manner, honor, reverence, and protect her with a deep sense of mystery and care.

In his commentary on chapter 1 of *Laudato Si'*, Peter Knox delves into the data of what is happening to our common home. He observes, however, that Africa is "data scarce," making it challenging to quantify the harm being done to our continent by the interconnected triple threats of pollution, climate change, and biodiversity loss. Sophisticatedly engaging the latest scientific evidence on the effects of these triple threats to Africa, Knox employs the tools of theological ethics to show the negative effects of these threats on people in their landscapes. Against a backdrop of social breakdown, global inequality, and weak responses, Knox maps out a road for the future by proposing a return to African ecospiritual values, which have been abandoned in the objectification, resource-ification, and commodification of God's gift of Creation.

9. Woldeyes and Belachew. "Decolonising the Environment," 64.

Stan Chu Ilo explores *Laudato Si'* as an important teaching on developing an African theology of creation, taking up some of the ecospiritual values that Knox writes about in the previous chapter. He proposes that the second chapter of *Laudato Si'* affirms a God-centered universe and the interrelatedness of all things as the bases for integral ecology. While bringing out the main themes of this chapter, he shows how they resonate with African ecospiritual ethics. He demonstrates how African cosmogonies, just like the creation account of Genesis, are wisdom traditions which offer some spiritualities and religiocultural traditions of abundant life. Through an appeal to a Trinitarian account of creation and the cries of Africa in the face of creation's destruction—particularly manifested in the rising amount of garbage in African cities—this chapter develops three ethical practices for respecting and promoting integral ecology for human and cosmic flourishing through an *Ubuntu* theology of creation. These practices are a recovery of a sense of beauty; a renewal of an ecoethics of participation and solidarity; and the ecospiritual practices of vulnerability and care.

In chapter 4, Evelyn Mayanja shows why making peace with the earth in Africa cannot be realized in the current global structures of injustice. Mayanja's prophetic critique of some development paradigms, exploitation of the earth and Africa's resources, and technological determinism are breathtaking and wide-ranging, critical, evidence-driven, and constructive. She lays out a plan for how peace with the earth, and peace among people in Africa and with Africa and the world, can be achieved. She makes an appeal to a new ecological ethics, while addressing the inexcusable poverty and suffering in the continent. She also bemoans the challenges of failed leadership, extractive states in Africa, and their global co-conspirators whose false ideologies of power have congealed Africa's resources and people in the frozen vaults of a few while ignoring the poor of the land and wounding and bruising the continent of Africa. This situation is the greatest driver of violence in the continent. There can be no peace in the world unless we make peace with the earth and with the earth's poor. Mayanja challenges the church in Africa to a prophetic role in meeting the challenges of the ecological crisis. She also challenges all people who care about the future of the continent to a new level of social engagement, solidarity with the earth and with the poor, and reconciliation with nature in order to save Africa and the resources of the continent for her peoples and the generations yet unborn.

In chapter 5, Odomaro Mubangizi continues the analysis of *Ubuntu* begun in Ilo's chapter with a discourse on an African account of integral ecology from the philosophical perspective of the *Ubuntu* ethic. His chapter tells the stories of the many real problems caused by human activity on the environment: for example, the rising water levels of Lake Victoria—shared by Kenya, Uganda, and Tanzania—which are submerging homes and lands around this lake and the fight over the damming of the Nile River between Sudan, Ethiopia, and Egypt. He concludes this engaging chapter on a note of hope and optimism by introducing some earth-keeping African practices particularly the Tadeo Nyebirweki Rwakazooba Forest (TNRF) found in Kabale, South Western Uganda, near the border with Rwanda. These examples demonstrate how small efforts and initiatives, grounded in African ecotheological principles, themes, and practices, offer lessons for Africa as well as the world and the wider church. His chapter is an important contribution to an emerging African integral ecospirituality, grounded in the *Ubuntu* ethic of praxis employing a narrative methodology.

Toussaint Karfahire, in chapter 6, continues the conversation begun by Mayanja but focusing more on interpreting the African ecological crisis through an interrogation of history and modernity. He looks at the global dimension of the ecological crisis and how the development paradigms have conspired to inflict death-dealing policies and realities for Africa. Through a decolonizing framework, Karfahire dismantles the structural concoction of the messy planet that development practices leave behind all over the world, especially in Africa. He uses the COVID-19 pandemic to demonstrate how the failure of justice, lack of respect for nature, and the uncritical assimilation of Western epistemological frames are turning the earth into a sick and deadly place to live, especially for the poor and the vulnerable. While Mayanja concentrates on the role of the church, Karfahire focuses on the role of the state, individuals (e.g., citizen participation), and social movements in fighting the good fight to save our common home.

In her commentary on chapter 7 of *Laudato Si'*, Kinikonda Okemasisi makes a case for ecological spirituality and education. In Africa, she argues, *Laudato Si'* resonates well with the traditional ecospirituality of social and environmental justice. Focusing on some of the recent disasters experienced in Africa as a result of human-induced global warming, she draws a road map for ecological education on the continent. She offers a triadic ecological education paradigm focused on teaching for mature functionalism. This system, Okemasisi proposes, offers pertinent methodologies that would bring about the conversion required, both at the individual and communal levels, for sustainable development. The chapter calls for integration of traditional and modern systems of education for integral ecology. This kind of education is particularly targeted to young people who should be socialized into an environmental consciousness that is typical in traditional African society and that embraces the care for creation as the purpose and vocation of our lives together.

The final chapter, by Emmanuel Katongole, moves from theory to performance. Katongole explains how *Laudato Si'* is being enacted in Africa through the Bethany Land Institute (BLI) which he pioneered in Uganda. BLI is a practical and impactful attempt to reverse what is being taken away from Africa and the world through climate change and global warming—our kinship with the land. BLI is a demonstration model of an alternate site of hope being developed as Africa's own *Magnificat*; it shows that, by putting *Laudato Si'* into practice, God can do great things in Africa when we all become caretakers of the earth, guardians of our common lives and our common home.

## Dying in One's Farm

I would like to finish this introduction with a sad story. On June 30, 2020, Anayo Iloabani, a sixty-seven-year-old man from my town, Achi, in Enugu State, Nigeria, went to his farm as usual to cultivate his ancestral land. He did not return home. When his family went in search of him, what they saw was his lifeless body in his farm with multiple machete wounds in his body and his severed neck. Eyewitnesses who came around reported to the community that they had seen some Fulani herdsmen, whose cattle were grazing in the area. A violent confrontation between my townspeople and these herdsmen was averted when the police intervened, promising to investigate this heinous crime. However, to date, nothing has really come out of the investigation.

Sadly, in the last decade, thousands of people have been killed by Fulani herdsmen in Nigeria in the fight for grazing rights between these nomadic people and their host communities all across Nigeria. Many people have often read these violent conflicts—as my community leaders have done—as an invasion of ethnic Fulani from northern Nigeria, which is predominantly Muslim-populated, into the predominantly Christian-populated southern Nigeria. There are a lot of conspiracy theories and catty insinuations in Nigeria about the intentions of the herdsmen, and these stoke fear of an Islamic agenda led by the federal government under the Islamic supremacist, President Buhari. There are other conspiracy theories and contested narratives that have also spread fear among the people. However, there are a few others who are beginning to see a larger ecological crisis and structural evil in these conflicts which have become more frequent and deadly in Nigeria within the last few years.

Whatever position or stand one takes in this argument, no one will deny the fact that Nigeria is experiencing severe ecological occurrences—the

Sahara Desert encroachment in the North, the drying of the Lake Chad basin, flooding in the South, erosion and landslides, the depletion of forests and ancestrally protected groves and parks. These are happening because of urbanization, industrialization, development projects and construction, and gentrification in the large cities, as well as severe and unpredictable weather patterns which have affected vegetation for animals, agricultural and food production, and ecosystems' health and harmony. Rather than address this ecological crisis, successive governments in Nigeria continue to play one group against the other, exploiting existing divisions and narrow ethnic and religious sentiments for political gains. In this kind of mistrust, even viable proposals like creating designated grazing areas for the cattle rearers in some states are pooh-poohed and rejected without any dialogue. What is happening in Nigeria is similar to what is happening in many countries in African Sahel and the rest of the continent.

The killing of Iloabani in his own farm by unknown gunmen is a metaphor of what is happening to our earth. We are killing the earth. Humans have made the earth a sick place. Because of anthropogenic factors, we are dying in this beautiful garden that God has given us. Our authors here show us why this killing of the earth is occurring in Africa, how it is affecting all of us, who the culprits are in this destruction, and what we can do collectively and individually about it. The volume also exudes hope about the future by pointing us back to our roots—African ecospirituality and an environmental ethics of life, participation, and cosmic flourishing. These signs of hope can also be found in places like the Bethany Land Institute in Uganda, the Songhai Farm in Benin, and the Green Belt movement in Kenya, as well as through many ecological movements and social and peace movements and among the earth keepers in Zimbabwe, where so many Africans are standing tall for the good of this earth, our common home.

# I

# United by the Same Concern: An African Womanist's Plea

Anne Arabome, SSS

## A. An African Ecological Story

On March 14, 2019, Cyclone Idai tore through coastal towns and cities of Mozambique, leaving in its wake a trail of death and destruction. Catastrophic occurrences like Idai are the consequences of anthropogenic climate change, like other multiple extreme weather-related events witnessed in recent times, such as heat waves, droughts, forest fires, and floods. An abundance of examples of such outcomes exists in Africa. Across eastern Africa and the Horn of Africa, a pernicious succession of locust infestations of biblical proportions has devastated food crops and cash crops, rendering millions of Africans food insecure while exacerbating the scourge of poverty. Most strikingly, there is credible evidence to suggest that climate change is to blame for this seemingly "natural" disaster.[1] In one sense, this destructive incident replicates and reenacts other such extraordinary and severe weather-related events. By way of example, the droughts of the 1980s in eastern Africa and the Horn of Africa come to mind. Decades later, the scars still run deep as evidenced in the broken lives and livelihoods of millions of people in the region. Studies show that the negative impact of these extreme climate happenings is writ large on the lives of many African women. These women shoulder the burden of climate change and are disproportionately affected as victims: "More specifically, women have much to lose, since not only their livelihoods, but also their responsibility for the survival and

---

1. Stone, "Plague of Locusts." See also Dunne, "Q&A."

health of their children, are linked to their natural surroundings."[2] Taken together, this reservoir of climate-related tragedies evokes, in the words of Pope Francis, the "intimate relationship between the poor and the fragility of the planet."[3] In a world where ecological degradation has become incontrovertibly evident, it is instructive that many scholars characteristically apply the appellation "Mother Earth" in reference to our planet.[4] This implies a profound recognition that the earth nourishes the human community as well as sustains the plants and animals, microorganisms, and inorganic matter, just like any mother would her beloved children.

Pope Francis renders the theme of "Mother Earth" as "our common home" in his groundbreaking encyclical, *Laudato Si'*. Francis opens the introductory section by drawing on the inspirational ecospirituality of St. Francis of Assisi. The pope reminds readers of the constitutive relational quality of creation. Sadly, he notes, creation moans and wails under the exploitative activities of human beings, and he categorizes such damaging activities as sinful. Furthermore, Francis situates his theological analysis in the long tradition of Catholic social teaching, dating back to Pope Saint John XXIII's 1963 encyclical, *Pacem in Terris*. Francis highlights the values and principles of this tradition, crafting a compelling message about the interconnectedness of natural and human ecology. The pope's concern for a planet in peril lies at the heart of his stirring appeal for an inclusive dialogue about the future of our common home and the imperative of a conversion of attitudes such as indifference, resignation, and technological hubris, in favor of greater ecological solidarity and responsibility. By purposing to underscore the shared fragility of the poor and the earth, Francis aims to inspire and recover an attitude of praise and reverence for the profound mystery of creation that originates in the inexhaustible love of God. In the following sections of this essay, I will expound on these ideas, first, by offering concrete examples of the ecological damages instigated by human activities in Africa. Second, I will identify specific aspects of the introductory section of *Laudato Si'* and their pertinence for the situation in Africa. And, finally, cognizant of the disproportional burden foisted on African women on account of climate change, I will develop some themes, principles, and practices derived from an ecofeminist perspective for a renewed, just, and balanced relationship between human beings and nature.

---

2. African Development Bank, "Climate Change, Gender, and Development," 7.

3. Francis, *Laudato Si'*, 16 (hereafter cited in-text as *LS*).

4. Onwurah, "Mother Earth in Igbo Religion," 42–49; McCall, "Mother Earth"; May and Söö, *Great Cosmic Mother*; Pettersson, *Mother Earth*.

When Francis speaks of the damage done to our common home, there is no dearth of examples of such destruction in Africa due to the exploitation of natural resources and the degradation of land resources taking place on the continent. The consequence is appalling: "In the whole of Africa, there is widespread poverty, deplorable living conditions, piling up of garbage, low-life expectancy, prevalence of diseases including the dreaded HIV/AIDS, destitution, unemployment, occurrence of orphaned and vulnerable children (OVCs), industrial and agricultural pollution, and immense climatic changes."[5] In light of the ecological damage identified in *Laudato Si'*, the areas of ecological devastation and their consequences in Africa can be summarized as follows:

*Deforestation and degradation.* The stark reality is that Africans depend on trees for every aspect of their lives! Yet, under pressure to survive harsh economic conditions, many are cutting down trees for fuel, for the selling of timber, and to make room for planting. Human beings are destroying their very habitat so that they might live in the short term. These "activities aggravate the environmental crisis leading to a vicious circle of poverty."[6] While the world's tropical forests are being lost at an alarming rate, largely due to agricultural expansion, so also the soil of the world is being destroyed with overplanting as well as the use of chemical fertilizers. This leads to "a net increase in greenhouse gases that contribute to global climate change, increased soil erosion, drought, and flooding. This environmental degradation forces farmers to clear even more land to grow food for their families."[7] My own country, Nigeria, has suffered severely from soil, air, and water pollution due to oil prospecting by multinational companies in the Niger Delta.

*Poverty.* Poverty is intertwined with ecological degradation. Poverty occurs as a result of an unfortunate convergence of insufficient natural resources, lack of education, and damage to the ecosystem. Obviously, "[w]hen the choice is between taking care of the environment and meeting basic requirements like food, shelter, and clothing, the poor of Africa will certainly choose the second option."[8]

*Pollution.* Pollution of water and air are major challenges to peoples who are already struggling with issues of survival. For example, in addition to the indiscriminate use of rivers for bathing and washing of clothing, the

---

5. Gitau, "Environmental Crisis," 309; see also the Union of Concerned Scientists' "Climate Hot Map" at http://www.climatehotmap.org/global-warming-solutions/africa.html.

6. Gitau, "Environmental Crisis," 311.

7. Chibuko, "Forestation—Deforestation—Reforestation," 193.

8. Gitau, "Environmental Crisis," 310–11; see Kanyandago, "Let Us First Feed the Children (Mark 7:27)," 172.

lack of proper environmental regulation means that industrial waste and effluents of all kinds are channeled into water sources.

*Overpopulation.* Increased population growth combined with influx into major cities creates a confluence of factors leading to smog and dirty air. In addition, motor vehicles of every kind emit carbon dioxide and other deleterious particles into the atmosphere.[9] Demographic expansion in Africa creates immense pressure on the earth's resources. Given the appalling reality of poverty, South African theologian Peter Knox has queried the sustainability of the current situation: "Are we trying to support too many people . . . ? If the wealth of Africa is its people, might we not be wealthier in a different sense if we had slightly smaller families?"[10]

Across Africa, these environmental catastrophes wreak incalculable damage on lives and livelihoods. As mentioned above, perhaps more than anywhere else, the Niger Delta region of Nigeria provides a somber and graphic illustration of the converging consequences of nefarious and environmentally damaging activities, in particular the pollution of water, air, and land.[11]

## B. *Laudato Si'*: A Message for the Church, the World, and Africa

It is not accidental that Pope Francis opens his programmatic encyclical, *Laudato Si'*, with gendered language in the tradition of his namesake, Saint Francis of Assisi, for whom "our common home is like a sister with whom we share our life and a beautiful mother who opens her arms to embrace us" (*LS* 1). Notwithstanding the beauty and poetry of this assertion, from an ecofeminist perspective, this approach allows us to query the fundamental link between ecological abuse and the abuse of women—and, in this case, African women. It may seem unfair to pose this question to the text of the encyclical. That *Laudato Si'* does not explicitly address it does not amount to saying it neglects the question. From the introductory section, it is clear that the encyclical provides an overarching framework for analyzing and confronting the deeper concerns of justice, albeit in the specific context of the global ecological crisis. Like the plight of women, Francis makes clear that Sister Earth laments and wails on account of the willful and incalculable damage visited on her by human beings (*LS* 2). In this situation, the foremost ethical imperative incumbent on the global community is a profound and transformative dialogue and acknowledgment of the urgency and challenge

---

9. Beckerman, *Economic Development and the Environment*.
10. Knox, "Theology, Ecology, and Africa," 169.
11. Solomon et al., "Environmental Pollution in the Niger Delta," 10–15.

concerning the interconnected fate of humanity and our common home (*LS* 3 and 15). This encyclical stands in the venerable tradition of Catholic social teaching, whose origins date back to the nineteenth century (*LS* 3–6, 15), although it is set apart by its uniqueness as a pioneering attempt to engage in a sustained analysis of the ecological crisis confronting humanity and our common home. It aligns with other trenchant voices of concern in multiple circles across the globe (*LS* 7).

In my opinion, any discussion of the ethical implications of the abuse of Mother Earth must go beyond a simple consideration of the concept of earth as being affected by global warming. This is because whether we designate it as "global warming" or "climate change," we are confronted by "an inconvenient truth" of the gradual and undeniable abuse of the earth. The threat is real, and it affects all parts of the world.[12] Unfortunately, the effects of this massive damage to the earth are especially evident in less-developed countries where entities from the West and China continually desecrate and abuse Mother Earth through unethical exploitation. Interestingly, Francis casts such acts of ecological abuse in the language of sin. Drawing upon the insight of Patriarch Bartholomew, Francis provides an inventory of sinful attitudes, behavior, and acts "against the natural world," ourselves, and God (*LS* 8). They include unbridled consumption, greed, wastefulness, and fear, all of which ought to be replaced with the virtues of sacrifice, generosity, a spirit of sharing, asceticism, and love. These virtues entail a radical shift away from self-centeredness to a sacramental communion with the world created and loved into existence by God (*LS* 9).

According to Pope Francis, the person who embodies and exemplifies these virtues in their fullest and most authentic sense is Saint Francis of Assisi. He is the icon, patron, and exemplar of an integral ecology that embraces the plight of the vulnerable and the pain of the earth with confidence and joy. Although Francis of Assisi lived in a different era, his attitude toward nature models for humanity the virtue of discovering and celebrating the beauty and goodness of every constituent being in our common home. In this perspective, the earth is born of the mystery of God, a mystery that invites praise and worship, reverence and care (*LS* 10–12).

Pope Francis outlines the purposes and intent of this encyclical as an urgent appeal for a new and inclusive dialogue about the fate and future of the planet. This honest, frank, and incisive conversation is the antithesis of the attitude of denial propagated by climate-change antagonists (*LS* 13–14). The fundamental principle of this dialogue is the idea of the

---

12. See Gore, *Inconvenient Truth*. In this documentary, former US Vice President Al Gore presents a compelling narrative and argument about the need to reassess humans' relationship with natural ecology in order to save our dangerously imperiled planet.

interconnectedness of everything in the world and the link between the fate of the world and the fragility of our common home (*LS* 16).

## C. Mother Earth: Ecofeminist Theological Principles, Themes, and Practices

Against the backdrop of the introductory section of *Laudato Si'*, Africa emerges as the place where Mother Earth has been weeping, mourning, and bleeding. The sacredness of life for Africans covers a wider range than for many other cultures of the world. Traditionally, Africans would not touch, cut, or destroy any part of creation without some thoughtful reflection and awareness of its sacredness and right to life. An anecdote from Nobel Laureate Wangari Maathai's book, *Unbowed*, illustrates this idea: "When my mother told me to go fetch firewood, she would warn me, 'Don't pick any dry wood out of the fig tree, or even around it.' 'Why?' I would ask. 'Because that's a tree of God,' she'd reply. 'We don't use it. We don't cut it. We don't burn it.' As a child, of course, I had no idea what my mother was talking about, but I obeyed her."[13] Africans and indigenous people learn early on that they are part of creation and, therefore, must respect what the Supreme Being has placed here *with them*. As Lynn White Jr. has argued, this attitude of ecological reverence dates back to antiquity. For people of such a pre-Christian era, every tree, every spring, every stream, every hill had its own genius loci, its own guardian spirit. Before one cut a tree, mined a mountain, or dammed a brook, it was important to placate the spirit in charge of that particular situation and to keep it placated. By destroying pagan animism, Christianity made it possible to exploit nature in a mood of indifference to the feelings of natural objects.[14]

The outcome, according to Rosemary Radford Ruether, is the singular ability of humans to dominate and exploit nature while maintaining an impersonal and objective distance from it.[15] Compare this with the attitude in Nigerian Yoruba cosmology, in particular as portrayed in Ifa divination.[16]

The Yoruba recognize the earth and the gift of abundance that she is to humanity. She is a mother, first and foremost, taking care of her children

---

13. Maathai, *Unbowed*, 44–45.
14. White, "Historical Roots of Our Ecologic Crisis," 1205–6.
15. Radford Ruether, "Religious Ecofeminism," 364.
16. Yoruba is a major ethnic group in southwestern Nigeria. Other smaller groups of Yoruba people are found in Benin and Togo, sharing a common language and some socioeconomic, cultural, and political features. The reference here is to the Yoruba of Nigeria.

and deserving of our respect. All things emerge from her. She is the one who brings balance and fairness to human interaction. She punishes those who hurt others. All things return to her womb at the end of their time.[17] Mother Earth bears life and allows life to end when it is time, as illustrated in this prayer of the Akan people of Ghana:[18] "O Mother Earth, we are fully dependent on you; it is you who receive us with your open arms at birth when we were yet naked. You supply our daily wants with your rich resources; indeed, you nurture us throughout our earthly life. And when the wicked death finally snatches us away, You will still be there to open up your womb and receive us all back."[19] This prayer is a beautiful commentary on the African traditional way of perceiving the earth as our mother. Although embedded in the African mind and heart, this seemingly natural empathy and reverence for Mother Earth do not always match reality, given several specific instances of abuse and damage of the natural ecology. Unfortunately, the need to survive the daily grind of poverty and related socioeconomic and political crises, combined with the exploitation of the continent's natural resources by local and global political and economic institutions, has had a terrible eroding effect on the peoples of Africa, as it did in other parts of the world.[20] Thus, without seeking to portray Africa as an idyllic paradise, a healthy balance has always existed between "subduing" and "preserving" the earth and its fertility as a source of life.

The symbol of a loving Mother Earth is exquisitely rendered in the sublime prayer of St. Francis of Assisi, who speaks lovingly of Sister Water and Mother Earth (*LS* 1). This metaphoric Franciscan-esque reference to the earth as "Mother" resonates well with African cosmological worldviews and spiritual perspectives precisely because African religions have a place for the feminine in divinity vis-à-vis the creative activity of the latter. In many African mythologies, the Supreme Being, earth, and creation are linked as one entity through a process of birthing and nurturing. African thought processes are symbolically reflected in circles, like a web of connections of dependence and interdependence among all the constituents of nature, including spirits and deities.[21] This is even seen in the circular shape of African huts or mud houses. The earth is the circle of life.[22] And

17. Olupona, "Spirituality of Matter," 78.
18. Akan is a major ethnolinguistic grouping of peoples who inhabit the Guinea Coast. Akan people live predominantly in Ghana.
19. Appiah-Kubi, "Oh Mother Earth," 61.
20. Berry, *Great Work*, 40.
21. Cf. Gebara, *Longing for Running Water*, 52.
22. Brown-Hinds, "Circle in African Tradition."

life comes from the womb of birth and is called forth into being—a life that continues even into death, providing the necessary mulch for yet new life. African religions reflect this life-giving feminine reality.

The Igbo people of Nigeria, Akan, and Yoruba have traditions that recognize the "Earth goddesses Ala or Ani."[23] Such traditions recognize, respect, and reverence the feminine quality of the earth. Before working the fields, consent to do so is sought. When the fruits of the harvest are ready, ceremonies are held to say "thank you" and to engage in acknowledgment of Ala's beneficence.[24] From the examples of the Igbo, Akan, and Yoruba, the underlying mindset in cultures that venerate the Earth Mother goddess affirms the sacredness of the earth and the circle of life as intrinsically relational. The earth, plants, and animals are not seen as disposable objects for human utility. The earth as mother functions as a life-giving metaphor and can be applied in an ecofeminist retrieval and reconstruction of the identity, travails, and place of the African woman today.

The African woman has always been the compelling energy for family food production: she prays for rain; she worries into the wee hours of the morning in hopes of harvest; she pours all of her soul into the growing of bitter leaf (*Ewuro*), African spinach (*Efo Tete*), and okra and tomatoes to feed her family and take to market.[25] "It is she who grows fruit trees around the family orchard and has very beautiful flowers around the yard. Her great passion for pets and livestock is amazing."[26] In short, the African woman is the one who sings to the fields and engages with the energies of life in the plants, in the animals, and in her family. She is the epitome of the earth goddess come to life in human form. Returning for a moment to Igbo culture, the presence of the earth goddess is acknowledged at the time of birth when "the baby is washed with loose earth to depict its connection with *Ala* and to announce to the ancestors that the baby has arrived safely."[27]

In sum, there is a significant gender quotient to the appellation of earth as Mother. When the earth is abused, women suffer from its terrible effects on account of their vulnerability to violence. This process is akin to the "pattern of domination of subjugated others/nature, both ideologically and practically."[28]

---

23. Onwurah, "Mother Earth in Igbo Religion," 42.
24. Onwurah, "Mother Earth in Igbo Religion," 43; McCall, "Mother Earth," 305.
25. See "Nigerian Leafy Vegetables."
26. Chirongoma, "Karanga-Shona Rural Women's Agency," 122.
27. Onwurah, "Mother Earth in Igbo Religion," 44.
28. Radford Ruether, "Religious Ecofeminism," 364–65.

In the final analysis, *Laudato Si'* connects intimately with "the central assumption of ecofeminist epistemology [that] is the interdependence among all the elements that are related to the human world."[29] This, too, is the core conviction of Pope Francis: "We are all related"; "everything in the world is connected"; we are dependent on one another; we are a "universal family"; "we are part of nature, included in it and thus in constant interaction with it" (*LS* 16, 42, 89, 91–92, 117, 120, 138–39, 141–42, 240). Thus, ecological damage cannot be separated from humanity's relationship with God (*LS* 8). A contemplative attitude is necessary to recognize the harm that we have inflicted on our common home and to assume our inescapable duty to heal Mother Earth and ourselves.

---

29. Gebara, *Longing for Running Water*, 51.

# 2

# Our Common Home: An African Cry of the Earth, Our Home

PETER KNOX, SJ

## A. Setting the Scene: Lack of Data

Living outside of an urban area in Africa means that one is likely to encounter some of the wild animals for which our continent is famous. In Nairobi, the capital city of Kenya, one might even have the misfortune of meeting a lion escapee from the Nairobi National Park. Most of these contacts are infelicitous, either for the human or for the animal. One or the other comes off the worse for the event. And with changing climate, the number of human-wildlife conflicts is steadily rising. An article by the *Agence France-Presse* itemizes such contacts in just one country: Zimbabwe. With drought ravaging the country, humans and animals are on the move in search for water. The article cites one man's encounter with a buffalo which had strayed out of the Hwange National Park, which left him crippled and almost emasculated. However, 311 such animal attacks occurred in 2019 alone, a 59 percent increase on the previous year.[1]

Africa is on a slow but steady trajectory of developing sustainable cities and economies. The future of our peoples depends on our ability to use the rich natural resources with which God has endowed us for the benefit of all people. We rely heavily on agriculture and the primary production of foodstuffs. The mineral wealth of the continent is famous. And many countries are dependent on tourism at our national treasures of immense beauty and rich wildlife. But these three pillars of African development suffer from

---

1. Mafundikwa, "Drought Ignites Human-Wildlife Conflict," para. 5.

interconnected vulnerabilities: Contamination of the land, air, and water is linked to the extraction of minerals, and to agricultural activities and unsustainable cities. Changing weather patterns result in floods, droughts, and locust swarms of biblical proportions, and are weakening the ability of our land to produce crops and sustain livestock. Many areas of immense natural beauty are losing their attractiveness as their usage is changed, or the herds of animals are slowly being wiped out. The complex interplay of these triple threats of pollution, climate change, and biodiversity loss is difficult to quantify.

There simply isn't sufficient hard data or accessible reliable information concerning what is happening on the continent. Regarding the Sustainable Development Goals (SDGs), the United Nations Environment Programme (UNEP) quotes the African Union's *Sustainable Development Report*:

> Six out of every ten SDGs indicators cannot be tracked in Africa due to severe data limitation. . . . There is . . . lack of regular credible surveys to capture changes . . . inadequate funding and limited autonomy of the national statistical offices to generate accurate, credible, timely and neutral data . . . poor data quality. . . . These limitations lead to persistent data gaps in key development indicators, mainly in social, environmental and governance indicators . . . impede the establishment of baselines. . . . Ultimately, this means that policy-making . . . is not informed by adequate data, nor the effects of policy adequately monitored.[2]

The UNEP *Measuring Progress* report reaffirms this in relation to SDG indicators in sub-Saharan Africa, stating: "[s]ome data is available, but not enough to analyse changes over time" or "[n]o data is available."[3] So, our governments and policymakers over time could be introducing legislation and structures that are based on local perceptions and hearsay, rather than on hard evidence. Or particular, local challenges might be generalized and local solutions imposed widely in contexts to which they are not applicable.

One issue that concerns ecologists, for which more data would be useful, is the human-wildlife conflict mentioned in our first paragraph. Conflict frequently arises as people encroach on areas that have been used for generations by wild animals, either as their habitual range, or as migration routes. Alternatively, because of changing climate, wildlife often have to go

---

2. African Union Commission et al., *Africa Sustainable Development Report*. The extract I have summarized is taken from United Nations Environment Programme (UNEP), *Measuring Progress*, 13.

3. UNEP, *Measuring Progress*, 12; see figure on this page.

beyond their habitual range in search of food and water. The need to house and feed ever-expanding human populations places pressure on previously natural areas. Predators might raid livestock, killing poultry, sheep, goats, or cattle. Or large herbivores may damage crops. Sometimes this interaction might be fatal if humans are killed by wild animals, but more frequently, the animals are on the receiving end of human wrath. The same solutions do not apply everywhere: In some places, elephants might be scared off by bees, and leopards or lions by Anatolian sheep dogs, averting the damage to crops and livestock. But while local challenges should be addressed with local solutions, the more information people have about what is occurring at different regions, and how it is affecting humans in their environment, the better interventions can be made at local, national, and regional levels.

## B. An Africa Thematic Commentary on Chapter 1 of *Laudato Si'*

Chapter 1 of *Laudato Si'* is so important because it introduces the encyclical with data by exploring "what is happening to our common home."[4] Before judgments can be made and actions proposed (the remaining two steps of the See-Judge-Act pastoral methodology), the encyclical begins with the all-important step of seeing and describing the current situation of planet Earth, the common home of every living creature. Pope Francis calls for more research to give a greater understanding of what is happening around the world, and the interdependence of all species, including humans.[5] A perusal of the footnotes to this first chapter[6] shows the pope's sensitivity to the experience of people around the world. He quotes the episcopal conferences of Latin America and the Caribbean, the Philippines, Bolivia, Germany, Patagonia, and the United States, just as he quoted the bishops of Southern Africa in paragraph 14. The goal of this review "is not to amass information or to satisfy curiosity, but rather to become painfully aware" (*LS* 19) of what is happening to our world and to grow in compassion, and thus to make a change.

The descriptions given in the chapter are perforce qualitative rather than quantitative. A papal encyclical could not possibly offer statistics or scientific data on which to base any policy decisions. In fact, at the end of the chapter (*LS* 60–61), Pope Francis avows that there is a variety of competing opinions, from the myth of technological solutions for every problem to the outright condemnation of humans as nothing but destructive creatures.

---

4. This is the title of chapter 1.
5. Francis, *Laudato Si'*, 42 (hereafter cited in text as *LS*).
6. These are footnotes 23 to 35 in chapter 1.

The way forward is going to require negotiation between these divergent outlooks. "On many concrete questions, the Church has no reason to offer a definitive opinion; she knows that honest debate must be encouraged among experts, while respecting divergent views" (*LS* 61). The church has no particular investment in one particular scientific theory. Indeed this is beyond her area of expertise or competence. As science advances, it would be foolhardy of the church to commit itself to one theory or set of explanations. Instead, the church has millennia of experience in human nature, and caring for human beings. This is her area of expertise. Insofar as the quality of people's lives and relationships with God, themselves, and their environment is affected by what is being done to the natural environment of which we are a part, Christians have a duty to make interventions. This cannot be left to nonchurch actors alone. It is the duty of the Church in Africa, as it is elsewhere, to address what concerns the lives of people across the continent. We need to reflect on the issues Pope Francis brings to our attention in this first chapter, and relate them to Africa and to the wider world.

## Pollution

In the first subsection of chapter 1 (*LS* 20–22), Pope Francis addresses the issue of pollution. He uses a shocking image: "The earth, our home, is beginning to look more and more like an immense pile of filth."[7] However, I maintain that this land-based image is only half of the picture. Rivers, lakes and oceans are also beginning to resemble one enormous cesspool. So much waste is flushed into waters that they are becoming hazardous for aquatic life and, ultimately, for the people who depend on these biomes.[8]

---

7. Apart from being unsightly, all around Africa, garbage poses great dangers for animals and, ultimately, human consumers of animal products. For example, livestock often eat plastic. This sometimes kills the animals, and at other times, it accumulates in their digestive system, carrying numerous poisonous chemicals into their bloodstream. Cf. Priyanka and Dey, "Ruminal Impaction Due to Plastic Materials," 1307–15.

8. In 2016, Craig Leeson brought the issue of marine plastic pollution to the attention of the public. His film, *A Plastic Ocean*, illustrates how plastic waste is found in every stratum of the world's oceans and how its toxic effects on all marine life work their way up in the human food chain. Pieces of plastic afloat around the seas and oceans are reduced in size by the effects of the waves, salt, and sunlight. Designed to be "indestructible," they never break down completely. These plastics are eaten by birds, fish, whales, dolphins, turtles, etc., blocking their digestive systems and leading to a slow and painful death. Many animals drown after getting ensnared in "ghost nets" and fishing equipment discarded by fishermen around the world. Most of the plastics floating around the seas have been brought down by rivers in countries that do not have adequate refuse treatment facilities in place. Cf. Leeson, *Plastic Ocean*.

Pope Francis attributes this "immense pile of filth" largely to a "throwaway culture." Indeed, as people acquire more and more, enticed by deceptive advertising campaigns of industries which require their endless supply of goods to be purchased, they simply have to discard what is broken or irreparable, outmoded, or superseded. Before we even use our new products, we have to dispose of the packaging in which they were delivered: metal, plastic, glass, and cardboard. In African cities, one sees all sorts of packaging disposed of on the roadside: shattered glass bottles, single-use water bottles, cardboard boxes, foil wrappers, plastic baskets. Since the onset of COVID-19, we now also see discarded surgical masks added to this mess. Our unwanted electronic goods are added to an enormous heap of e-waste generated every year, leaching toxic chemicals into the soil, rivers, or oceans where they were disposed of. And we are blissfully unconcerned as we enjoy our new cell phone or the latest computer games. The few moments of happiness these products might bring us are outlived thousands of times by the remnants of our acts of consumerism.

In paragraph 20 of *Laudato Si'*, Pope Francis writes:

> Some forms of pollution are part of people's daily experience. Exposure to atmospheric pollutants produces a broad spectrum of health hazards, especially for the poor, and causes millions of premature deaths. People take sick, for example, from breathing high levels of smoke from fuels used in cooking or heating. There is also pollution that affects everyone, caused by transport, industrial fumes, substances which contribute to the acidification of soil and water, fertilizers, insecticides, fungicides, herbicides, and agrotoxins in general.

Pope Francis had anticipated by two years the outcome reported by the *Lancet* Commission on Pollution and Health:

> Pollution is the largest environmental cause of disease and premature death in the world today. Diseases caused by pollution were responsible for an estimated 9 million premature deaths in 2015—16 percent of all deaths worldwide—three times more deaths than from AIDS, tuberculosis, and malaria combined, and 15 times more than from all wars and other forms of violence. In the most severely affected countries, pollution-related disease is responsible for more than one death in four.[9]

---

9. Cf. Landrigan et al., "*Lancet* Commission," 462.

The Commission reports: "The highest population-based estimates of premature deaths and disease due to pollution are seen in the low-income countries of sub-Saharan Africa."[10]

Pope Francis compares the linear economy of extraction-production-sale-disposal of manufactured goods to the circular economy of nature in which waste and by-products are absorbed and recycled (*LS* 22). In general, people have not taken seriously enough the end-of-life issues related to everything we consume. Relatively simple technology exists to treat solid waste—by reusing, recycling, or repurposing it—even in Africa. But we frequently don't have the political willpower to deal with waste. It is too easy to turn a blind eye, to see it as somebody else's problem, or simply to burn junk on the sidewalk outside our property, making a stinking, smoldering mess for our neighbors.

Around the world, confronted with this enormous issue of what to do with waste, people have come up with innovative solutions. In the so-called developed world, people incinerate municipal waste as a source of energy for electricity production. Alternatively, with extended producer responsibility programs, manufacturers might be compelled to take back the waste of the products that they have produced. Another approach is to attach sufficient value to waste to make it profitable to take care of it. Finally, and tragically for us, discarded goods from the "developed world" are shipped to Africa and Asia. The examples are numerous and include the following: "Computers 4 Africa";[11] British plastic dumped in Turkey; dead ships sent to India for breaking; secondhand cars which are considered ecologically unsafe in their countries of manufacture; container loads of used clothing for resale, undercutting local African garment industries;[12] and nuclear waste and hazardous chemicals that can always find a home in the desert in some distant African country (*LS* 51). If enough bribes are paid, international conventions on importing hazardous waste can easily be ignored.[13]

---

10. Landrigan et al., "*Lancet* Commission," 474. Here, the authors are citing another *Lancet* study of twenty-five years of risk factors: Forouzanfar et al., "Global, Regional, and National Comparative Risk Assessment."

11. Dominic Rizzo's article, "Computers 4 Africa: Where Our Technology Is Going and How It's Being Used," examines the limitations of the philanthropic model of Computers 4 Africa, a charity that collects, refurbishes, and delivers used information and communication technology to African recipients. Rizzo highlights issues regarding cultural rejection of Western technology, the skills gaps, and the issue of e-dumping.

12. See UNEP and IWMA, *Global Waste Management Outlook*, 88: "Many of the higher-quality garments are sold in Eastern Europe. Lower-quality wearable items from Europe and North America tend to go to Africa."

13. For example, the Basel, Rotterdam, and Stockholm Conventions establish obligations relating to the trans-frontier movement of hazardous waste. The Bamako

Where African authorities or entrepreneurs do collect municipal rubbish,[14] it is taken to monstrous landfill sites where the poorest of the urban poor often eke out a living picking through the rubbish, collecting rags, plastics, metal, glass, or the edible food that nobody else wants. The people who are unfortunate enough to be involved in the recycling of our waste are frequently doing so in the most dangerous of conditions—breathing the toxic fumes from burning plastics or using their bare hands on chemicals that would never be handled in developed countries without layers of protective clothing.[15]

Most of what has been discussed so far concerns municipal solid waste, but the pope is also acutely aware of the pollution caused by industries. Extractive industries across Africa often use potent and hazardous chemicals such as cyanide, acids, and mercury. In the gold mines around South Africa, these are stored above ground in the so-called "mine dumps" that dot the country's industrial hub of Johannesburg. Frequently carried by the wind as fine dust particles, these chemicals are inhaled, leading to some of the highest rates of respiratory disease in the world. Chemical manufacturers pump tons of toxic gases into the atmosphere, often within close proximity to residential areas. Even when they are stored with extreme caution, gases can still escape and kill people in the vicinity.[16] The pollution released by the oil industry is notorious and affects oil-exporting nations such as Nigeria, Libya, and Angola.

## Climate Change

As a former chemist, Pope Francis is aware of the damage done to the earth's protective ozone layer by several classes of industrial gases. In addition,

---

Convention, in force since 1998, bans the import into Africa, and the trans-boundary movement of hazardous waste, and specifically prohibits the import of radioactive waste into Africa.

14. Apparently, nineteen of the world's fifty biggest dumpsites are in Africa—see UNEP and IWMA, *Global Waste Management Outlook*, 16.

15. See UNEP and IWMA, *Global Waste Management Outlook*, 17: "Among the most impactful e-waste dumpsites [in the world] is the Agbogbloshie dump in Accra, Ghana which receives around 192,000 tonnes of e-waste annually and pollutes soil, air and water and causes serious health impairments in the 10,000 scavengers gaining their livelihood from sorting and recycling."

16. This happened in the notorious Union Carbide disaster in Bhopal, India, in 1984, when an estimated 3,787 people were killed from one toxic gas leak. See Taylor, "Bhopal." In 1995, a brush fire caused the release of clouds of toxic sulfur dioxide, injuring more than 100 people outside Cape Town in South Africa. See "Chemical Fire Sends Toxic Gas over Cape Town Community."

despite climate change denialists, the pope goes with "a very solid scientific consensus" (*LS* 23) concerning the effect of so-called "greenhouse gases" in changing the earth's climate. It is not only industries that produce these harmful gases. Every time we use a fossil fuel, chop down a tree, or eat beef, pork, goat, lamb, chicken, or eggs, we have contributed in our own way to the buildup of greenhouse gases. Pope Francis subscribes to the broad scientific consensus of anthropogenic climate change—i.e., that human activity is largely responsible for the changing climate of the past two centuries. His primary concern in paragraphs 23–26 of *Laudato Si'* is not the science but the effects that climate change are having on people around the world—rising sea levels and extreme weather events like storms, floods, and droughts with consequent starvation, migration, and the breakdown of social stability. It is the poorest people around the world—those most dependent on natural cycles—who are already suffering most from these effects.

The pope recognizes climate change as "one of the principal challenges facing humanity in our day." The challenge is on a global scale. This is one area in which our planet is crying out for every one of us to commit to an "ecological conversion" (*LS* 216–21). It calls for economic migration away from technology that is clearly damaging our common home. What is of great concern is the lack of solidarity with the rest of the human race displayed by people who can afford to, and should, make a difference. The most hardcore among them deny the reality of climate change, "green-wash" the problem, or conceal the symptoms. This is often because they are so invested in industries related to fossil fuels that they cannot countenance a shift towards more climate-friendly energy and modes of transport, construction, heating, etc. The irony is that these new "clean" technologies promise soon to be even more profitable than outmoded "dinosaur" technologies and may provide up to five times more jobs than coal-based industries.

## Water

In paragraphs 27–31, the encyclical considers the twin aspects of the quality and quantity of water as the most basic ingredient for life. Along with agriculture, industries have a parlous reputation concerning gases and solid waste. They also have an insatiable appetite for water—clean water—which can never be purified once it is contaminated with chemicals, fertilizers, and petroleum. Where regulations do not exist, or are loosely enforced, waterways easily become the sewers into which industries sluice their waste. Water is also contaminated with domestic waste from detergents, sewage, pharmaceuticals, and other persistent organic pollutants that make it unsuitable for agriculture or drinking. Iconic of the destruction of fresh and ocean water is the pollution of the Niger Delta with leaked petroleum products.[17] People are living there, yet they can no longer fish, bathe, pasture their flocks, irrigate their fields, or even drink. Not only is climate change making less water available in many places, but "[w]ater poverty especially affects Africa where large sectors of the population have no access to safe drinking water or experience droughts which impede agricultural production" (*LS* 28).

Certain areas of the continent are historically prone to cycles of drought and are marginal agricultural locations—for example, the Sahel region and areas adjacent to the Kalahari and Namib Deserts and the Karoo semi-desert. Frequently on the fringes of deserts or semi-deserts, these areas have unreliable rainfall patterns. Wealthier farmers can afford the land which has a more constant water supply. However, even this is no longer certain. For example, in 2019, South Africa's Western Cape Province, home of the deciduous fruit cultivation and the best wine production on the continent, suffered from a water shortage, and Cape Town became the first world city in modern times to run out of water. This was partly due to inadequate and ill-maintained infrastructure, characteristic of most of the continent's cities. But it was an indication of the future fate of many cities.[18]

Pope Francis affirms that safe drinkable water is a "basic and universal human right" (*LS* 30) and thus decries its privatization or conversion into a commodity which becomes too expensive for ordinary people to afford. They can only afford to buy in small quantities. A further problem arises with the privatization of water, when it is sold in plastic bottles which are used once and then discarded. Single-use plastic bottles litter our cities, countryside, and even the remotest villages. They are a recent phenomenon that have become a "must-have" at every social event. Ironically colored blue, to suggest the purity of the contents, these very bottles damage the quality of water all over the world. Plastic water bottles represent one face of the throwaway culture that needs to be challenged.

## Biodiversity Loss

Africa might seem to be the last paradise left on earth with pristine wilderness and herds of large animals migrating across its infinite plains. The seasonal migrations of zebra and wildebeest in Kenya, Tanzania, and Botswana come to mind, conjuring up images of a world that is still in good

17. See, for example, "Price of Oil."
18. Cf. Cartwright, "Cape Town 'Day Zero' Water Crisis."

shape. Nothing could be more deceptive! For a host of reasons, species are disappearing from Africa at an alarming rate.[19] The International Union for the Conservation of Nature (IUCN) maintains a "Red List" of threatened species around the world. An insatiable appetite for so-called "bush meat"—basically, any mega-fauna that can be eaten—is contributing to the decline in numbers of species of large mammals, reptiles, and birds. The "traditional medicine" industry both in Africa and Asia accounts for the killing of thousands of lions, rhinos, pangolins, and primates—and the almost certain imminent extinction of these species. But even more catastrophic are the desertification of once fertile lands, the destruction of tropical forests of the Congo Basin as well as the mangrove coasts, and wetlands such as the Sudd Basin in South Sudan. These habitats are home to thousands of species, some of which are not even known to "science" and are being obliterated from the face of the continent. Without their niche habitats, hundreds of species are dying alongside their homes.

Pope Benedict XVI captures the human agency of this drama when he writes in *Africae Munus*, "Some business men and women, governments and financial groups are involved in programs of exploitation which pollute the environment and cause unprecedented desertification. Serious damage is done to nature, to the forests, to flora and fauna, and countless species risk extinction. All of this threatens the entire ecosystem and consequently the survival of humanity."[20] These lines are gleaned from what he had heard participants discussing at the Second African Synod in October 2009. The world is currently undergoing the "sixth great extinction," and the loss of habitats and species is directly attributable to human interference in the natural order.

Landscapes are fragmented by human settlement or agricultural or monocultural forestry or mining activity, restricting the range of animals. It takes great foresight to leave biological corridors for plants, insects, and other animals. This is why the precautionary principle must be exercised and thorough environmental impact assessments made before any changes are made to land usage. Often, however, commercial interests override any concern for potential environmental damage.

In paragraphs 32–42 of *Laudato Si'*, Pope Francis attributes the plundering of the earth to a utilitarian mentality, which regards everything on

---

19. For further information, consult the Red Lists of Threatened Species on the International Union for the Conservation of Nature (IUCN)'s website: https://www.iucn.org/resources/conservation-tools/iucn-red-list-threatened-species. These lists are used to monitor the progress of the United Nations Convention on Biological Diversity (cf. https://www.cbd.int/).

20. Benedict XVI, *Africae Munus*, 80.

the planet as a resource for human consumption. Nothing is recognized as having intrinsic value or giving glory to the Creator by its mere existence. The spiritual value of the world is forgotten and, with it, our sense of being created, contingent beings. Often, people do not realize that they are part of the web of life and depend on the rest of creation for their own survival. As we destroy other species, we are slowly killing ourselves. Even bugs and microorganisms that are killed by "pesticides" have an important place in every ecological system.

Humans "seem to think that we can substitute an irreplaceable and irretrievable beauty with something we have created for ourselves" (LS 34). We are making the planet more grey and lifeless. Africans claim to have a concern for the living, the "living-dead," and the still-to-be-born. Yet we stand by uselessly as our natural world is demolished. What are we leaving for future generations? Where is our intergenerational solidarity?

In paragraph 37 of *Laudato Si'*, the pope recognizes that some countries are reserving sufficient land and sea space for other species to survive. We are rightly proud of the many and vast protected areas on our continent. Yet members of our governments permit prospecting for minerals in national parks;[21] endorse the construction of major dams in our game reserves;[22] and allow the hunting of threatened species in the game reserves.[23] The passing promise of profit is more alluring than the sacred trust that government officials receive from their people when they assume office. They seem to have forgotten their baptismal promises to reject Satan and all his empty works and all his empty promises, and to choose to live in the freedom of the children of God.

In paragraphs 40 and 41, Francis returns our attention to the world's oceans and their intimate connection to what happens on land. The oceans' rising temperatures and acidity threaten coral reefs, the breeding grounds of fish, on which about 2.5 billion people around the world depend as their source of protein. Fishing can be a very destructive and wasteful industry. Some fishing nets do immeasurable damage to the coral, pulverizing it beyond recovery. Other types of nets do not discriminate between fish large

---

21. For example, in South Africa, there have been serious attempts to mine coal and iron ore in the famous Kruger National Park, and only public outcry stopped the mining of titanium in South Africa's iSimangaliso Wetland Park, a UNESCO World Heritage site. Cf. Jones, "Dune Mining for St Lucia?"

22. For example, in 2020, construction began on the Stiegler's Gorge Dam in Tanzania's Selous Game Reserve, another UNESCO World Heritage site. Cf. "WWF Reaction to Stiegler's Gorge Hydropower Dam Construction Launch."

23. For example, the promotion of the hunting of elephants, lions, and rhinoceroses in some South African national parks. Cf. Martindale, "Opinion."

enough to be used and those that are too small to be of any use. Dynamite and cyanide kill all species instantly. With long-line trawling, many birds and "undesirable" species of fish are killed and discarded as bycatch. Some fishing companies poach in other countries' territorial waters, knowing that those countries are too poor to take legal or military action. Already, some African nations have experienced the depletion of their offshore fisheries by illegal European and Asian fishing.

Social Breakdown

In paragraphs 43–47, the pope shows that his concerns about our common home are not limited to the natural world. Cities and urban areas can also be very unhealthy places, particularly as they grow in an uncontrolled and unplanned manner. They can have very high concentrations of toxic gases from vehicles' exhaust emissions, generators, industries, cooking, and heating. Surrounded by concrete jungles and greyness all year long, people can suffer from deprivation of natural spaces, parks, or greenery. And on the other end of the economic scale, people live in gated communities and "eco-parks," secluded from many of the challenges of urban life and the realities of "the disposable of society" (*LS* 45).

As people are cut off from each other, alienation, exclusion, unemployment, and disparity of opportunity and advantages contribute to the disintegration of society. This can lead to mistrust, drug dependency, social aggression, violence, and other forms of lawlessness. Social media can often be used to contribute to the stereotypes we have of one another; for example, on social media, people might receive and/or distribute more noxious images and messages, further entrenching suspicion and fear. And the lure of the instant message and instant solution discourages people from profound thought and reflection. Often, a glut of information is mistaken for wisdom, and people don't know what to do with all the data at their disposal. Pope Francis coins the term "a sort of mental pollution" (*LS* 47) for this information overload and resultant confusion. This media malaise removes us from profound identification with other people and their joys, hopes, and complex personal experiences. Ironically, the more access we have to social media, the more disconnected and isolated we can become.

Global Inequality

The heart of Pope Francis's message in *Laudato Si'* is that the cry of the earth *is* the cry of the poor. Issues that affect the earth always have a human dimension. The suffering of the earth involves the suffering of the poorest people who, among other inequalities, die younger, live with pollution, become involved in conflicts over shortages of resources, or are forced to migrate. Often this suffering is not deemed newsworthy, and so it does not reach the headlines of the international media. In paragraph 49 of *Laudato Si'*, the pope discusses the unequal access that people have to the media and the diametrically different worlds occupied by the wealthy and the poor. Even the environmental stories covered by the mainstream media reflect pitifully on the suffering whales and elephants, the ozone layer, or global warming, and yet seldom touch on the human story.

In paragraph 50, Francis argues forcefully that population control is not the solution to the world's problems. The unequal distribution of resources is responsible for the problems of the poor, and this might be relieved through more creative ways of sharing the benefits of the earth. If extreme consumerism were curtailed, then there would be greater equity in the lives of people across the world. This paragraph points out that about one-third of all food produced worldwide is wasted, "stolen from the table of the poor." None of this can be denied. However, it is also undeniable that the earth is a limited resource; as the title of the 1972 Club of Rome study announces, there are *Limits to Growth*.[24] The human population and economy cannot grow indefinitely. And the planet has boundaries, as contemporary scientific theory is pointing out. Planetary boundary theory highlights nine geophysical conditions that sustain life on Earth,[25] and eight of these are cited directly in *Laudato Si'*.[26] The quantification of these boundaries is still somewhat imprecise, making it a matter of judgment where they lie. In a similar way, it is a matter of judgment whether the world is capable of bearing still greater human populations. I tend to err on the side of caution on this question.

In paragraph 51, the matter of international inequities is discussed within the context of imbalanced international trade and resource extraction. Wealthier countries have an "ecological debt" due to their consumptive lifestyle and the accumulation of pollution over the centuries. With a history of exploitation come differentiated responsibilities, requiring the powerful

24. Cf. Meadows et al., *Limits to Growth*. See also Meadows et al., *Limits to Growth: The Thirty-Year Update*.

25. Cf. Rockström et al., "Planetary Boundaries." This seminal article was updated in 2015 with some real quantities: cf. Steffen et al., "Planetary Boundaries."

26. These are global climate change, ocean acidification, biogeochemical changes (C, N, and P cycles), biosphere integrity (biodiversity), land-system change (desertification, deforestation, etc.), freshwater use, ozone depletion, and novel entities (nanotechnology and nuclear technology.) Cf. Knox, "*Laudato Si'* and *Veritatis Gaudium*."

to do more for the weak and vulnerable. Pope Francis points out that people in poorer countries, such as those of Africa, are bearing the brunt of the resultant global climate change. This is true. However, it is important that Africa not be portrayed only as a victim. It is incumbent on Africans to assume greater agency for their own escape from the cycles of victimhood. For example, debt is an easy trap to fall into and is also used by wealthier nations as a way of controlling poorer ones. With the global economic shift towards China, this Asian country will soon be the financial superpower to which debts are owed and which will control the economies of smaller nations, imposing odious mining contracts, etc.

## Weak Responses

In paragraphs 53–59 of *Laudato Si'*, Pope Francis examines the reasons for the continuing deterioration of the environment, despite people knowing better. They boil down to a lack of culture of care for the world (*LS* 53); ineffectual multilateral organizations and vested economic interests (*LS* 54); enticement of consumptive habits (*LS* 55); and economic power and denialism (*LS* 56). The way things are going, it is predictable that wars will be fought over precious resources. And these wars may be worse than previous ones because of the arsenal of new, destructive chemical, biological, and nuclear technology at the disposal of the belligerents. In 2020, we saw what havoc one virus can wreak on the world. It is almost unimaginable how disruptive a deliberate engagement in biological warfare might be. Nations are developing biological warfare agents and allowing potential enemies to know that they have these in their arsenal. However, at the same time, most nations adhere to the relevant UN conventions;[27] while politics demands that nations do not appear weak, diplomacy is required to avert conflicts.

In paragraph 58, the pope acknowledges the achievements of people whose efforts to improve their natural and built environment have been successful. For example, rivers have been cleaned up, landscapes beautified, native woodlands restored, beautiful buildings erected, clean energy and public transport produced.[28] These success stories are indicative of a will to work in harmony with nature, a solidarity among people of that particular region, and the fact that we are created for love. However, we must not be deluded by "green-wash" or lulled with a false or superficial ecology that can only lead to complacency. Despite appearances to the contrary, the

---

27. See, for example, UNODA, *Biological Weapons Convention*.

28. In another context, the pope also celebrates the production of artists and poets in evoking the beauty of nature; cf. Francis, *Querida Amazonia*, 41–46.

challenges remain urgent. Lifestyles and structures of consumption and production must change. We cannot continue with "business as usual" and delay the inevitable painful decisions.

## C. An Ecotheological Principle: Traditional Spirituality and its Breakdown

In his opening homily for the Second Session of the Special Assembly of the Synod of Bishops for Africa—and again, twice in the postsynodal exhortation for this Second African Synod—Pope Benedict XVI identified Africa as a "spiritual lung" for the world: "A precious treasure is to be found in the soul of Africa, where I perceive a 'spiritual lung' for a humanity that appears to be in a crisis of faith and hope, on account of the extraordinary human and spiritual riches of its children, its variegated cultures, its soil and sub-soil of abundant resources."[29] There is no denying that many African people do have a "spiritual" rather than "scientific" engagement with reality. Indeed, John Mbiti once famously wrote, "Africans are notoriously religious, and each people has its own religious system with its set of beliefs and practices."[30] In the very title of his book on African spirituality, Laurenti Magesa asks rhetorically, "what is not sacred?"[31] His answer is that everything is sacred. Everything has the potential to communicate the benevolence of the Creator. Thus, all spaces and outcrops, rivers and lakes, forests and groves, hills and mountains, animals and persons, etc., must be treated with awe and reverence, because they are occasions for sacred communication. The sacred permeates everyday life, and nothing should be treated as merely mundane or profane.

However, particular activities and locations have been identified as particularly sacred. In particular, over generations, taboos have been attached to areas of natural importance or to species of plants or animals. For example, members of a certain clan may not hunt certain animals; in some cases, their very names may not be pronounced. Frequently, only elders are permitted to eat certain parts of an animal, thus restricting the hunting of that animal. Some groves in a forest might be identified as the home of spirits (either malevolent or benevolent), and nobody is permitted to traverse these groves or pick any plants from them. In South Africa, a rocky outcrop might be identified as the home of some ancestors, and only people with specific ritual status (or clearance) are permitted to venture

29. Benedict XVI, *Africae Munus*, 13.
30. Mbiti, *African Religions and Philosophy*, 1.
31. Magesa, *What Is Not Sacred?*

onto the outcrop. Breaching any of the abovementioned taboos might bring misfortune or incur the wrath of the ancestors, who are able to punish and reward their descendants.

Unfortunately, many people in contemporary Africa have become secularized to the point of having a total disregard for such traditions.[32] There are no longer sufficient guardians of the old ways to ensure the protection of species and biomes through observance of the taboos. Everything is commodified and exploited. Everything has a price. People are trafficked; forests and lumber are sold; geological anomalies like outcrops, frequently indicators of precious underground minerals or water, are exploited.

However, this is not a new phenomenon. Already in the 1995 *Ecclesia in Africa*, Pope John Paul II observed that there is "tragic mismanagement of available scarce resources."[33] Indeed, the colonial and postcolonial periods, which blighted the past 500 years of African history, are marked "by the dishonesty of corrupt government leaders who, in connivance with domestic or foreign private interests, divert national resources for their own profit and transfer public funds to private accounts in foreign banks."[34] John Paul II continues: "This is plain theft, whatever the legal camouflage may be." The common patrimony, which should be applied for the advantage of the majority of Africa's population, is being completely stripped for the benefit of the few. It seems nothing has changed from the plunder economy of the colonial age. It is sad that Africa's elites have given in to their most selfish instincts.[35]

The assignation of taboos may be regarded as a religious equivalent to the modern scientific identification of biodiversity hotspots, migration corridors, Important Birding Areas (IBAs), or the International Union for the Conservation of Nature (IUCN) catalog of vulnerable and endangered species. In modern conservation strategy, these areas are recognized as warranting extraordinary attention and are set aside for special protection. Members of environmental movements of young African people[36] are more

---

32. Cf. Shorter, "Secularism in Africa."

33. John Paul II, *Ecclesia in Africa*, 40. Here, he is quoting the *relatio ante disceptationem* speech of Cardinal Hyacinthe Thiandoum at the beginning of the so-called First African Synod.

34. John Paul II, *Ecclesia in Africa*, 113.

35. For example, the "Panama Papers" have disclosed how many African politicians, military leaders, and businesspeople are plundering their respective countries. This corruption keeps millions of people in poverty as taxes are unpaid and wealth flows offshore. Cf. Hairsine, "Panama Papers."

36. I have in mind networks like CYNESA, the continent-wide Catholic Youth Network for Environmental Sustainability in Africa, or any number of nonfaith-based organizations.

likely to be persuaded by Western-style scientific reasoning and demonstrations than by taboos. In the interest of safeguarding Africa's natural heritage, the religious and scientific discourses need to coexist, respecting each other as a means of communicating knowledge and concern to their respective participants.

As the ministry of Pope Francis invites us all to mercy and conversion—spiritual, pastoral, and ecological—this first chapter of *Laudato Si'* indicates why an ecological conversion is so necessary. Our world, our common home, is suffering from abuse and human depredations. The superabundant diversity of biological life is being diminished. The climate on which humanity has depended for millennia to support our very existence is changing due to our own human activity. Pollution is making our home unsafe for many poor and vulnerable people. Every one of us is responsible in some small way for the suffering of our planet and, thus, for our fellow creatures. We can all grow in empathy towards our home and our fellow citizens. We should acknowledge and be grateful for the gift of life that we enjoy and try to extend that life to others. This will demand changes in our lifestyles. By reducing our use of fossil fuels, being more careful of our attitude toward waste—both how we create it and dispose of it—and by using fewer animal products, we can all make a difference.

# 3

# The Gospel of New Creation: An African Ecotheological Ethics for Human and Cosmic Flourishing

STAN CHU ILO

## Introduction

What kind of African theology of creation will shed light on the complex challenges of climate change in Africa and the world? This is the task that I wish to undertake in this chapter's commentary on chapter 2 of *Laudato Si'*. The second chapter of *Laudato Si'* affirms a God-centered universe and the interrelatedness of all things as the bases for an integral ecology. While bringing out the main themes of this chapter of *Laudato Si'*, I will show how these themes resonate with African ecospiritual ethics. Just like the two creation accounts of Genesis, African cosmogonies are wisdom traditions which offer some spiritualities and religiocultural traditions of abundant life. Through an appeal to a Trinitarian account of creation and the cries of Africa in the face of the destruction of creation particularly manifested in the rising garbage in African cities, this chapter will develop three ethical practices for respecting and promoting integral ecology for human and cosmic flourishing. These practices are a recovery of a sense of beauty; a renewal of an ecoethics of participation and solidarity; and ecospiritual practices of vulnerability and care.

## This Was Our Home, All That We Had . . .

This is how Vijay Kolinjivadi of the *New Internationalist* captured the Qoshe, Addis Ababa landfill disaster which received very minimal local and international attention:

> Ethiopia is booming, or so they say. Addis Ababa is a rapidly urbanizing city of more than four million people and is the showcase for the modern Ethiopia that the government wants to project. The construction sites around the African Union headquarters, the light rail system (among the first in sub-Saharan Africa), and freshly paved roads provided by Chinese investment in the country represent the changing geography of a city that claims double-digit economic growth and a 30 percent reduction in poverty since 2000. However, as debt-inducing mega infrastructure projects mushroom around the city to project an outward image of development, the basis of human well-being—such as health, education, housing, sanitation, water supply, nutrition, and human rights—remain among the very poorest in the world. But disaster lurks just beneath the country's thin decorative veneer of modernism.
>
> On March 11, 2017, a part of the Qoshe landfill collapsed, burying houses and killing at least 115 people.[1]

Qoshe is a symbol of the contradictions of modernity, progress, and development which many African cities face. It is also a metaphor for the devastation and decay that humans have brought on the environment and, particularly, on the world's poor. Most of the people who live around the Qoshe landfill are poor, and they survive by "treasure hunting" in the landfill. Some of them live in this toxic filth because such an indecent, unsafe, and polluted environment is the only affordable "home" that they can find with their meager resources. As Girma Seifu, a former member of the Ethiopian parliament, said after the landfill's collapse: "The idea that they died buried in dirt, just like they lived in dirt, is heartbreaking."[2] Perhaps, the most heart-wrenching cry was that of Mrs. Hannah who said, while pointing to the stench-filled collapsed dump, "[T]his was our home. We don't know how such a thing could happen. Hopefully, someone can tell us and find a solution for the future."[3]

According to a World Bank Report, *What a Waste 2.0*, 69 percent of Africa's solid waste is dumped in empty land, landfills, and canals. Nearly 20

---

1. Kolinjivadi, "Inside Addis Ababa's Landfill Disaster," paras. 1–2.
2. Ahmed and Fortin, "As Trash Avalanche Toll Rises."
3. Ahmed and Fortin, "As Trash Avalanche Toll Rises."

percent of the world's fifty biggest dumpsites are in Africa. The report shows how solid waste is contributing to climate change globally and in Africa because it is contributing to greenhouse (GHG) emissions and exposing many Africans to serious health risks. The report noted particularly that only 7 percent of Africa's waste is recycled, while the rest is burned. The risks of the burning of waste, improper waste disposal, inadequate waste collection, and inappropriate siting of dumpsites are high. This is because these sites expose whole populations to scavenging or lead exposure and black carbon. The report goes further: "When waste is burned, the resulting toxins and particulate matter in the air can cause respiratory and neurological diseases, among others. Piles of waste produce toxic liquid runoff called leachate, which can drain into rivers, groundwater, and soil. Organic waste entering waterways reduces the amount of oxygen available and promotes the growth of harmful organisms."[4]

Africa continues to suffer from the adverse effects of pollution, environmental decay, depletion of natural resources, dumping of substandard goods, high carbon-emitting secondhand cars, toxic wastes, and toxic processed foods among other pollutants. These death-dealing dumps, and e-wastes, ignore any industrial emissions standard. They expose Africans to those hazardous industrial chemical emissions, which are illegal in Western countries. In Africa's oil-rich countries like Nigeria, they pollute the environment through oil exploration and spillage, as well as gas flaring and fracking, which are no longer acceptable outside Africa.[5]

When I think of a similar site in my home country, Nigeria, the Olusosun dumpsite—the world's largest—in Lagos, on a 100-acre plot of land, I wonder how African leaders have allowed these kinds of sites to exist. The Olusosun dumpsite generates millions of dollars to a few business people by sending recyclable materials to China. It is sustained by the exposure of many young "pickers" to health hazards, potentially leading to their early deaths. According to an exclusive report by the *Washington Post*, the Olusosun dumpsite is seen by the locals as a goldmine because it provides jobs to over 4,000 people. However, for many environmentalists, this site, just like the Qoshe landfill in Ethiopia or the Kiteezi landsite in Kampala, is an unmitigated environmental disaster. According to the report:

---

4. Kaza et al., *What a Waste 2.0*, 76 and 118.

5. For a comprehensive report of the devastating ecological impact of oil exploration in Nigeria, see Human Rights Watch, *Price of Oil*; Singh et al., *Defining an Environmental Strategy for the Niger Delta*; Moffat and Linden, "Perception and Reality"; Jones, *ERA Handbook to the Niger Delta*.

Africa, the fastest-urbanizing continent, is full of cities struggling to balance their extraordinary growth with sustainable waste management. Every year, improper garbage disposal contributes to devastating epidemics of mosquito-borne malaria, yellow fever, and other potentially fatal diseases. This year, Lagos has had two outbreaks of Lassa fever, a sometimes deadly virus, spread by rodent urine or feces, that has been linked to poor sanitation.[6]

When I read of the Lagos State Commissioner for the Environment describing the Olususun dumpsite as "an eye sore;" and of an Ethiopian resident of Qoshe landfill who lost his friend and "all that he had" to the disaster, say that "no one cares about us because we are invisible,"[7] I am challenged to embrace seriously the call of Pope Francis for "ecological conversion" and for a movement away from "an economy that kills."[8] This is the backdrop for this chapter, especially the need to expose the power differentials that create the unjust structural basis for the ecological crisis of our times and the need to develop the systemic and structural changes which are needed for an integral ecology that benefits everybody, and not just a few.

Integral ecology calls us to a return to beauty. According to the Swiss theologian Hans Urs von Balthasar, the crisis of our modern times is the eclipse of beauty.[9] Those famous words of Fyodor Dostoevsky are still very true: "Only beauty can save the world."[10] There is an urgent need to recover this sense of beauty. Considering the pollution in the world and the rising slums and waste dumps in Africa's big cities, as well as the frightening environmental degradation facing the world and the havoc wreaked on our common home by the devastating effects of climate change, I see ugliness and suffering; I do not see beauty and flourishing. The image of a police officer asphyxiating George Floyd was as ugly as it can get. The images of seniors abandoned to die in nursing homes during the COVID-19 pandemic represent an ugly side of a lack of human connectivity and compassion. The images of a starving child and destroyed cities after wars, the stories of the pain of people who are sexually abused, and women suffering abuses and rape, tell me why humanity needs to rediscover beauty, virtues, and the values of compassion, hope, dignity, respect, reverence, and solidarity with the poor who are vulnerable and silently crying out to God in their desolation.

6. van Lohuizen, "Drowning in Garbage."
7. van Lohuizen, "Drowning in Garbage."
8. Francis, *Evangelii Gaudium*, 53 (hereafter cited in text as *EG*).
9. Hans Urs von Balthasar, cited in Thiessen, *Theological Aesthetics*, 321–22.
10. Cited in Scanland, *Dostoevsky*, 147.

It is ugly when falsehood, lies, and injustice are perpetuated in human affairs, especially through politics, businesses, marriages, or in the church.

In a sense, the coronavirus pandemic has exposed our human vulnerability and fragility. COVID-19 has shown that humans are tied together by the same garment of destiny. COVID-19 somehow reflects the calamitous human journey of over a century in a world that has lived on false values and ideas, and on deceptive and destructive notions of human progress and exclusionary practices. How many human lives have been lost in the last century by wars, violence, hunger, diseases, and the destructive economies of scale that kill? In reading *Laudato Si's* "Gospel of Creation," I think of the birth of a new creation, because this present creation is not the best possible world, and a new one in the making is possible if we all embrace the central theological aesthetics of this chapter—humans are in this together, and we can see and be with God by being one with each other and with nature.

In the rest of this chapter, I will first look at the theological aesthetics which form the framework for interpreting chapter 2 of *Laudato Si'*; then I will proceed to unpack the themes of the chapter, develop these themes through an African ecotheological reading, and conclude with proposing three ecoethical practices for a new creation and a new earth.

## The Theological Aesthetics and Trinitarian Foundation of Integral Ecology in *Laudato Si'*

The key to interpreting any aspect of Pope Francis's teaching is his theological aesthetics. When he writes that "everything is, as it were, a caress of God" (*LS* 84), one sees the key to understanding the structure of this theological aesthetics. We are invited into contemplation on how all things are seen in the light of God and how God is seen through all things. The inner word of creation is a gift which gives life to all things. This life is a dynamic force of love and energy which potentiates creation and, within and through creation, initiates the movement of one to another in harmonies of relationships which all enrich life with goodness, beauty, love, and truth. To see God in creation and all things in God is an affirmation of a truth which the Christian religious faith and all faith traditions embrace. It is not a form of panentheism or pantheism. Rather, it is an incarnational thrust inviting us into the sites and places in which we are located in order to ponder the realities of things our eyes could be opened to and a fuller knowledge of the "the precious book" of God that is nature (*LS* 85). God's face is revealed in various manifestations in creation, and we can only grasp this truth of being by seeing our place in the universe and how all things are related. This contemplative attitude will lead to a recovery of beauty, the unity of being, and the cultivation of the ecological virtues needed to address the ecological crisis of our times (*LS* 88).

Theological aesthetics begins with seeing the beauty of God in the created world, and encountering God in the loving embrace of God's creatures. Pope Francis's writings are filled with instances of where and how God is to be found. This is particularly evident in his constant emphasis on a culture of encounter—that is, this insistence that people need to be in touch with reality in its concreteness as a beginning of a deeper encounter with God (*EG*, 167). Pope Francis often uses phrases like "gaze upon," "openness of heart," "spiritual encounter," "the art of listening," "contemplation with wonder" (*EG*, 170–71; *LS* 238), and the "gaze of Christ" (*LS* 96) in inviting people to appreciate the different forms of beauty in their lives, in the lives of others, and in the world of nature.[11] For Pope Francis, the culture of encounter with nature and with others becomes the starting point of ecological consciousness, just as it is for all people the beginning of authentic humanity and a rich inter-subjective communion with the *other*.

The culture of encounter opens up a sense of mystery which moves people to appreciate beauty even in the complexities of life. Through contemplation of nature, one can grasp a deeper level of truth in the sublimity of being and all things. As Pope Francis rightly proposes, modern society should be wary of the new forms of Gnosticism, which, by its nature "seeks to domesticate the mysteries—God, nature, people, and others."[12] Theological aesthetics invites people to embrace the path of mystery as they behold the works of God in creation, to regain a sense of awe and sacredness of the earth as our common home, and to be open to the surprises and beauty in all things. The sense of wonder and sacredness imbued in nature is the greatest inspiration against the spirit of pride or domination that have often clouded human relationships with one another and creation.

## A Trinitarian Structure as Form for Integral Ecology

Two seminal principles emerge from *Laudato Si'*, which I propose are central to building both an ecotheology and an ecoethics to mitigate and adapt to the current ecological crisis. In an African ecotheological ethics and social context, these principles serve as hermeneutical keys for the theological aesthetics of nature and the gospel of creation as articulated in chapter 2 of *Laudato Si'*.

11. Ilo, *Poor and Merciful Church*, 201.
12. Francis, *Gaudete et Exsultate*, 20 (hereafter cited in text as *GE*).

The first principle is an ecotheology built on the relationality and interconnectedness of creation modeled by God, who is revealed in history as a Trinity. The second is an ecoethics for integral ecology through daily choices that promote and respect the connectedness and participation of all things in the bond of life. This connection is often ruptured by sin, understood in this chapter as human ideologies, mentalities, choices, and cultural systems and patterns that are opposed to God's will for creation, and thus undermine human and cosmic flourishing. In a general way, this teaching of *Laudato Si'* finds strong resonance in an African theology of participation, or *Ubuntu*. The African understanding of abundant life as human and cosmic flourishing offers a foundation for an integral ecology that I will employ in the second part of this chapter. While I cannot, in a short essay of this kind, fully develop this link between the central message of *Laudato Si'* and the African notion of abundant life, I hope to deepen this linkage in a systematic way. I will identify key theological principles for a global ecological ethics gleaned from a dialogue between *Laudato Si'* and an African ecospirituality of participation, within the larger context of God's centrality in the rhythm and life of creation.

In calling humanity to embrace beauty, Pope Francis unifies the insights from both the Eastern Orthodox tradition and the West in recognizing where God is present in history. Ecumenical Patriarch Bartholomew shows how this notion of beauty and creation emerged in the history of Orthodox theology and spirituality. He points out that, as early as the third century, Anthony of Egypt, the father of monasticism, had described nature as a book that teaches us about God's creation. And he notes that Saint Maximus the Confessor speaks of the sacramental dimension of creation and that the whole world is a "cosmic liturgy."[13]

Orthodox Christians thus affirm "a theological and liturgical vision of the world": "Creation is a sacred book, whose letters and syllables are the universal aspects of creation, just as scripture is a beautiful world, which is constituted of heaven and earth and all that lies in between."[14] Inviting people to allow themselves to be enraptured and encounter God in nature, Pope Francis writes in *Gaudete et Exsultate* that "God infinitely transcends us; he is full of surprises. We are not the ones to determine when and how we will encounter him; the exact times and places of that encounter are not up to us. Someone who wants everything to be clear and sure presumes to control God's transcendence" (*GE*, 41). Pope Francis's *LS* contains many

---

13. Chryssavgis, *On Earth as in Heaven*, 128.
14. Chryssavgis, *On Earth as in Heaven*, 128.

indications of this theological aesthetics of creation, but we will draw out three aspects of this aesthetics within a Trinitarian narrative of creation.

## God as Creator

The central Christian affirmation, which is the first article in the profession of faith, is that God is the Creator of all things. Creation is not a necessity on the part of God. As Pope Francis teaches (*LS* 77), creation did not emerge as a result of "arbitrary omnipotence, a show of force, or a desire for self-assertion." The earth, our common home, is the result of God's free act of love to bring creation into being. Pope Francis underlines this theistic origin by highlighting God's action in nature: "Every creature is thus the object of the Father's tenderness, who gives it its place in the world. Even the fleeting life of the least of beings is the object of his love, and in its few seconds of existence, God enfolds it with his affection. Saint Basil the Great described the Creator as "goodness without measure" (*LS* 77). Pope Francis further elaborates: "In the Bible, the God who liberates and saves is the same God who created the universe, and these two divine ways of acting are intimately and inseparably connected" (*LS* 73). But this God who is creator is also a community of persons as a Trinity whose being is prior to creation. *Laudato Si'* makes a clear distinction between creation and nature, a distinction which is very important in order to move away from any form of immanentism in which the infinite transcendence of God is narrowed to the created order. God as the One, True, Good, and Beautiful Source of all things always offers us more, and God is always more in power and agency. Nature, according to *LS* 76, is "a system which can be studied, understood, and controlled."

Here, Pope Francis maintains the Catholic position which goes back to the Aristotelian-Thomistic notion of science and nature. This is not unexpected given the fact that he begins chapter 2 with an affirmation that his teaching on the gospel of creation is an invitation to "intense dialogue" (*LS* 62) between science and religion that "no branch of sciences and no form of wisdom can be left out including religion and the language particular to it," which is the language of faith (*LS* 63). As a system that can be studied, understood, and controlled, nature is scientific. Science, in the Aristotelian sense, is the knowledge of things through their first principles or causality. So, a scientific knowledge always involves knowing the origin of matter, for instance, and how it operates or interacts with other realities in realizing the proper end for which it exists. To give another example, having a scientific understanding of the human person will mean knowing the origin and destiny of the human person, who we are, what we are doing here on earth, and the things or realities that sustain and shape humanity's ultimate future.

Human scientists exercise their intellect by seeking the origin and causes of things, their relationship with other things, and their proper ends or their utility. For instance, in discovering the truth, origin, purpose, and principles of matter, scientists are thus cocreators with God in fostering beauty, purpose, and order within creation, all of which are conducive to human and cosmic flourishing. In an African sense, scientific knowledge in this related account seeks to understand the rhythm of things by understanding the vital principle within nature and respecting the right order of relationships and mutual participation in each other's lives in order to sustain and promote those life bonds which make for an abundant life. In this hermeneutic, the false application or abuse of created things for a means that produces an unwholesome end for creation is considered destructive and harmful and, in Christian terms, sinful and unethical.

Creation, unlike nature, invites us into the realm of mystery. In the teaching of Pope Francis, creation can only be understood "as a gift from the outstretched hand of the Father of all, and as a reality illuminated by the love which calls us together into universal communion" (*LS* 76). Viewed in this light, our interaction with nature must be governed by the same sense of care, gentleness, contemplation, and compassion with which God the creator made all things (*LS* 77). The order in nature is specified by love, and the human encounter with nature in creation should not be driven by the myth of material progress (*LS* 78) or of domination and subjugation of nature in a way that undermines countless forms of relationships and the participation (*LS* 78) of all things in an evolving order of creation (*LS* 79).

The affirmation of a Creator who is all-powerful calls humanity to humility, the lack of which often has led human beings to treat nature simply as a disposable material, subject to our whims and caprices as if we have an "unlimited right" to trample on creation (*LS* 75). Rather, human beings are invited to treat nature and creation as God does—with love and respect. This is patterned after God, who is all-powerful and almighty and yet bends down to creation, as we see in the second creation narrative (Gen 2:5—3:25) where God enters into the world of nature and mingles with humans and all things in an immanent and respectful manner.

Pope Francis also deconstructs the image of God which has, in some biblical exegeses, given rise to the "dominion theology" of stewardship that created the kind of anthropological imaginary of human beings as occupiers and conquerors of creation. If our human knowledge of creation is limited to that of nature lying there to be exploited, trampled, and dumped on, we will continue to live and act like bulls in a china shop. If, however, we humans see all things as creation with a divine caress, then we will not divinize creation or apotheosize and exaggerate our human stewardship (*LS* 90). The image of God presented in *Laudato Si'* as Creator of all things is relatable and corrects some images of God that are still predominant in some Christian teaching and can be found in some of the other Abrahamic faiths.

The challenge for Christianity—and indeed, all religions—has always been to present an adequate and relatable image of God which can govern ethics, spirituality, morality, politics, ecology, and eschatology. The quest here is to discover and encounter an image of God that could help us account for human nature and human destiny, as well as discover the pathway for realizing the mission of God in human and cosmic life. This image also specifies how we view nature and reality in general. Unfortunately, the image of the Trinity, which was developed in some versions of divine immanence, painted a false picture of a divine celestial being who is remote from creation and from people, showing only the influence of various dimensions and qualities of some of the Greek pantheon—those gods who were angry, feuding, vengeful, and punishing, for example. In some other cases, Christians influenced by particular cultures embraced images of a divine power or force which Richard Rohr calls an "abstruse conundrum," a "divine threatener," "a static and imperial image," "a Monarchical pyramid," "a critical spectator," and a Supreme being who is remote from history.[15] Rohr, therefore, proposes a Trinitarian Revolution as a spiritual paradigm shift which could make people appreciate how God is present in history in such a way that

> every vital impulse, every force toward the future, every creative momentum, every loving surge, every dash toward beauty, every running toward truth, every ecstasy before simple goodness, every leap of *élan vital*, as the French would say, every bit of ambition for humanity and the earth, for wholeness and holiness, is the eternally, flowing life of the Trinitarian God.[16]

There are also some currents which tended to deny the "otherness" of God and sometimes made God indistinguishable from creation. Pope Francis, however, presents a Trinitarian image which emphasizes dynamism, interconnection, and relationality: "The Father is the ultimate source of everything, the loving and self-communicating foundation of all that exists. The Son, his reflection, through whom all things were created, united himself to this earth when he was formed in the womb of Mary. The Spirit,

---

15. Rohr and Morrell, *Divine Dance*, 36–37.
16. Rohr and Morrell, *Divine Dance*, 37–38.

infinite bond of love, is intimately present at the very heart of the universe, inspiring and bringing new pathways" (LS 238).

In this Trinitarian image, we see some important truths necessary for reading the book of creation and human place in creation: (i) God is Trinitarian and has left God's mark on all creation; (ii) the world was created by three divine persons acting as a single divine principle, united in an intimate relationship of love; (iii) each creature bears in itself a specific Trinitarian structure; (iv) the Trinitarian relationship in which the three persons are so united in action and essence forms the model of the mutual relationship and solidarity which should exist in the created world (LS 239–40). Integral ecology is a reflection of the integral harmony and union between God the Father, the Son, and the Holy Spirit. The relationship between the three divine persons is characterized by love, friendship, respect, mutual relationship, indwelling, solidarity, reciprocity, collaboration, partnership, service, generosity, compassion, and relationality that is governed by recognition, diversity of means, multiplicity of action, unity of essence, and self-donation.

The Christian faith affirms that creation was born as a result of this kind of relationship, which in theological language is called *perichoresis*: an intimate and intricate web of relationships that are inseparable and indistinguishable. Creation, being the gift from God and bearing God's imprint and nature, receives and manifests these Trinitarian qualities. Harmony in creation is a gift that is intrinsic to it. It is not a gift that humans confer on creation, but rather a value which humans must recognize in creation. In doing this, we honor God and enjoy, in our own way, the fruits of this reality: human and cosmic flourishing.

## Theological Aesthetics of Relationality as the Basis for Integral Ecology

The second aspect of this theological aesthetics in chapter 2 of *Laudato Si'* is relationship. According to Sean McDonagh, "in many ways *Laudato Si'* is an attempt to redefine the relationship between humans and the rest of creation, so that we can soon reach a point where the basic needs of all humans will be met in a way that does not endanger the rest of creation or irreversibly damage it."[17] Relationality, in my judgment, is the hermeneutical key for understanding Pope Francis's vision of integral theology in *Laudato Si'*. This relationality is grounded on a theological aesthetics of seeing all things in God and seeing God through all things. In chapter 2 of *Laudato Si'*, Pope

17. McDonagh, *On Care for Our Common Home*, 16.

Francis uses the word *relationship* twenty times to reflect different degrees of interconnection between all things; this interconnection can be grouped into five themes:

(i) The first is the affirmation of the three fundamental relationships of human beings with God, with their neighbors, and with nature (*LS* 66).

(ii) Second is the proposal that Pope Francis makes in which he affirms that these three fundamental relationships should be harmoniously governed by care, humility, solidarity, mutuality of responsibility, caring, overseeing, preserving, and all the attributes which we find in God, who models creation after his exemplary nature (*LS* 67).

(iii) Third is the recognition of what Pope Francis calls "three vital relationships" (*LS* 66) which have become fractured and ruined. What emerges today is "a ruptured relationship" (*LS* 70), and a "conflictual relationship" (*LS* 76) rather than "a relationship of mutual responsibility between humans and nature" (*LS* 67). This rupture has occurred because human beings disregard their duty to each other, to God, and to the environment. We have failed to be guardians of one another and of creation by failing to care for the sick, the poor, and the vulnerable of the earth (*LS* 48).

(iv) Pope Francis proposes that, when these relationships are governed by sound ethical principles and spiritual practices of care, compassion, tenderness, and solidarity, they give birth to harmony and peace in creation, as well as fraternity, justice, and faithfulness to others (*LS* 70). However, when they are disfigured by sin and the violation of the law of nature, life itself is endangered.

(v) *Laudato Si'* invites humanity back to "respect the laws of nature and the deliberate equilibria existing between the creatures of this world" (*LS* 68). In order to understand and respect this harmonious relationship, there is a need for human beings to understand our place in creation and respect the fact that "in this universe, shaped by open and intercommunicating systems, we can discern countless forms of relationship and participation. This leads us to think of the whole as open to God's transcendence, within which it develops. Faith allows us to interpret the meaning and the mysterious beauty of what is unfolding" (*LS* 79).

The nature of this relationship—God-humans-nature—is such that God is personally involved in the "emergence of a personal being within a material world" (*LS* 81). Creation, Pope Francis teaches, is not the result of "pure chance" (*LS* 66) but is the result of God's creative act conveyed in symbolic ways through the wisdom of the Creation stories in Genesis. God does not dominate humans or the earth through some form of arbitrariness, but rather God's relationship with creation is built on freedom and respect and demands the affirmation of the "otherness" of humans as well as nature. This respect for human subjectivity and freedom on the part of God invites human beings not to dominate nature and obligates humans to respect and affirm nature and creation's integrity. In some African cultures and eco-traditions, nature is said to have an eye, meaning it can perceive and see. In this light, one can aver that people can come to a new level of understanding of integral ecology and relationships in creation through a greater dialogue with each other and dialogue with nature (*LS* 62–63; 67–68).

This new understanding based on embracing the gospel of creation will bring about greater respect for the laws of nature imbued in creation, so that all other creatures can move forward with humans towards God. God is the common point of arrival in the ultimate ordination of all things to God (*LS* 83)—a relationship which always bears within it a transcendent dimension (*LS* 119). Solidarity with nature's fragility and the recognition of human fragility through an ethics of care become a necessary response to healing the broken interrelationship in creation between human beings and nature, and among human beings themselves (*LS* 86).

## The Gospel of Creation as an Invitation to Solidarity

The third aspect of this theological aesthetics in chapter 2 of *Laudato Si'* is solidarity. An adequate theological aesthetics should lead to solidarity. Pope Francis refers twice to the basis for solidarity in two sentences: "Everything is connected" (*LS* 91) and, later, "Everything is related" (*LS* 92). It is this connected and related bond which unites humans as one family and also unites humans and nature as one family, sharing one home. This sense of bondedness should lead people to act with tenderness, compassion, and concern toward one another, and especially directed to those "mired in desperate and degrading poverty" (*LS* 90). It should move people to fight for the rights and dignity of every person, including the right to labor, land, and lodging, and it should move people to fight as well for the rights of animals. It is this connection of all things in creation which is the basis of integral ecology.

Integral ecology takes into account all aspects of the created order. It offers a total-picture approach to looking at the movement of history and the choices people make relative to the ordination of all things to their proper end. Seen in this light, integral ecology is also an invitation to intersectional discourse, because Pope Francis is calling humanity to see the ruptures in our human relationships, which are the result of social hierarchies and exclusionary practices. Violating the earth through what he calls "tyrannical anthropocentrism" (*LS* 68) and arbitrary human domination (*LS* 82) is a form of violence and abuse of power wherein the human who claims superiority over nature disposes of and abuses nature without any sense of moral rectitude or restraint.

The same analysis of power can apply to all forms of social evils that humanity faces in the world today, including the global health inequality that the poor experienced during the height of the COVID-19 pandemic, racism, sexism, homophobia, religious bigotry, nativism, nationalism, and gender violence. Integral ecology offers the intersectional key for understanding the movement of history. We cannot separate respect and reverence for the environment from reverence and respect for cultural differences and the social, moral, economic, and religious dimensions of human lives vis-à-vis the life of nature and the environment. Every ethical choice we make that hampers or harnesses the environment or humanity has implications for all other relationships, intersections, and interconnections in life. Integral ecology looks at the present crisis of climate change and other related problems in the world through "a broader vision of reality" (*LS* 138) in order to identify and heal the human moral failings which have created such disconnection in reality and brought death and destruction to the earth and humans (*LS* 220).

As a final remark in this section, however, it must be noted that the idea of integral ecology is not new. Perhaps there is a new awareness of integral ecology that has been brought into sharper focus, due to the fact that Western modernity and technologism have steered creation onto the wrong path. However, integral ecology might be new in the language of the church and Western societies, but it is not new in the African world or in the Mayan world of the ancient kingdom of the peoples of Mexico and Central America. The Mayans have a saying, *Lak'ech Ala K'in*, which means, "If I do harm to you, I do harm to myself; if I love and respect you, I love and respect myself." The Mayans possess a wisdom that says "I am another you," and this is the basis of the relationship with everyone and with creation in general. So, in this way of thinking, nature and the entire cosmos and every human being has something of *me*, and I am not complete except when I am united in a healthy way with *you*.[18]

---

18. See Gallardon and Kingdon, "Applying Latina/o Psychology," 93–98.

### African Re-Presentation of the Message of Chapter 2 on Relationship

There are three points of conversation between the message of *LS* chapter 2 and African ecotheology. The first is the striking resonance between the message of relationality and the African notions of relationship as vital principle and mutual participation. The second relates to the three propositions in the chapter which reflect some limitations of Catholic social teaching and its foundation in natural law. And third are some concluding ethical principles which can be developed when chapter 2's message is enriched with some wisdom traditions from Africa vis-à-vis Africa's own vulnerabilities.

In *LS* chapter 2, at the end of his analysis of the two creation stories of Genesis, Pope Francis writes as follows regarding the wisdom of these cosmogonies: "These ancient stories, full of symbolism, bear witness to a conviction which we today share, that everything is interconnected, and that genuine care for our own lives and our relationships with nature is inseparable from fraternity, justice, and faithfulness to others" (*LS* 70). Elsewhere in *Laudato Si'*, Pope Francis highlights the values and wisdom of indigenous knowledge and cultural ecological knowledge (*LS* 143–46). Africans have many cosmogonic myths—like that of the Creator god *Unumbotte* among the Basari of northern Togo and northern Ghana—which are very similar to the biblical accounts insofar as the consumption of forbidden fruits.[19] Loreen Maseno proposes that the wisdom traditions in African myths of creation offer significant, deep insight into African ecospirituality and ecoethics. She argues that African wisdom traditions offer frameworks which can be reinterpreted and appropriated to uphold "the wholeness and health of the planet earth."[20]

Jacob Olupona proposes that these cosmogonies offer "an indigenous hermeneutics" for understanding the African worldview on ecology, spirituality, nature, proper relationships, and vital participation for human and cosmic flourishing.[21] Ernst Conradie argues that African cosmogonies also emphasize the aspect of vital participation as the dynamics of this relatedness when he writes:

> There is a sense of wonder at the fecundity of life, for the land, and all the creatures that live from it, for the cycles of the seasons. There is an almost overwhelming emphasis on notions of interrelatedness, mutual dependence, reciprocity, ecological

---

19. Olupona, *African Religions*, 11.
20. Maseno, "Towards an African Inculturated Sophiology," 136.
21. Ilo, "Fragile Earth, Fragile Africa," 131.

balance, wholeness, the integrated web of life, and, especially, community. The world exists as an intricate balance of parts. Human beings must recognize and strive to maintain this cosmic balance. Everything, from hunting to healing, is a recognition of affirmation of the sacredness of life.[22]

One can appreciate the richness of this ecological spirituality and morality through the African *Ubuntu*: the spirituality and ethics of connectedness of all things in a bond of life. Teddy Sakupapa's work on the different understandings of *Ubuntu* across different African countries brings out important dimensions of this notion among many African peoples, including *umunthu*, among the Chewa people of Zambia; *obuntu*, among the Ganda of Uganda; *obunu*, among the Jita of Tanzania; and *unhu*, among the Shona of Zimbabwe.[23]

According to Sakupapa, *Ubuntu* has been used in African discourse in three ways—as a signifier of a quality of being human (that is, a form of ethical theory on how to be human); as a notion of relational cosmology (a form of social ethics of being-with—that is, intersubjective relations among humans as well as the mutual relations between all creatures); and as an African communitarian philosophy of how to participate in the bond of life. This is well captured in John Mbiti's articulation of the notion: "I am because we are; and since we are, therefore, I am."[24] This "we" does not simply refer to humans alone but to all creation in its relatedness.

Sakupapa proposes that, in all three of these different meanings and in the task of developing an African ecclesiology, what is consistent in the application or appropriation of *Ubuntu* is the primacy of community, communion, and interrelatedness. I also apply these three meanings in what follows in this section of the essay.

*Ubuntu* is ideal. It may never have been realized in any African setting in the past, but it is a spiritual vision and a common dream rooted in African culture, social relations, and ecological consciousness. It specifies the kind of theological principles and concrete ethical choices African communities desire through the promotion of vital participation and vital force in strengthening the bond of life among all creatures. It is also a vision and a dream at the heart of African culture of how to promote and preserve this bond of life for sustainable human and cosmic wholeness. Thus, *Ubuntu* is projected here to be the basis for a life-centered and God-centered ethics that enhances human and cosmic flourishing.

22. Conradie, "Approaches to Religion," 440.
23. Sakupapa, "Ecumenical Ecclesiology," 8.
24. Sakupapa, "Ecumenical Ecclesiology," 8.

*Ubuntu* highlights the concrete dimensions of sound ethical choices that people need to make in their relationships with God, others, and nature. These ethical choices promote mutual participation of all creatures in the bond of life in order to bring about human and cosmic flourishing. Thus, emphasis is placed on this African notion of good acts, ethical choices which promote the life of all creatures of God. At the same time, those acts which injure people or harm the earth and nature are to be considered evil, because they diminish vital force and abundant life.[25]

*Ubuntu* is thus Africa's moral tradition of cosmic *koinonia*; the ethics which affirms the sacredness and sublime integrity of the earth and all creatures. It can be seen, then, as a form of cosmic liturgy, because the practice of *Ubuntu* generates a vital bond of peace and harmony in creation when all things relate in a healthy and wholesome manner. Such harmony and peace emerge when there is a just and respectful order maintained through the recognition of the beauty and value of all creatures. It is sustained by a conscious and deliberate effort on the part of human beings to heal the earth of exploitation, evil, injustice, poverty, violence, and suffering and all that diminish life and bring death and decay. *Ubuntu* offers a fitting ethical motif for re-presenting the centrality of relationality as the basis of integral ecology in *Laudato Si'* in Africa in many ways.

*First*, it reveals a world in which human and nonhuman forms of life have a sacramental and mutual relationship that is mimetic of the divine. As Pope Francis highlights in many places (*LS* 21, 69, 82, 164), the earth is our planetary homeland; humanity shares an interconnected homeland with all creation. In Africa, every member of the created world is regarded as having life. Here, life is not understood as simply sensitive, vegetative, or intellectual existence (as, for instance, we can relate to with regard to humans, animals, plants—each in its own way). *Life is seen as a force, a causative spiritual dynamic which inhabits creation in general and is translated and transmitted through every reality in such a way that sickness is seen not as something that resides in the body but as a reflection of imbalances in the multiple chains of relationships in the community.*[26]

African traditional ecospirituality and morality agree with the teaching of *Laudato Si'* on the intrinsic value of all things (*LS* 9) and the order in nature defined by laws and harmony (*LS* 75; 84). In many African cosmogonies, human activity is governed by certain natural laws and a certain order and cycle, all of which work together for the good of all creation, of which the human is only a very tiny, though important, member. The human must

---

25. Sakupapa, "Ecumenical Ecclesiology," 8.
26. Olupona, *African Religions*, 3.

respect and reverence creation's natural cycle in order to survive here on earth and maintain the sustainable evolution of the cycle of creation for future generations. At a deeper level of cultural understanding, African myths of origin reveal that, in this infinite majesty of creation, humans arrived later into an infinite and sacred universe. This understanding rejects any form of what Pope Francis calls "excessive anthropocentrism" that arises from currents of modernity (LS 116). These currents of modernity have often been promoted by an inadequate Christian anthropocentric understanding of stewardship as lordship. The renewal of nature will lead to the renewal of humanity (LS 118), just as human acts of violence against and neglect of nature lead to violence against and neglect of the poor by fellow human beings (LS 119).[27]

## The Gospel of a New Creation

Perhaps the title of chapter 2 of *Laudato Si'* should have been "The Gospel of a New Creation," because when I look at this present creation, I think that it is a dying creation from which a new creation can be born. As a result, the vision of integral ecology should be framed as the conditions for a new earth and a new heaven. This is why it is important to highlight two important propositions in the chapter which could be enriched through an African representation.

The first is that some of the chapter's proposals present a problematic idea of creation, sin, and restoration in its account of history (LS 80). While the chapter affirms the traditional Catholic teaching on the autonomy and instrumental nature of earthly realities and the common destination of earthly goods (LS 93–95), the notion of history is still embedded in a Greco-Judeo account of progressive history. The account we find in the analysis of the two cosmogonies of creation in Genesis proceeds in a triadic movement. First, a good creation is formed and given to humans by the Creator; then the rupture in creation occurs as a result of human sins, and then God comes in the person of God's Son to save the world and bring harmony to creation (LS 82).

There is also a second limitation that can be identified in the chapter's account of creation, which has to do with an insufficient christological and pneumatological account of the new creation. I will concentrate on the christological limitations, especially the absence of a theology of the cross. *Laudato Si'* teaches that, "in the Christian understanding of the world, the

---

27. See a more detailed discussion of these five dimensions of African ecological consciousness and ethics in Ilo, "Fragile Earth, Fragile Africa," 134–36.

destiny of all creation is bound up with the mystery of Christ, present from the beginning" (*LS* 99). Some citations in the encyclical are taken from the Pauline corpus, which shows that the One Person of the Trinity (*LS* 99) who entered the cosmos and who threw his lot even to the point of death on the cross is present from the beginning of creation. *LS* rightly shows the sacrificial nature of the death of Christ and how Saint Paul rightly makes a link between the cross and redemption of creation; however, how the cross plays a decisive role in birthing a new creation is not identified, rather it is passed over in silence. How the Spirit is present in the beginning and continues to be at work is also not given sufficient treatment in the development of the Pauline corpus in *LS*. This One Person is also the Risen One who is "mysteriously holding" all creatures to himself and directing them to the fullness proper to their end. As a result, creatures are not to be seen as natural guises but as beings with the "radiant presence" of the Risen One to be contemplated and admired. In this, the theological aesthetics of the chapter come to full circle (*LS* 100) without a cruciformic or pneumatological account of the new creation.

The weakness of this argument is that it is *telling* rather than *showing*. It makes general claims about Christ but does not show how Christ is actually present with the Spirit—in the struggles of humanity, for instance, or the limitations of the entirety of creation, suffering in and along with it. It doesn't show how the moral and ethical dilemma of humans in their relationship with creation can be resolved or how to bridge the distance and dualism projected in the text between what is divine and what is human. While there is a strong rejection of dualism, which *LS* 98 describes as "unhealthy," the christological account does not help us to see how this new creation is emerging. Nor does it help to resolve the progressive and evolutionary deterministic account of history, the notions about heaven and earth which create such dualism. We still find traces of this progressive evolutionary account of history in *Laudato Si'* as it struggles to chart a new course in Catholic social teaching, away from the stranglehold of modernism and previous papal teachings' notions of progress and development (*LS* 81).

Because *Laudato Si'* projects an inevitable movement to an end of time when the Risen Lord will "deliver all things to the Father" (*LS* 100),[28] there is also the danger of a christological reductionism here which limits an interfaith dialogue. This eschatological thrust can be re-presented through an African ecotheology that can overcome this dualism and answer questions

---

28. See my discussion of the development of Catholic theological ecological ethics and natural law and order in nature in Ilo, *Church and Development in Africa*, 96–100.

as to how the Risen Lord participates in the bond of life, how the cross is a model and source of the ancestral life force, which can strengthen what *Laudato Si'* calls "the unseen bonds" in creation (*LS* 89).

## The Gospel of New Creation through an *Ubuntu* Reading of What Jesus Did on the Cross

My proposal is that it is possible to apply the African communal ethics of *Ubuntu* as *a theological grammar,* which offers a good ethical framework for a *theology of creation.* In this expanded reading, creation is a vast and continuing story, in which our human choices that define individual and collective stories in our cultures, systems, institutions, and corporate affairs are all intertwined in shaping our collective destiny. Thus, our daily choices must be inserted into the larger and continuing story of the world in order to see clearly how those choices are good or bad, relative to how they enrich or impoverish the human and cosmic story in its inner enrichment and external thrust towards God, the source and telos of human and cosmic flourishing. History, in this sense, is not a movement towards an ultimate point but a dynamic web of life stretching into God's infinite horizons and boundless recreating, sanctifying, and saving love in which all creations—past, present, and future—are intimately tied in a common story that is always in the making. This web of life is redemptive, not because of a prior condition of chaos or decay, but because of the presence of the creative, saving, and energizing love of God, which has been lived as an unmerited gift by our human ancestors, and for whom Christ as Proto-Ancestor is the exemplar par excellence.

In this kind of reading, there are no cyclic movements of sin, punishment, and redemption. Rather, what is important is a new consciousness of our common responsibility for this earth and everything in it as well as our reverence for the work that God does in creation and beyond creation. We need only to embrace this work of God with sacred awe, conscious of human finitude and temporality and God's infinite horizon beyond space and time. Individual responsibility is also collective responsibility writ large. This does not deny individual autonomy but rather specifies the end proper to it. This is because *Ubuntu* affirms that the choices of individuals are ethical to the extent to which they bring about abundant life for the wider community. Sound ethical choices are those that strengthen the bond of life, opening wider the possibility of participation in the common good for everyone so that all creation can flourish and share in the good things of life. *Ubuntu* orients human actions to solidarity, community, collaboration, and cooperation in strengthening the web of life and creating better possibilities for the realization of the common good for all. Having this kind of spirit is a choice which people make from the perspective of a communal and global consciousness, rather than out of fear of divine punishment.

Viewed in this light, when we stand at the foot of the cross and gaze upon the poor man of Galilee, we see the expression of the communal *Ubuntu* at its highest level. This is why the most significant title in Africa for Christ is the "African Ancestor of Humanity." Why? Because he is a perfect exemplar of the ethics of *Ubuntu*; his death, as interpreted by Christians, enhanced the possibilities for human and cosmic flourishing. His life blood is a vital circuit in the value chain enacted in history by all those who, like him, live beyond themselves and, thus, fructify the earth by ethical choices that strengthen our human and cosmic participation in the life of one another and nature. At the foot of cross, we see the design of a life—or, rather, a love—that is the divine-human life so totally poured out that nothing remains unused or unrealized, but all is given. This is not a *kenosis*, really, for what is given does not belong to the individual. *Ubuntu* shows that because I belong to the community, and the community shaped me, what I give to others is simply my sharing with others what I have received from the community. So, in giving I am increasing my own vital force, and enriching the same common vital source that enriches my life and the life of the earth, our common home.

The manner of giving specifies in itself the proper manner of receiving—this embodiment in creation of a divine-human talent in the Crucified Son's treasured life is offered as a path for a new creation to the extent that this life is received and relived in time by humans. This life, which is given away totally on the cross, is the fructification of this treasure. In humans who follow this exemplar act, it potentiates the grace—resilience—of giving themselves fully to God, and to one another, as a way of realizing the end proper to each person's treasure or talent for increasing the vital force of our common home.

In the garden of Eden, Adam and Eve violated the spirit of *Ubuntu* and lost the harmony in creation. An African ecotheology metaphorizes the curse imposed on our first parents and the punishment of the flood as a way of capturing the chaos brought to the human and cosmic harmony when we refuse to live for and with others. In its orientation to relationality, African ontology always moves away from the dualism of curse and blessing, earth and heaven, human and cosmos. On the contrary, the garden of Eden is a loss of what ought to be there—that is, a world characterized by justice, beauty, peace, and abundant life. On Calvary, the Son replicates, renews, and recreates humanity and a cosmic emergence. His cross models the way to realize this treasure of the divine-human life which can bring to birth in creation a new life and a new ethical model for giving totally all that one has received. Through this total giving, his cross also models how to bring creation into a new space for the fecundity which comes from participation in the gift of another.

When we listen to our stories and allow ourselves to be touched by other people's stories, and when we ourselves share our own stories with others, we find that all our stories help us to understand our connection and that we all are facing similar situations and circumstances. In the story of everyone, in the stories of the cries of the earth and the cries of the poor, I can hear and see my own story. It is only by paying attention to how our human and cosmic stories are connected that we can see how our stories can be redeemed by God's love and our love for everyone. In this way, we also see how that unconditional manifestation of love on the cross—through the pain, suffering, and death of the poor man of Galilee—becomes a unique exemplarity of what happens in every good and life-giving choice that we make.

Calvary shows what can happen when the closed narrative of humanly designed unjust structures and institutions are exhausted when a good steward of our collective patrimony breaks the cycle of decay. Calvary shows how the resilience, sacrifice, and commitment to our common good in a common home, even to the point of death, becomes a boundary between good and evil and the limit beyond which evil cannot go. It is what happens when the treasure of one life becomes the treasures of all lives—or, to put it in the words of Pope Francis, this is what it takes for one person to restore hope (*LS* 71).

## Cry of Africa, Cry of Creation

On his plane returning to Rome after his 2015 visit to Africa, Pope Francis gave a press conference where he decried the social injustices that Africa suffers, including malnutrition, exploitation, slave labor, and death from poor sanitation, and the lack of drinking water, food, or housing. He pointed out that these social injustices are "a big wound" for Africans, along with environmental injustices, which he referred to as a form of "suicide." As a result of social injustice, greed, and the arms trade, Africa faces what he called "tragic maladies provoked by man." He concluded his press conference with these moving words and this diagnosis of African and global injustice: "Africa is a victim. Africa has always been exploited by other powers. From Africa, people came to America, sold as slaves. There are powers who seek only to take the great wealth of Africa, which is perhaps the richest continent."[29] Sean McDonagh agrees with this assessment of the cry of Africa when he writes,

> Pope Francis is aware that the poor suffer most from environmental damage. Africa, for example, has done least to cause climate change through the emission for greenhouse gasses, and yet it suffers most in terms of the impact of extreme weather on the environment and on people. Severe weather does enormous damage to crops in African countries where population levels are rising dramatically.[30]

Let us go back to the stories of the two dumpsites with which I began this chapter; I would like to relate them to the oil pollution that is destroying the lives, environment, and livelihood of millions of people in the oil-rich Niger Delta region of Nigeria. While we do not have the space to explore in detail this painful and calamitous situation, the words of one of the prominent advocates for the region's rights capture the full extent of the devastation and the same lament of the residents of Qoshe and Olusosun. Lamenting the oil exploration in the Niger Delta, Chief Leton, an Ogoni[31] royal, says

> We have woken up to find our lands devastated by agents of death called oil companies. Our atmosphere has been totally polluted, our lands degraded, our waters contaminated, our trees poisoned, so much so that our flora and fauna have virtually disappeared. We are asking for the restoration of our environment; we are asking for the basic necessities of life—water, electricity, education—but above all, we are asking for the right to self-determination so that we can be responsible for our resources and our environment.[32]

The ugly face of environmental pollution in the oil exploration occurring in Nigeria and the countless pipeline explosions and continuous gas flares that have killed thousands of human and aquatic lives illustrate how our common home is being destroyed through an unethical and unjust exploitation of the poor. Here, one sees the absence of the *Ubuntu* spirit.

---

29. Francis, "Meeting with the Muslim Community"; see also Francis, *Laudato Si'*, 48.

30. McDonagh, *On Care for Our Common Home*, 18.

31. The Ogoni people are one of the minority indigenous peoples of the oil-rich Niger-Delta region in Southern Nigeria.

32. Cited in Steyn, "Oil, Ethnic Minority Groups," 62.

What have we done to God's creation in Africa? How can a new creation be born in Africa? Indeed, in concluding this review of chapter 2 of *Laudato Si'*, I think that Pope Francis is calling African theologians—and all people interested in the future of this continent, which is often called Mother—to do more than we have done so far. African theologians must demonstrate how the human and material resources of Africa have been developed or exploited throughout the continent's checkered history. This discourse should be explored vis-à-vis what the late African scholar, Ali Mazrui, with reference to "resource curse" and "African predicament," characterizes as the reality of "the garden of Eden in decay."[33]

## Conclusion

This chapter developed both an African ethics for an integral ecology and a theological aesthetics for appreciating the beauty of creation through a review of Pope Francis's Trinitarian theology of creation. I showed that both approaches to ecological ethics share a common vision and propose common practices based on the relationality and interconnectedness of all God's creatures. The African concept of *Ubuntu* is proposed as an organizing ethical motif for a new vision of cosmic and human flourishing and for inspiring people to make daily choices to heal the earth. This is also particularly presented as an act of solidarity with our fragile earth and the fragile, vulnerable peoples of the earth who are on the margins of life. In a special way, Pope Francis has a solicitude for Africa, a continent that continues to suffer even though it is potentially one of the richest places on earth. He invites the world to embrace the spirit of *Ubuntu* as expressed in the message of the Bishops of South Africa which he cites: "Everyone's talents and involvement are needed to redress the damage caused by human abuse of God's creation" (*LS* 14). Here, at the end of my dialogue with chapter 2 of *Laudato Si'*, I propose three practices with inspiration from the African *Ubuntu* spirituality and ethics as well as from the African bishops, who affirmed that everyone is needed to play an important role in healing the earth and making it more beautiful and life-giving:

First is a *recovery of a sense of beauty and wonder*. *Laudato Si'* drew its inspiration from the songs of praise written by Francis of Assisi about creation. In Africa, as I have shown, nature is highly esteemed. Africa remains the most visited continent in the world by those who are looking for a deeper connection with nature, found especially in African safaris. Humanity must again recover the sense of beauty and awe it has forgotten. Faith is

---

33. Mazrui, *African Condition*, 1–22.

a way of beauty, because through faith we can immediately discover that we are not the center of the universe or the center of reality, but rather that we are essential parts of a large and beautiful universe. Preserving nature, creating gardens, cleaning and refusing to litter, disposing of waste, and building ecological villages are some of the ways to help the beauty of creation shine through and help humanity celebrate and luxuriate in the harmony between us and nature.

Second is a *renewal of an ecoethics of participation and solidarity*. Solidarity is both a social and moral principle for a better world, because *Ubuntu* affirms that we are related in a bond of life that is often frayed through ecological sins. Solidarity is also social, because it is required in our relationships with one another and with nature in order to support, uplift, strengthen, and heal the bonds of relationships. Solidarity is needed to restore the order of justice, which is often toppled by exploitation and widening power differentials among people based on race, nationality, sex, religion, and other exclusionary categories in the world today, categories which perpetuate suffering and poverty among many people. As a moral principle, solidarity moves the human heart to see clearly the devastating effects of wrong human choices, which have created structural violence and structures of sin and injustice, and also to see the need for conversion—economic, moral, spiritual, social, cultural, and ecological as developed in *Querida Amazonia*—toward God, nature, and our fellow human beings.

Finally, I propose some *ecospiritual practices of vulnerability and care*. An ancient Christian wisdom, which we find in all ages, is the recognition that, through the incarnation, God has become near to humanity and the entire cosmos. The nearness of God to creation and God's covenant with the earth was an act of humility on the part of God—a self-emptying. God always bends down to creation; God always accommodates Godself to creation as a way of filling creation with love and energy so that it can move and have its being in God. This divine action on the part of God is both a model and a mission for humanity. Ecotheological ethics today must deepen a sense of vulnerability and humility in human beings. Vulnerability is not a sign of weakness; rather, it is the recognition of the value of humility in daily choices, and this reflects God's own humility as displayed in the vulnerability on the cross.

With a strong emphasis on healing, caring, restoring, and reverencing the other as a co-participant in the bond of life, the African concept of *Ubuntu* could help develop this global ethics of vulnerability, away from an obsession with power and domination. Vulnerability also brings to the fore the notions of incompleteness and finitude as inner dispositions that should move people to seek ways to improve connections, communality, and sharing among all. Thus, when Africans care for sacred groves, preserve and prune ancestral trees, or protect those species regarded as heavenly emissaries, they are speaking through their actions. They are saying that there is a sacred bond tying all things together, and also that, in preserving these species and reverencing these sacred spaces, people recognize what Patriarch Bartholomew once wrote on the beauty, connection, and bond between all things. His moving words bring together what I have written in these concluding proposals: "God invites us to share in and to enjoy beauty. For, everything that lives and breathes is sacred and beautiful in the eyes of God. The whole world is a sacrament. The entire created cosmos is a burning bush of God's uncreated energies. And humankind stands as a priest before the altar of creation, as microcosm and mediator."[34]

---

34. Chryssavgis, *On Earth as in Heaven*, 152.

# 4

## The Human Roots of the Ecological Crisis: An African Ecotheology of Peace on Earth

Evelyn Namakula Birabwa Mayanja

### Introduction

Gold dazzles the eye. It is a symbol of wealth and glory. Around 643 BC, Romans started using gold in worship and glorification of gods. They used it in jewelry-making and adopted golden rings as a shining symbol of marriage love. To this day, gold fires dreams of wealth and glory. But so do platinum, diamond, coltan,[1] tin, copper, cobalt, uranium, and other minerals and metals used to make high-tech items such as iPhones and electronic cars. On every continent, geologists and corporations hunt for minerals and metals. But there is a dark side to these coveted minerals and metals.

Africa happens to possess many of them, and their extraction has wreaked havoc on local populations and the environment on which the livelihoods of many depend. From Mali to the Central African Republic, South Sudan, Darfur, Liberia, Sierra Leone, and the Democratic Republic of Congo (DRC), armed conflicts are waged to access those resources. The movie *Blood Diamond* depicts bloody conflicts driven by the desire to have access to Sierra Leone's diamonds. Since 1996, the eastern DRC has been embroiled in wars and armed combat motivated by the exploitation of minerals and other resources.[2] Since 2012, whenever I visit South Kivu, I am

---

1. Coltan (colombite tantalite) is a raw material used in manufacturing electronic capacitor that holds high electric charges in cell phones, laptops and other electronic devices.

2. See Prunier, *Africa's World War*, and Reyntjens, *Great African War*.

flabbergasted by Banro Mining Corporation's destruction of communities and the environment. Banro displaced people living around the villages of Luhwindja and Luciga from their homes, land, and sites where they mined to earn a living. Approximately 800 families were relocated to a mountainous and rocky area called Cinjira where they have no access to water and cannot cultivate. Mineral extraction and cleaning expose people to dust and toxins that contaminate the land surface and underground water. To separate gold from other impurities, Banro uses cyanide acid, which causes cancer in a population that has no access to medical care.[3] The cost of new roads and infrastructure, along with mineral extraction, results in deforestation, the loss of biodiversity, and erosion. Life-sustaining thick forests and clean water have been destroyed. Toxic spills, sinkholes, tailing ponds, open pits, and acid mine drainage contaminate the soil, as well as ground and surface water, exposing local populations to skin diseases, tuberculosis, and increased outbreaks of malaria. Aquatic life and land animals alike are endangered. As the minerals and metal leave Africa, so do money and development. Nothing is returned to Africa. Many people remain poor and oblivious of the high-tech devices invented from their resources.

This chapter examines the human roots of the ecological crisis following sections 101 to 135 of *Laudato Si'*. A brief exploration of the critical roots of the crisis is followed by an analysis of its implications for the world and the universal church. In order to establish an African ecotheology of peace on earth, I consider the encyclical's implication for Africa and the church in particular.

## The Human Roots of the Ecological Crisis

Chapter 3 of *Laudato Si'* explores the human roots of the ecological crisis, "so as to consider not only its symptoms but also its deepest causes."[4] Pope Francis highlights the joys and perils of the "technocratic paradigm . . . the place of human beings and human actions in the world" (*LS* 101). Technological progress has improved living conditions, as well as created amazing things such as the aircraft, robotics, nanotechnologies, and medicine (*LS* 102–4), but it has also "brought us to a crossroad" (*LS* 102). While humans have, for generations, respectfully interacted and received what nature offered, the technocratic paradigm extracts "everything possible . . . ignoring or forgetting the reality in front of us" (*LS* 106). The once-friendly human-nature relationship "has become confrontational" (*LS* 106). The ideology

---

3. Dang et al., "Physician Beware."
4. Francis, *Laudato Si'*, 15 (hereafter cited in text as *LS*).

of "infinite or unlimited growth" and "infinite supply of the earth's goods," adored by economists, financers, and technology experts has stretched the planet beyond its capacity (*LS* 106).

The ecological crisis springs from individuals and societies making science and technology their "epistemological paradigm" (*LS* 107). Technological progress has assumed "an undifferentiated and one-dimensional paradigm" that exalts the individual who uses "logical and rational procedures, progressively approaches and gains control" over the planet as if it were "formless, completely open to manipulation" (*LS* 106). Those with technological and scientific "knowledge and especially the economic resources to use them" dominate "the whole of humanity and the entire world" (*LS* 104). A different paradigm that considers technology as a means is almost inconceivable, and choosing a lifestyle "independent of technology" appears impossible (*LS* 108).

Technological prowess has blinded us to the bigger picture of human life and planetary integrity. Constant novelties make it difficult to "pause and recover depth in life" (*LS* 113). Technology is perceived as the key to meaningful existence, though its negative symptoms, including "environmental degradation, anxiety, a loss of the purpose of life and community living," are obvious (*LS* 110). The technological paradigm perceives "nature as an insensate order, as a cold body of facts, as a mere 'given,' as an object of utility, a raw material to be hammered into useful shape; it views the cosmos similarly as mere 'space' into which objects can be thrown with complete indifference."[5] Humans have failed to find their true place as stewards in the world and instead have compromised it cosmic "intrinsic dignity" (*LS* 115).

The technocratic paradigm dominates politics and economics as well. Global policy makers have limited ecological integrity to "partial responses" to "pollution, environmental decay, and the depletion of natural resources" instead of implementing a comprehensive approach that incorporates new ways of thinking, policies, education, lifestyles, and spirituality for resistance against "the technocratic paradigm" (*LS* 111). Global economics "accepts every" technological progress with the sole aim of profiting, and without concerns for "potential negative impact on human beings" (*LS* 109). Some people believe that economics and technology suffice to resolve the global problems of hunger, poverty, and inequality, dismissing any consideration for "balanced" production levels, wealth distribution, environmental protection, and "the rights of future generations" (*LS* 109). There is an imbalance between the super economic prowess of wastefulness and consumerism in developed nations, dehumanization and deprivation in developing nations.

---

5. Guardini, *End of the Modern World*, 55.

We are "too slow in developing economic institutions and social initiatives" that can provide the poor "regular access to basic resources" (*LS* 109).

Modernity has been characterized by "excessive anthropocentrism" which prevents understanding and "efforts to strengthen social bonds" (*LS* 116). Christian anthropology is partly responsible for this discrepancy. It has misrepresented the relationship between humans and the world as one of "mastery" and "dominion," rather than "responsible stewardship" (*LS* 116). Diseased with the pathology of a superiority complex, humans have neglected to monitor "the harm done to nature and the environmental impact of our decisions" (*LS* 117). The pope warns that when humanity "declares independence from reality and behaves with absolute dominion, the very foundation of our life begins to crumble" (*LS* 117).

The technological paradigm is in "a constant" schizophrenic state, disvaluing "lesser beings," including fellow humans (*LS* 118). The pope notes that "when we fail to acknowledge as part of reality the worth of a poor person, a human embryo, a person with disabilities . . . it becomes difficult to hear the cry of nature itself; everything is connected" (*LS* 117). There cannot be ecological reconciliation—"renewal of our relationship with nature"—without anthropology, the "renewal of humanity itself" (*LS* 118). He emphasizes that "the ecological crisis" signifies "the ethical, cultural, and spiritual crisis of modernity, we cannot presume to heal our relationship with nature and the environment without healing all fundamental human relationships" and "much less the transcendent dimension of our openness to the 'Thou' of God" (*LS* 119).

A misplaced ecological and anthropological paradigm creates a "misguided lifestyle" of "practical relativism" (*LS* 122) and "use and throw away" that generates "so much waste" (*LS* 123). This relativism places some people "at the center," treats others as "mere objects," gratifies "immediate convenience," allows "forces of the market to regulate the economy," and "consider[s] their impact on society and nature as collateral damage" (*LS* 123). Lack of respect for human labor, employment, and "a correct understanding of work" (*LS* 124–25) is a real danger. Human work is "a vocation" (*LS* 128). Replacing human labor with artificial intelligence "to gain greater short-term financial gain is bad business for society" (*LS* 128).

Satisfying "desires and immediate needs" spurs the evils of "human trafficking, organized crime, the drug trade, commerce in blood diamonds . . . buying of the organs of the poor for resale or use in experimentation," (*LS* 123) and "genetic manipulation by biotechnology" (*LS* 132). These evils are aggravated by "the absence of objective truths or sound principles" to guide technological progress and modernity (*LS* 123).

Finally, to shed "new light on the problem[s]" (*LS* 135), the pope recommends interdisciplinary, comprehensive, "broad, responsible scientific and social debate" that considers "all the available information" and calls "things by their names" (*LS* 135).

I concur with Pope Francis that technology has contributed to human progress. However, the abuse of power and capitalist greed are transforming technological progress into a monster that dominates, controls humanity, and destroys nature through unregulated extraction and wastes. This is because technological progress has not been accompanied by education on and ethics for using power and doing business in a manner that puts people and nature over profit. Economists, financiers, multinationals, and tech experts believe in the ideas of unlimited growth, consumerism, the market, and maximizing profit. This paradigm of domineering technology is based on the lie that the earth supplies goods infinitely. But this squeezes the planet beyond its limits. As the pope notes, this paradigm also results in increased inequality as well as both economic and environmental crises.

Pope Francis, however, fails to acknowledge the role the church has had in preaching the gospel of exploitation, colonization, and conquest, as opposed to stewardship, love, and respect for nature and all people regardless of race, gender, and creed. Genesis 1:28 proclaims that God told humanity to "fill the earth and subdue it," ruling over all creatures. In Africa, missionaries were emissaries of exploitative colonialism. In contrast, Africa's spirituality and religions believe in the well-being of all people. The ideology of "I am, because we are" testifies to this belief. Equally, nature is perceived as a mother, provider, and a life force that sustains all beings.[6] Africa's technological advancement was coupled with frameworks for sustaining both nature and the common good. For example, the Buganda kingdom of Uganda followed advancement in wood usage and backcloth-making with nature-preserving laws. Every tree that was cut was replaced, and failure to do so was punishable. The belief was that, without caring for nature, technological advancement could become a curse, instead of a blessing, on the common good. Sadly, missionaries considered such beliefs of respecting nature to be animism and paganism.[7] Although times have changed, I believe that African traditional wisdom can contribute to overcoming the human roots of the ecological crisis.

---

6. Mbiti, *African Religions and Philosophy*.

7. Idowu, *African Traditional Religion*.

## Implications for the World and the Whole Church

In 2000, the cofounder and chief scientist at Sun Microsystems, Bill Joy, published an article in *Wired* entitled "Why the Future Doesn't Need Us."[8] In the article, Joy expressed concerns about scientific and technological advancement in artificial intelligence, nanotechnology, and genetic engineering. Aware of the potentials of these technologies, he also noted the ethical questions they would pose and our unpreparedness to handle both the technologies and their ethical implications. Joy wrote, "We are being propelled into this new century with no plan, no control, no brakes. Have we already gone too far down the path to alter course? I don't believe so, but we aren't trying yet, and the last chance to assert control—the fail-safe point—is rapidly approaching."[9] Nothing changed after Joy's warning. Fifteen years later, Pope Francis wrote *Laudato Si'*. And as I write this chapter, seven years after its publication, nothing has changed in the world or the church. In 2016, world leaders signed the Paris Agreement to combat climate change. But as a global society, we are still grappling with climate change, exacerbated by unregulated resource extraction and consumerism in the name of progress. The environmental activist Greta Thunberg has excoriated leaders for their inertia in the face of the environmental crisis.[10] Instead of listening to the cry of the people and the land, they want to look to politics, economics, and technology to find solutions to global problems like climate change.

A key contributor to the ecological crisis is capitalist extraction to augment technological progress. Although science and technology have contributed to alleviating global problems (*LS* 103–4), they portend real and numerous disastrous ramifications for humanity and the environment. The essence of being human is at risk of being destroyed in the name of advancement that increases our dependence on technology rather than human relationships. How we are engineered and engineer others in return are the most challenging questions of the twenty-first century—and not without several implications.

The first implication is valuing profit and things over people. Technology is dominated by an individualistic and capitalistic paradigm that values profit rather than people's well-being, human dignity, and planetary integrity. The capitalist economic system of profit above people has created inequalities in almost every society. The rich benefit from exploiting the vulnerable without the sting of conscience. Those "with technological

---

8. Joy, "Why the Future Doesn't Need Us."
9. Joy, "Why the Future Doesn't Need Us."
10. Gajanan, "'You Have Stolen My Dreams.'"

knowledge and especially the economic resources to use them" dominate fellow humans and the planet (*LS* 104). For example, in 2019, Apple CEO Tim Cook's annual pay was over US $125 million,[11] while Chinese workers who assemble Apple iPhones receive about US $3.15 an hour.[12] The artisanal miners who provide the minerals Apple uses (cobalt, coltan, copper, and gold) in the DRC and other developing nations hardly earn a dollar a day. During the first weeks of the COVID-19 pandemic, approximately twenty-six million Americans lost their jobs, and the 1-percent billionaires increased their wealth by US $308 billion in a month.[13] This level of inequality is threatening global security. As the pope notes, "We should be particularly indignant at the enormous inequalities in our midst, whereby we continue to tolerate some considering themselves more worthy than others" (*LS* 90).

Businesses believe in "infinite or unlimited growth" (*LS* 106) to satisfy the wants of a few, while leaving the majority lacking basic needs. This modus operandi is unacceptable. It is also "a lie" (*LS* 106). We are realizing more and more that the planet cannot sustain insatiable global demands and greed. Resources are shrinking, threatening human and ecological security. Primitive accumulation has blinded us to environmental deterioration and the suffering of vulnerable people but also to corporeal vulnerability and the shortness of life. We have a global scenario where those in affluent societies are becoming obese while others—including those living in places where minerals used in technological devices are mined—suffer from malnutrition. Many people are caught up in the culture of buying and spending even when they do not need to. We "fail to see the deepest roots of our present failures, which have to do with the direction, goals, meaning and social implications of technological and economic growth" and assume "more balanced levels of production, a better distribution of wealth, concern for the environment, and the rights of future generations" (*LS* 109). The pope exhorts us to seek "true joy and peace" through a "prophetic and contemplative lifestyle, one capable of deep enjoyment free of the obsession with consumption," to be "spiritually detached from what we possess and not succumb to sadness of what we lack" (*LS* 222). After all, corporeal vulnerability is a reality. We come into the world with nothing and return to dust with nothing.

The second implication is equating consumerism with development and modernity. The mentality of "use and throw away" (*LS* 123) is

---

11. Leswing, "Apple CEO Tim Cook's Total Pay."
12. Nicas, "Apple's Plan."
13. Rushe and Chalabi, "'Heads We Win,'" para. 2.

so pervasive that we hardly question planetary sustainability in relation to human exploitation and greed. The pope warns: "Once the human being declares independence from reality and behaves with absolute dominion, the very foundations of our life begin to crumble" (*LS* 117). Consumerism benefits producing groups (elites, developed nations, corporations) and creates classes of the super-rich and the poor at the margins of society. To alleviate poverty, the UN and developed nations resort to foreign aid, which William Easterly calls the "white man's burden."[14] Without questioning the capitalistic economy that benefits the 1 percent and impoverishes the other 99 percent, inequality and poverty will increase.

The third implication is the negation of personal and responsibility because of the invisible and destructive forces of neoliberal capitalism, with its culture of consumerism and exploitation of the poor. It appears that those who control technology play on the psychology of people's buying power. Least known is the fact that "our freedom fades when it is handed over to the blind forces of the unconscious, of immediate needs, of self-interest" (*LS* 105). Consumerism points to something deeper—inner emptiness that a person tries to fill with things. Pope Francis notes, "The emptier a person's heart is, the more he or she needs things to buy, own and consume. It becomes almost impossible to accept the limits imposed by reality . . . [and] a genuine sense of the common good also disappears" (*LS* 204). Consumerism by the affluent few when the rest are impoverished has created scenarios such as the mass migrations from Africa, the Middle East, and Latin America into Europe and the United States. The deaths of millions of African youth in the Mediterranean Sea and the separation of children from their parents at the Mexico-US border when they are fleeing poverty are permanent scars on the conscience of humanity.

Sadly, technological progress has not been accompanied by education for responsibility, ethics, and values, including stewardship and care for the planet. We have certain mechanisms and laws[15] but no sound ethics to monitor and regulate technological progress. We lack "a culture and spirituality genuinely capable of setting limits and teaching clear-minded self-restraint" (*LS* 105). Humans are fascinated by technology but have forgotten the maker of human intelligence which spearheads technological progress. Similarly, technological progress has not been accompanied by a sound spirituality and reflection on the meaning of life and material things. In Africa, we are trapped by copying Euro-American tech practices and the colonial legacy of considering whatever is African as archaic and useless.

---

14. Easterly, *White Man's Burden*.
15. Guruswamy and Zebrowski Leach, *International Environmental Law*.

For example, traditionally, one's private life was not supposed to be known to the public. Instead, today, Africans use Facebook, Instagram and other apps to make their private lives known to the whole world.

The fourth implication is that technology has complicated the war landscape. From the September 11 attacks in New York to biological warfare in Syria, we witness the dangers of technological progress and war. Killing by pressing a computer button has not only increased the numbers of deaths but also has dehumanized war. The dead are faceless. Yet, the global war machine and arms trade are highly lucrative businesses, worth about US $100 billion annually.[16] Nations invest in weapons more than in education and health care.[17] In 2019, African governments spent US $41.2 billion,[18] yet they are choked with debt and poor infrastructure for health care and education. In some African nations, children still learn under trees, and pregnant mothers have no access to medical facilities. The 2016 movie *Shadow World* provides a relevant account of the devastations of the global arms trade, though nations invest more in wars than in people. Whenever a war is waged and natural resources exploited, the magnitude of environmental destruction is alarming. Examples of such destruction can be seen in Iraq, Yemen, Syria, the DRC, Mali, Darfur, and the Central African Republic.

The fifth implication is that technology is also taking away our privacy and depersonalizing the dignity of work. Technology is depriving us of the "vocation" to create (*LS* 128). Artificial intelligence (AI) is believed to perform better than humans and has left many unemployed. It is projected that by 2030, AI will replace about 20 million factory jobs.[19] Unemployment portends a nexus of health, security, and environmental degradation.[20]

The sixth implication is the destruction of human and planetary integrity. Technological progress is dependent on resource extraction (e.g., of minerals, metals, oil, gas). In the absence of green resource extraction, human and planetary integrity are destroyed, as the *Laudato Si'* epigraph highlights. But many consumers, mesmerized by technology, appear to have no knowledge—or at least insufficient information—about the dangers associated with resource extraction. Many people fail to ask such questions as: Where do the raw materials used in making modern electronic devices come from? How are they accessed? What happens to those communities

---

16. Stockholm International Peace Research Institute, "Global Military Expenditure."
17. Feinstein, *Shadow World*.
18. See "African Military Spending," para. 1.
19. See "Robots 'to Replace.'"
20. Duraiappah, "Poverty and Environmental Degradation."

where we get our raw materials? These questions and many others remain inadequately addressed by technological experts, governments, and even the United Nations. In the globalized world, environmental calamities know no borders. The whole world is gradually paying the price for the greed of capitalist resource extraction. The pope recommends that we transcend "an undifferentiated and one-dimensional paradigm" (*LS* 106) and be concerned about what is happening to every person and the planet everywhere.

Pervasive corruption is part of this technological paradigm, witnessed when powerful nations and their mining companies loot Africa's resources, evade taxes, and destroy the environment with impunity.[21] These nations are UN members with veto power at the Security Council. Can we trust them to design and implement laws to mitigate ecological damage accruing from resource extraction? The pope exhorts us "not (to) think that political efforts or the force of law will be sufficient to prevent actions which affect the environment because, when the culture itself is corrupt and objective truth and universally valid principles are no longer upheld, then laws can only be seen as arbitrary impositions or obstacles to be avoided" (*LS* 123). The ecological crisis signifies an "ethical, cultural, and spiritual crisis of modernity," and "we cannot presume to heal our relationship with nature and the environment without healing all fundamental human relationships" (*LS* 119). There cannot be "renewal of our relationships" with nature and each other "without renewal of humanity itself" (*LS* 118). It is my contention that a relationship with people and nature requires a renewed spirituality and theology.

## *Laudato Si'* and Africa

In this era of globalization, Africa is on the fringes of technological development but the hardest hit by the ecological crisis. Societies and the church in Africa have ecological causes and consequences that are Africa-specific, rooted in colonial exploitation and persistent capitalist extraction of resources. From the pneumatic tire to electronic cars, technology has progressed on the backs of human capital and resources looted from Africa. Patrick Bond captures this fact:

> Trade by force dating back centuries; slavery that uprooted and dispossessed around 12 million Africans; land grabs; vicious taxation schemes; precious metals spirited away; the appropriation of antiquities to the British Museum and other trophy

---

21. Engler, *Canada in Africa*.

rooms; the nineteenth-century emergence of racist ideologies to justify colonialism; the 1884–85 carve up of Africa, in a Berlin negotiating room, into dysfunctional territories; the construction of settler-colonial and extractive-colonial systems—of which apartheid, the German occupation of Namibia, the Portuguese colonies and King Leopold's Belgian Congo were perhaps only the most blatant.... Cold War battlegrounds—proxies for US/USSR conflicts—filled with millions of corpses; other wars catalysed by mineral searches and offshoot violence such as witnessed in blood diamonds and coltan (colombo-tantalite, a crucial component of cell phones and computer chips); poacher-stripped swathes of East, Central, and Southern Africa now devoid of rhinos and elephants ... societies used as guinea pigs in the latest corporate pharmaceutical tests ... and the list could continue.[22]

In light of this account, it is obvious that African resources have been siphoned away for centuries, yet Africa lacks industrial, scientific, and technological development. Africa continues to lose many of her resources even today. This unfortunate situation has denied Africa the opportunity to spearhead technological progress (given Africa's human and resource potential) and to mitigate the effects of climate crisis through her own rich, traditional ecowisdom. Africa thus risks losing her children's twenty-second-century progress. As the resources for making the highly demanded technological devices are becoming scarce, the search for what is left has become violently competitive, embroiling Africa in incessant wars. As of February 2021, out of the United Nations' twelve peacekeeping operations, six are in Africa's natural resource-rich nations of Mali, the Central African Republic, the DRC, Abyei, South Sudan, and Western Sahara. When considered alongside other recent conflicts across the continent, everyone can recognize natural resource extraction as the origin, driver, and sustainer of these conflicts. Although the looting of Africa's resources—which includes human trafficking and the harvesting of human organs—has never been interrupted, scholars have termed the current multifaceted looting as "the new scramble for Africa."[23] Western powers, along with Russia and China, are all competing to win the hearts of African leaders and warlords in order to access the continent's resources. China appears to be winning, controlling people and resources in every African nation, with potential for becoming the next colonial power. Chinese colonization could be lethal for Africa,

---

22. Bond, *Looting Africa*, 2.
23. Carmody, *New Scramble for Africa*.

given China's poor human rights record[24] and racism.[25] Colonial and recent extractors of Africa's resources have destroyed the environment. Reviewing the devastation of capitalist extraction and bloody conflicts, Nnimmo Bassey concludes that Africa is being cooked.[26]

We have cycles of resource extraction, wars, armed conflicts, and ecological damages exacerbating poverty, underdevelopment, and environmental degradation as livelihood resources shrink. Floods, droughts, locust invasions, desertification, earthquakes, increased cases of disease (malaria and cholera), and a food-and-water shortage have become continental phenomena. Yet, international agreements and UN conferences on climate change have not seriously considered current and historical resource extraction or wars on the continent as critical ecological destroyers. If they did, and if there were a global ethics, the first step in mitigating climate change should be to call out the nations and corporation for robbing Africa. Bassey asks, "What makes possible the lack of regulation in Africa's extractive sectors, the open robbery, and the incredibly destructive extractive activities? Leading the multiplicity of factors are unjust power relations that follow from and amplify the baggage of slavery, colonialism, and neocolonialism."[27] Policy makers capitalize on money to save Africa's environment. The Paris Climate Agreement of 2017 promised US $100 billion per year to developing nations by 2020. Money, though important, cannot be equated with the treasure of forests, fresh water, and vegetation Africa is losing. As Bassey argues, "There is a climate debt that must be recognized and paid. The payment is not all about finances but principally about decolonizing the atmospheric space and redistributing the meagre space left. Developed countries already occupy 80 percent of that space."[28]

What enables the unregulated extraction of Africa's resources and the destruction of the environment? Where are the African leaders when extraction, looting, and wars devastate people and the environment? Why have African leaders failed to tap continental resource wealth that would transform the continent into a super power? Reflecting on who is responsible for Africa's underdevelopment, Walter Rodney pointed to the imperialists and African compradors.[29] The crisis of leadership has exposed Africa to global

---

24. Webster, "China's Human Rights Footprint," 626–63.
25. Sui, "China's Racism."
26. Bassey, *To Cook a Continent*.
27. Bassey, *To Cook a Continent*, ix–x.
28. Bassey, *To Cook a Continent*, 110.
29. Rodney, *How Europe Underdeveloped Africa*, 27.

exploitation and humiliation. Leaders are not only looting resources;[30] their corruption levels include embezzling climate change funds[31] and making policies that remain on paper. Africa will overcome climate change and play its part in fostering a holistic technological development that is human- and ecologically friendly to the degree that we overcome the crisis of leadership and resource governance. We also discern the void of ethics where, for centuries, looting Africa's resources and consequent deforestation and poisoning water sources has not been considered a crime. If looting were considered a crime in international law, corporations leading the looting and militarization machineries in Africa would have been prosecuted. Equally, politics and economics without an Afrocentric ethics and ideology—for example, of fostering the common good—are contributing to corruption, stealing our very resources and destroying the environment on which the livelihoods of many people in Africa's communities depend. Ethics in the African worldview implies creating cosmic unity or an order of bondedness by being in harmony with oneself, God, the community, and nature. This order is destabilized by wrongdoing, unethical practices, and/or social injustice.[32]

The church must play its prophetic role and speak the truth to power. For example, where political leaders are corrupt and side with corporations looting Africa's natural resources and ecological destruction, the church must be the moral voice. Sadly, the church is becoming an institution that associates with political elites who fund its economic projects instead of the poor. Clerics are caught up in materialism and consumerism. The desire to own the most sophisticated phone and car (believed to be symbols of technological progress, derived from looting Africa's minerals) is driving clericalism instead of service and relationship with Jesus's *anawim* (*the poor*).

In the absence of political leadership, and with the church failing at its prophetic role, what can Africans do? "If people do not take responsibility for their resources and the environment, we will continue on the path laid out by elites, a path that brings us ever closer to the brink."[33] It is important to remember that some resources are not renewable, and restoring ecological integrity is complex and, in some circumstances, impossible. How will we restore the disappearing forests, shrinking lakes, degraded landscapes, vanishing glaciers, extinct species, and biodiversity of wildlife, flora, and fauna? We have to recognize that slave trade and colonialism led to identity

30. Burgis, *Looting Machine*.
31. Fredriksson and Neumayer, "Corruption and Climate Change Policies."
32. Bujo, *Foundations of an African Ethic*.
33. Bassey, *To Cook a Continent*, x.

and cultural genocides in Africa. Chinua Achebe's books, *Things Fall Apart* and *No Longer at Ease*, attest to what happened to Africa. Africans lost their belief in themselves and their indigenous knowledge. Africans look at themselves and their values with indignation, consuming technological devices and Western worldviews as if they cannot establish Africanized technology guided by African values. Contrary to the African worldview and spirituality of cosmic wholeness, we blindly follow Western worldviews that separate nature from humans, racializes and classifies humans, and considers superior races to be in control of nature. Conversely, African worldviews focus on interdependency between humans and nature.[34] African morality requires caring for the common good—people and nature.[35] Under the pretext of globalizing and becoming civilized, affluent Africans have become greedy, individualistic, and wasteful. Yet the levels of inequality and poverty remain high. Often, inequality breeds violence. To pursue the global drive for technological development without an African ideology, ethics, and worldview is perilous and liable to increase inequality and violence.

## Conclusion

Technological progress cannot afford to be unsustainable and imported. Africans have begun suing oil, gas, and mining companies over environmental destruction. On February 11, 2020, seven Tanzanian citizens—including a village chief in North Mara, Mwita Marwa—filed a lawsuit against Acacia Mining (also known as Barrick Gold Tz Limited). During its ten years of extraction in Tanzania, Acacia polluted water sources, produced toxic tailings, and made breathing difficult for many people. Forests and bushes became extinct, and open pits have claimed lives of both people and animals. In May 2019, Acacia was fined US $2.4 million.[36] When I talked to Mwita Marwa over the phone about his motivation and courage to sue Acacia, he said:

> I care for the common good of my people. For over ten years, we endure indignity and environmental destruction. I am an African Christian who believes in living out the gospel by doing justice. As an African, I am connected to all people and nature. Nothing should be exploited. I value the well-being of my community and the importance of creating a clean environment for my children, grandchildren, and everyone.[37]

34. Mbiti, *African Religions and Philosophy*.
35. Mbiti, *African Religions and Philosophy*.
36. Casey, "Tanzania Fines Acacia $2.4M."
37. Author's telephone conversation with Mwita Marwa, February 2020.

Mwita is an example of an authentic African who combines African and Christian values, values that must be "harnessed and combined with other values to support common principles aimed at addressing a deepening global socio-ecological crisis."[38] Although individuals like Mwita are doing their part, the church needs to develop ecotheological principles and practices to guide Africa through the threats posed by technology and environmental degradation. Unfortunately, church leaders and followers alike are caught up in capitalistic accumulation. In Uganda, for example, every new bishop receives a car from the president, well aware of the engraved corruption that pockets even climate change and COVID-19 money.[39] Church ministers associate with the rich and less with the poor. Throughout Africa, the church is like a corporation, controlling huge chunks of land, believing that humans are entitled to control nature (Gen 1:28) rather than be stewards of it. We need to confront the realities of the ecological crisis, social injustices, political oppression, and resource exploitation with words and examples. As Harvey Sindima notes, "We must repent of some aspects of the Christian experience that have been exploitive or destructive to peoples and to nature."[40] Corporate exploitation poses huge environmental threats to Africa, yet it has not become a key component in the church's message. A combination of African and Christian principles and faith that banks—as Mwita does—on the interconnection of people among themselves and with nature is crucial. The challenge is that people like Mwita are becoming fewer and fewer in the African society and church. Sadly, the church is not helping people to translate faith into concrete practices for social justice and community well-being. Transforming the destructive status quo and the irreversible drive to technology means transforming the church's ministries—worship, preaching, pastoral care, and general involvement in people's lives—so that believers and clerics alike may become more life-giving, empower believers, and be leavens and salts in the world. Christian personal responsibility and ethics help to mitigate ills, including ecological damages, consumerism, and injustices leading to inequalities in society.

The church must listen to the cries and joys of people like Mwita, those affected by Banro Mining Corporations and other mining enterprises in Congo, and other African nations devastated by resource extraction and wars. It is also crucial to listen to the cries of the land and expediently design Africanized interventions to problems emanating from technological progress, environmental damages, and economic exploitation. Similarly, unless

---

38. Le Grange, "Ubuntu/Botho as Ecophilosophy and Ecosophy," 307.
39. Tenywa, "Climate Change"; URN, "Court Orders MPs."
40. Sindima, "Community of Life," 138.

it recovers its traditional values, ethics, and approaches to environmental integrity and innovativeness, Africa will continue to adopt foreign measures without success. This requires coming to terms with Africa's past as well as decolonizing the mind from colonial greed and consumerism to care, and from individualism to community. And above all, it requires reclaiming African identity and worth, destroyed when Africa was named *terra incognita* and its people as primitive beasts who never grow to attain the maturity of other races.[41] As Sindima states,

> People's emotions and relationships become conditioned by a new "reality." If a people's thought system is corrupted, their value system is destroyed; the "world" or cosmology that informs their way of life has been ruined. This corruption continues as long as the people do not come to a realization of who they are. Without such self-consciousness, a people cannot reject the disorienting language, that is, the process of alienation becomes total. This is what Western cultural imperialism sought to do to Africans.[42]

We need to recover the African ethics of communion, where "what falls on one, falls on all. In such a relationship, the issue is the re-establishment of community, the re-establishment of the circulation of life, so that life can go on transcending itself, go on bursting the barriers, or the intervals, the nothingness, go on being superabundant."[43] For example, the church could spearhead programs that empower those communities dehumanized by corporate mining to demand their rights and hold corporations accountable as Mwita did. They could launch tree-planting and similar projects, as Odomaro Mubangizi, SJ, did when he established the Pope Francis Botanical Garden in Addis Ababa.

The church has an irreplaceable role in crafting theology and spirituality to meet the challenges of technological progress. This theology and spirituality must be embedded and practiced in the mainstream of society and not simply the prerogative of theologians and clerics. For example, the church teaches that faith and science are complementary. In the late twentieth century, the church embraced ecotheology in response to the environmental crisis and ecological destruction. However, for over 2,000 years, the church preached the imperialist gospel of "fill the earth and subdue it" (Gen 1:28), which has misled the world towards planetary predation. Even after the publication of *Laudato Si'*, the church is still enmeshed in the imperial

41. Mamdani, *Citizen and Subject*.
42. Sindima, "Community of Life," 138.
43. Boulaga, *Christianity Without Fetishes*, 81.

aura that sides with dominant politics, economics, and the rich at the center of technological progress and ecological destruction. Why? The challenges we face in Africa require the church to live in solidarity with the groaning creation (Rom 8:22) in Africa, especially by shaping local and global policies which are ecofriendly. What is preventing the church from influencing government policies? While in African traditions there was no dichotomy between politics and religion, the sacred and the profane, colonialism and Christianity have presented a mechanical and divisive view of society, where governments, nature, and the church are disconnected. We need to recover the African heritage of interconnectedness of life—politics, economics, religion, and nature. Therefore, the church's presence at all levels—in local political councils, national parliaments, the African Union, and the United Nations—must be prioritized. The church needs to be a beacon of politics and policy.

Moreover, teachings about social justice and ecology, including *Laudato Si'*, must become part of the church's message. Faith does justice in everyday living. Unfortunately, in Africa, encyclicals are not common knowledge. For example, how many people at the grassroots level know of *Laudato Si'*? With an ignorant population of followers, the church remains influenced by a Western worldview of individualism, consumerism, racism, tribalism, imperialist politics, and an economics of conquer-and-exploit. We will transform the world to the degree that Christians know the church's teachings, such as *Laudato Si'* and ecotheology, and embody them in their daily practices.

Although secularism and sexual scandals have weakened the church's credibility, technological progress and the ecological crisis present a new opportunity for teaching and exemplifying a technoecological theology. This is a twofold theology of rediscovering the ecological wisdom in Christian traditions to respond, on one hand, to the environmental crisis and to technological threats on the other. Ecological theology involves "a critique of the cultural habits underlying ecological destruction and an ecological critique of Christianity,"[44] while offering Christians an opportunity for renewal and transformation. As creation groans (Rom 8:19–23), the church needs not only to preach the message of "a new creation" (2 Cor 5:17) but also to embody the theologies of ecology, responsible stewardship, and anti-consumerism.

Similarly, technological progress requires a technotheology which involves the critique of technological destruction, consumerism, and injustices against the poor. In the era where ecological genocide and "world

---

44. Conradie, *Christianity and Ecological Theology*, 3.

apartheid"[45] are emanating from myopic technological progress, Christians need "a transformation of ourselves from within our innermost being to accept all others as sisters and brothers. Our growth to a planetary dimension is an invitation to spiritual deepening, a purification from selfishness to a more universal communion in real life. . . . Insofar as we do so, we shall become truly civilized."[46]

In order to recreate a new humanity and a new cosmos (Rev 1–7), the church needs to discern how to champion an Africanized and holistic civilization, as well as how to champion globalization and technological development that prioritizes people and the planet. The challenges we face require the church to shift from worldly standards (such as racism, consumerism, and siding with the rich) to Jesus' paradigm. Besides teaching with example, the church also needs to be a witness to a simple lifestyle, not operating like a corporation hoarding wealth and resources, including land, in great quantities. As Pope Francis stated, clericalism and wealth and prevent the church from preaching and witnessing to Christ.[47] Believers preach with life more than words.

Following Christ requires being on the side of the downtrodden, those crushed by ecological damage, technological progress, and capitalist economics. We cannot respond to the ecological crisis without transforming the church, as well as the hearts of the oppressors and environmental destroyers and the structures they create for their benefit. We need a theology that awakens the oppressor and the oppressed to the groanings of both people and the land.

---

45. Balasuriya, *Planetary Theology*, 28.
46. Balasuriya, *Planetary Theology*, 95.
47. Esteves, "Clericalism, Wealth Prevent."

# 5

# Integral Ecology: An African Ecotheology of *Ubuntu*, Participation, and Our Common Sharing in the Bond of Life

Odomaro Mubangizi, SJ

## Introduction

No papal encyclical in recent times has attracted as much global attention and discussion as Pope Francis's *Laudato Si'* on the environment or "our common home." Reasons abound for this sensation about *Laudato Si'*. The obvious one is "fame by association"—an encyclical by the first Jesuit pope in history, in itself a brand. The next obvious reason is the choice of topic: climate change, or the environment, is the hottest topic of all time, only recently overtaken by COVID-19 (this too, by the way, is linked to ecology, since the COVID-19 virus, as some informed claims suggest, might have escaped from some animals).[1] Climate change is indeed a global crisis, and the destiny of humanity is under threat.

This chapter is a commentary, from the philosophical perspective of the *Ubuntu*[2] ethic, on the integral ecology section in *Laudato Si'*. But the point of departure is a story of one of the real problems human activity causes for the environment: the rising water levels of Lake Victoria (shared

---

1. For the scientific explanation that COVID-19 virus crossed from animals to humans, see https://www.who.int/health-topics/coronavirus/origins-of-the-virus.

2. *Ubuntu* is a Zulu word commonly used to express the proverb that "a person is a person because of other persons." A whole philosophy has been developed around this concept to include values of kindness, reciprocity, compassion, care, and reconciliation. It is also invoked to support care for the environment.

by Kenya, Uganda, and Tanzania) which is submerging surrounding homes and land around. It is important to observe that there is a critical debate looming regarding the building of a dam on the Nile by Ethiopia, with Egypt claiming that this dam will affect the volume of its share of the water received from the Nile. By way of conclusion, I will end with another story, this time of hope and optimism, but also a pedagogical one that demonstrates how small efforts and initiatives that are grounded in African eco-theological principles, themes, and practices offer lessons for Africa, as well as the world and the global church. Some theologians such as Joseph Healey and Emmanuel Katongole have suggested a new approach to theology that is narrative in nature.[3] This chapter is a contribution to an emerging African integral ecospirituality, grounded in the *Ubuntu* ethic of praxis and narrative methodology. The *Ubuntu* ethic is best narrated in stories, and that is why this chapter contains two narratives linked to the environment.

### Story: "More Displacements in Uganda as Lake Victoria Swells"[4]

The largest inland lake in Africa, Lake Victoria, which is bordered by parts of Uganda, Kenya, and Tanzania, has experienced a continuous rise of its waters since October 2019. The reason for the rise is climate change, which has caused an unexpected increase in heavy rains in the surrounding countries whose rivers feed the lake. As examples, River Kagera brings water from Uganda, Tanzania, Rwanda, and Burundi, and River Nzoia brings water from Kenya. Due to Lake Victoria's rising water levels, neighboring areas in Kenya, Uganda, and Tanzania have been submerged; these locations include five-star hotels as well as fishing and landing sites. Seven thousand people have been displaced, and 169 have been killed by the floods from backflows and rivers bursting their banks.[5] Bridges have been washed away as well. The supply and distribution of electricity has also been affected, because Lake Victoria supplies water to the Owen Falls Dam, the main source of hydroelectricity for Uganda.

According to engineer Callist Tindimugaya, "The lake level is the highest level the lake has reached in history (13.12 meters), the highest having

---

3. See Healey, *Towards an African Narrative Theology*. For another version of this kind of theologizing that prizes human experience as lived and narrated by ordinary people, see Donders, *Non-Bourgeois Theology*. For Emmanuel Katongole's use of stories of exemplary men and women who have worked for peace and reconciliation, see *Sacrifice of Africa* and *Journey of Reconciliation*.

4. See Kamoga, "More Displacements in Uganda."

5. See Kamoga, "More Displacements in Uganda," para. 8.

occurred in 1964. With the expected heavy rains in the second half of April and May, the situation is expected to get worse."[6] Tindimugaya went further to say that "[w]e are however trying to manage the situation by increasing the amount of water released at Jinja through River Nile, but it will still not solve the problem fully. The people to be affected are those that have constructed within two hundred meters around the lake as they encroached on the lake protection zone where the water used to be."[7]

As Tindimugaya explains, this solution to release more water through River Nile at Jinja raises another concern: "The concern, though, is that we shall cause impacts around Lake Kyoga, Albert, and along the Nile. So we are cautious as we release more water." He follows with a threatening warning: "It is a big concern next to Corona virus [sic]. Certainly Kampala (the capital city of Uganda) can easily be flooded if the rainfall and inflows continue to increase." What is the major cause of this environmental crisis around Lake Victoria? Tindimugaya says that in addition to the increase in heavy rainfall, "[t]he wetlands and forests that used to store the water and control the rate of flow of the water have been destroyed, and we are paying the price."[8]

Another well-informed expert, Peter Atekyereza, who has done some research on the areas, confirmed the human factor in the crisis:

> On this issue, I was doing a study on urban agriculture in Entebbe (where the Entebbe International Airport is located) in 2006–8 and found that many people had started encroaching on the lake reserve because water levels had dropped then. Most of these were government officials. I remember warning the Municipality leadership about the future effect when water levels rise again and indeed this is happening fifteen years after.[9]

This story confirms key elements of the environmental crisis, that it is clearly man-made and the result of short-term economic gains and also that what happens in one ecosystem affects and is affected by others. The whole Lake Victoria Basin that includes River Nile, River Kagera, and Lake Kyoga

---

6. Dr. Callist Tindimugaya is Uganda's senior hydrologist; he shared his views on this crisis via social media on April 12, 2020. This discussion took place on Whatsapp, under the group "Emperors 1981."

7. Dr. Callist Tindimugaya shared his views on this crisis via social media on April 12, 2020.

8. Same social media as in footnote 7.

9. Prof. Peter Atekyereza teaches social anthropology at Makerere University in Kampala; he also took part in this discussion about the Lake Victoria environmental crisis via the same social media in footnote 7.

is interconnected. Flooding impacts all of the following: fishing, housing, transport (roads), agriculture, and tourism.

Some of the key themes and ideas that will be explored as we comment on *Laudato Si'* can be discerned in this introductory story. The entire cosmos is interconnected. When humans encroach on the environment, Mother Nature hits back, almost to confirm the famous law in physics that for every action, there is an equal and opposite reaction. The flooding around Lake Victoria is Mother Nature's way of saying, "You tried to invest by encroaching on my space; I will push you back, and you will lose even the little you thought you had invested and much more!"

## A Thematic Commentary on the Integral Ecology of *Laudato Si'*: A Message to the Whole Church and to the African Context

I can, without hesitation, propose that the central message of *Laudato Si'* is to be found in chapter 4—namely, an integral ecology that is informed by both the methodology and major themes of Pope Francis's landmark encyclical. The idea of an integral ecology logically follows from the holistic approach that Pope Francis took in addressing the issue of the environment, but it is also in continuity with the whole corpus of Catholic social doctrine informed by Vatican II and the teachings of previous pontiffs on ecological concerns.[10] Pope Francis acknowledges that the church does not have a monopoly of opinion on issues of climate change and, therefore, takes note of "the reflections of numerous scientists, philosophers, theologians, and civic groups, all which have enriched the Church's thinking on these questions" (*LS* 7). It takes a humble pope to admit that all nonecclesiastical scholars have some say on the issue of ecology. This is part of Pope Francis's attitude of servant leadership symbolized by "foot washing."[11] It is important to observe that this pope, who has a Master's in Chemistry, would be more appreciative of what the scientists have to say on a crucial issue such as climate change.

What are the main themes and message of chapter 4 of *Laudato Si'*, for the world and the church? From the start, it is important to point out how difficult it is to compress scientific, philosophical, and theological perspectives on ecology into one chapter. It makes the text extremely dense for an ordinary reader, but Pope Francis tries his level best to make the content accessible. The main message of integral ecology is that humanity is an integral

---

10. Francis, *Laudato Si'*, 3–6 (hereafter cited in text as *LS*).

11. For a discussion of Pope Francis's exemplary leadership, see Reid, "Foot Washing," 9–23.

part of the universe and should not be opposed to, or separated from, the rest of creation. Then, Pope Francis connects human ecology to the famous concept of the common good (*LS* 156). He rejects the instrumentalization of creation and assigns it its own value (*LS* 140). Most previous papal documents can be accused of anthropocentrism—putting human beings at the center of creation and often assigning humans the role of stewardship and custodian, a role that is usually abused in the name of progress. Again, this is consistent with Pope Francis's humble approach of servant leadership. Human beings cannot put themselves above the rest of creation.

The chapter on integral ecology can be summed up in three main themes—namely, the interrelated nature of all things and their intrinsic value, cultural ecology, and the common good. The chapter's opening words are telling: "[E]verything is closely interrelated and . . . today's problems call for a vision capable of taking into account every aspect of the global crisis." (*LS* 137).

### The Interrelated Nature of All Things and Their Intrinsic Value

The planetary view that Pope Francis takes is quite relevant for today's world which tends to have a fragmented view of reality, focusing on economics (if one is a policymaker or politician), science (if one is a biologist or physicist), or theology (if one is a clerical or professional theologian). The planet has physical, chemical, and biological aspects; similarly, living species are intimately linked within this complex network, and human beings cannot fully comprehend this complexity (*LS* 138).

Furthermore, since all things are interrelated, the environment has intrinsic values. As Pope Francis points out, "We take these systems (ecosystems) into account not only to determine how best to use them, but also because they have an intrinsic value independent of their usefulness. Each organism, as a creature of God, is good and admirable in itself" (*LS* 140). While addressing the United Nations in 2015, Pope Francis talked of "the right of the environment" and has come close to suggesting that creation itself is the subject of rights. I think we need such a radical paradigm shift if the current crisis of climate change is to be addressed. Whether the United Nations will, in the near future, come up with the Universal Declaration of Creation Rights (UDCR) is yet to be known. If that were to happen, as it should, it would be the most concrete step towards ending the current regime of anthropocentrism that has dominated world events and systems for millennia.

From an integral view of the environment follows a new epistemological outlook which Pope Francis articulates: "It follows that the fragmentation of knowledge and isolation of bits of information can actually become a form of ignorance, unless they are integrated into a broader vision of reality" (*LS* 138). The current rigid division of labor and excessive specialization in scholarship, according to Pope Francis, is very problematic. This is partly why it is hard to find solutions to contemporary problems such as global poverty, global insecurity, and now climate change—each expert sees the problem from their narrow academic perspective. Due to the integral vision of reality under consideration, Pope Francis speaks of environmental, economic, and social ecology, so that comprehensive solutions can be found (*LS* 139). Fighting poverty, restoring human dignity, and protecting nature are considered triple concerns to be addressed simultaneously.

Integral ecology can be traced back to some leading Western thinkers such as Teilhard de Chardin (1881–1955) and Alfred North Whitehead (1861–1947). Taking a metaphysical understanding, Valerian Mendonca has done a commendable job of combining Teilhard de Chardin and Alfred North Whitehead to try to "produce a new intersubjective relational understanding of God, the world, and the human community" and, by so doing, laying "a metaphysical foundation for the vision of an integral ecology."[12] It is important to note that both Pope Francis and Teilhard de Chardin share the Ignatian spirituality whose unified cosmic and mystical view of reality can be discerned in the *Spiritual Exercises* of Saint Ignatius of Loyola, especially regarding the purpose of human existence and the created universe.[13]

The application of this integral ecology to environmental impact assessments is well-noted in this chapter. Ecosystems are interrelated, as illustrated by "dispersing carbon dioxide, purifying water, controlling illness and epidemics, forming soil, breaking down waste" (*LS* 140). These complex epidemiological and chemical processes involve systems that are closely interrelated: carbon dioxide from animals that plants take in, swamps helping to purify water, clean environments helping to prevent pandemics, and plants decomposing to form soil. The new concept that Pope Francis brings is "economic ecology," arguing that the integral approach to reality should be introduced in economic decisions as well. This approach will also affect how families, social institutions, and economic activities are organized, bearing in mind that one activity affects others (*LS* 141). A very compelling case is made for a global or international approach to social ecology, since

---

12. Mendonca, "Metaphysics of Intersubjectivity," 749.

13. For a discussion of the nature and meaning of the Spiritual Exercises of St. Ignatius of Loyola, see O'Malley, *First Jesuits*, 37–50.

issues such as trade, drug production, violence, and rights (for instance, the right to life is linked to rights to employment, health, and shelter) are also interconnected (*LS* 142). The rich nations of the world need to think of the impact their trade and investment policies have on the poorer countries.

## Cultural Ecology

The other novelty in Pope Francis's integral ecology is the dimension of cultural ecology, which connects the issue of environment to living spaces, national heritage sites, consumerism, and indigenous communities (*LS* 143–46). Development partners who mainly focus on profit when deciding where and how to invest will do well to take note of this issue of cultural ecology. Many countries rely on tourism that involves sacred and historical sites, which are part of a people's culture. Development projects that destroy such cultural sites in the name of profit and economic growth contravene the norms of integral ecology. At times, some global religions have tended to despise or look down on indigenous traditional religions. From the perspective of cultural ecology, this too is a violation of integral ecology. This is the same reason why a global economy that undermines local cultures is also challenged (*LS* 144). The other issue is that of multinational corporations (MNCs), especially those that manufacture weapons, neglecting ethical and cultural dimensions (since their main motive is profit) at the expense of life and people's well-being.[14]

Taking local cultures seriously demands from the universal church a respectful and appreciative engagement with various cultures, unlike in the past (and, to some extent, even today) when indigenous cultures were considered pagan and backward. Some attempts have been made to inculturate the gospel in local cultures, but the process is slow and oftentimes faces some resistance. The popular general perception is that the Western dominant culture, with its education, philosophy, and theology, is the norm for other cultures in developing countries to emulate.

This approach by some Western scholars to disparage and despise African worldviews is well documented, and Anne Arabome, one of Africa's up-and-coming women theologians, highlights this challenge, reflecting on Laurenti Magesa's book, *What Is Not Sacred? African Spirituality*:

> Missionary Christianity characteristically misunderstood African religion as animistic and pagan. For Christian missionaries, such belief systems did not merit being labeled religion, an

---

14. For a discussion of this issue, see Alva, "*Laudato Si'* Challenges Irrational Rationalization," 711–12.

appellation they reserved for Christianity and other so-called world religions. Indigenous religion stripped of any rational foundation was easy to caricature; its adherents could be demonized, and those opposed to it could systematically work toward to its elimination.[15]

Even when leading church authorities have made calls for an African Church, as was the case with Pope Paul VI on July 31, 1969,[16] Paul Béré observes that "the Catholic Church in Africa has not yet developed a genuine African face."[17] At an institutional level, the challenge is still there, since the theological curriculum of priestly formation is still the standard one set for the universal church, with small modifications. One cannot find a full-fledged African theology program, with African approaches to Scripture, theology, spirituality, liturgy, church history, and ecology. The church struggles with the tension of preserving unity in diversity.

It is important to note how in the African worldview, even what seems to be a purely material entity, like land, is imbued with spiritual value. See for instance how Pope Francis takes a radical view even regarding the way land is perceived by indigenous people: "For them, land is not a commodity but rather a gift from God and from their ancestors who rest there, a sacred space with which they need to interact if they are to maintain their identity and values" (*LS* 146).

Another aspect of cultural ecology is that of "daily life," whereby attention is paid to the way space is used and maintained to enhance decent living conditions through architectural designs, landscaping, and urban planning (*LS* 147–51). If badly designed, overcrowded, and noisy, urban places can create conditions which can contribute to the stress and unrest that produces violence and antisocial behavior (*LS* 149). In what can be considered the psychology of architecture, Pope Francis rightly argues that construction should take into consideration people's mindsets and thought processes, since there is "interrelationship between living spaces and human behavior" (*LS* 150). This perspective even has implications for the way churches are designed. Oftentimes, churches are built according to the standard designs from the West, which reflect alien aesthetic and artistic sensibilities. It is not uncommon to hear ordinary people complain of a local architectural design like the typical round-hut shape that is proposed. The

15. Arabome, "African Spirituality," 145.
16. On this day, Pope Paul VI was addressing the African Bishops when the Symposium of Episcopal Conferences of African and Madagascar was established, during a visit to Uganda.
17. Béré, "Old Testament Sources," 123.

same negative attitude is sometimes expressed about church vestments and sacred vessels with local designs. All of these go to demonstrate the failure to integrate cultural ecology with the ecology of daily life. But at times it is a matter of preference, with some people preferring exotic products and designs, since they associate them with prestige and high class.

Ecology of daily life covers other key challenging aspects of urban life such as poor housing (*LS* 152), transport that leads to traffic congestion (*LS* 153), and national heritage sites that need to be preserved for posterity (*LS* 151). No previous encyclical has ever gone to such great detail explaining the challenges of urbanization with such specifics. The theme of respect for human dignity is applied to the typically neglected aspect of society, namely rural areas, where living conditions are usually very poor "and where some workers are reduced to conditions of servitude, without rights or even the hope of a more dignified life" (*LS* 154).

Human ecology considers the appreciation of one's body to be a gift from God. This follows the concept of the "ecology of man" coined by Pope Benedict XVI, who insisted that there is a nature that man has that cannot be manipulated at will.[18] Pope Benedict was alluding to biomedical engineering, which is currently being explored with the aim of genetic engineering, cloning, and other complex bodily alterations that the church considers morally unacceptable. Again, true to his love for details, Pope Francis explains how to care for one's body: "Learning to accept our body, to care for it, and to respect its fullest meaning, is an essential element of any genuine human ecology" (*LS* 155).

Keeping physically fit through sports, taking walks, jogging, and a good massage, for example, are simple practices to take good care of the body, which is considered sacred and a temple of the Holy Spirit. This approach clearly challenges certain dualistic tendencies in Western tradition dating back to Plato that consider the body to be a prison where the soul is enslaved. It also challenges certain mystical traditions that see the body as a source of sin and temptation. Such negative attitudes toward the human body have even infiltrated liturgical practice, where certain bodily expressions are deemed inappropriate because they carry some immoral or indecent connotations in certain cultures. For example, even today, in some churches, liturgical dance is not welcome.

---

18. Benedict XVI, "Listening Heart."

## Common Good

Sections 156–58 of *Laudato Si'* are dedicated to the principle of the common good, which is at the heart of Catholic social teaching (CST). The common good is defined as "the sum of those conditions of social life which allow social groups and their individual members relatively thorough and ready access to their own fulfilment."[19] Several other important themes and principles are also compressed in these sections: respect for the human person, family, subsidiarity, social peace, and distributive justice (*LS* 157). Whose duty is it to defend and promote the common good? Pope Francis assigns this duty and obligation to society and the state. I wish to add that the church, too, has an obligation to make sure that this common good is well-known so that citizens can make their governments accountable when it comes to implementing the practical imperatives. The church is promoting the common good as well in its various social programs such as education, health, and work for justice and peace. And when the church engages in such work, governments should not feel threatened but rather see this as an opportunity for collaboration.

The section on the principle of the common good is quite dense and covers all the main principles of CST with rare precision. Pope Francis ends his discussion of it by relating it to the three other crucial principles of CST—namely, solidarity, the universal destination of goods, and the preferential option for the poor (*LS* 158). With the world richer now than ever before, it is a scandal and great injustice to find millions of people lacking basic needs. Here, the appeal is clear that the rich nations of the world, together with the universal church, need to work for the promotion of the common good that gives special preference for the poorest of the poor. This is an ethical imperative.

Pope Francis links the cry of the poor with the cry of the earth, and for this reason which Sandie Cornish rightly points out: "The poorest people and communities are often the most affected by ecological issues, and their poverty may influence behavior that contributes to them."[20] It follows, therefore, that when addressing environmental issues, the related social issues of inequality and poverty must not be left out.[21] More often than not, development agencies—even many faith-based organizations—tend to address social issues in isolation of environmental issues. Unless one is doing environmental studies or ecology, rarely do we find an educational

---

19. Paul VI, *Gaudium et Spes*, 26.
20. Cornish, "*Laudato Si*," 616.
21. Cornish, "*Laudato Si*," 616.

curriculum at all levels that addresses issues of ecology in all courses. And theological curricula are not spared from this sin of commission. Apart from some few individuals who have been taking personal initiatives to reflect and write on ecological issues, mainstream theological formation still largely concentrates on traditional theological issues: sin, grace, salvation history, revelation, Scriptures, moral theology, church history, patristics, liturgy, sacraments, and canon law. A few seminars here and there may deal with environmental issues, but ecological conversion is still a long way off, even in the intellectual formation of pastoral agents of evangelization.

The final paragraphs in the discussion of integral ecology, Part V under "Justice Between the Generations," deals with the need to think of future generations and the call for sustainable development. These are concrete ways of promoting the common good. Pope Francis makes an emotional appeal to the current generation, that they should reflect on what legacy they will leave for the generations to come, given the individualism and wasteful consumption habits that mark today's capitalist system (*LS* 159–62). Here again, the entire world and the universal church are in the spotlight. The global capitalist system that has given rise to competition, manufacturing needs through advertising, and massive production of goods, many of which are not essential for human flourishing, has been accepted as the norm. But it is time to rethink this unsustainable model of development.

### Integral Ecology: Towards an African Ecotheology of *Ubuntu*

Chapter 4 of *Laudato Si'* highlights the themes of integral ecology, cultural ecology, and the common good as central to the call to care for our common home. I appreciate this holistic view of reality, because it resonates well with African cosmology; however, this approach is still framed in a Western conceptual framework. The African themes of *Ubuntu* and *ubushingantahe* can help to enrich this holistic view of the environment. The main goal of this section is to contribute to the development of an African ecotheology of *Ubuntu*, with participation in the common sharing in the bond of life as its main pillar. At the heart of African philosophy and theology is the notion that life is a primary good. That is why the concept of vital force,[22] coined by Placide Tempels in his discussion of Bantu philosophy, has remained an operative term whenever African philosophy, theology, and spirituality are

---

22. This concept of vital force briefly states that all beings that exist are permeated by a spiritual force that gives them various degrees of energy to perform their respective functions. Even inanimate beings like stones have vital force that enables them to be used as building materials or to provide medicines.

discussed.[23] This vital force is also found in nature as the animating force, and since both animate and inanimate beings have force, vital force is the African metaphysical foundation for integral ecology. Whatever people engage in—be it rituals, prayers, work, celebrations, hunting, dance, you name it—the overall concern is the enhancement of life in its entirety.[24] Thus, the theme of integral ecology rings a bell in most African ears.

What are the elements of *Ubuntu* that can help to construct an African ecotheology? What vital force is to African ontology, *Ubuntu* is to African ethics and social relations. However, in African philosophy, ontology also determines ethical behavior, and this sharp categorical difference does not exist between the ontological and the ethical. To show how ontology and ethics are intimately connected in the African worldview, consider the often-quoted adage that summarizes the *Ubuntu* ethic: "A person is a person only with other persons, alone one is an animal."[25] An individual is shaped by community. Mogobe Ramose, regarded as the chief proponent of *Ubuntu* philosophy along with Desmond Tutu, observes that "to be a human being is to affirm one's humanity by recognizing the humanity of others and, on that basis, establish humane relations with them."[26] Here, the point of reciprocity and mutuality is emphasized as key to the *Ubuntu* ethic. We can extend this point of reciprocity and mutuality to ecology. Just as a human being wishes to be recognized and affirmed, so also does creation need to be recognized and affirmed.

Concretely, how does a person with *Ubuntu* qualities behave? How does an *Ubuntu* theological ethics inform the integral ecology of *Laudato Si'*? And equally important, what does integral ecology add to the *Ubuntu* ethic? The qualities of *Ubuntu* that Desmond Tutu has identified include openness, availability, affirmation of others, self-confidence, empathy, not feeling threatened by the success of others, and the sense of belonging to a greater whole.[27] Laurenti Magesa sums up the other related virtues of *Ubuntu*, thus completing the whole *Ubuntu* ethical system: tolerance, patience, generosity, hospitality, cooperation, integrity, and solidarity.[28] These are the social virtues that make sharing in the common bond of life possible and effective. When we apply these virtues to integral ecology, it is easy to

---

23. See Magesa, *What Is Not Sacred?*, 33–34, 170.

24. For a discussion of this worldview, see Magesa, *What Is Not Sacred?*, 27–32, 61–80, 89–98.

25. Magesa, *What Is Not Sacred?*, 12.

26. Ramose, "Philosophy of Ubuntu," 271.

27. Tutu, *No Future Without Forgiveness*, 34–35.

28. Magesa, *What Is Not Sacred?*, 13.

see how the two ethical systems can fit together. Because people are interrelated, together they can work for the common good that includes care for the environment. The virtues of generosity and hospitality that we generally associate only with human beings can be extended to the environment. The way human beings treat each other is the way they will treat Mother Nature.

While an *Ubuntu* ethic and ecotheology sound rosy and inspiring, the reality in some parts of Africa is far from inspiring. Theology and ethics are not a description of reality but an expression of an aspiration of the anticipated ideal that all hope for and work towards. The concept of *Ubuntu* developed in South Africa, but this nation is also home to xenophobic attacks on fellow Africans and all forms of violence against women. The Great Lakes region of the continent is home to the equivalent concepts of *ubupfura* or *ubushingantahe* (Rwanda/Burundi)[29] or *obufura* (Uganda) that refer to generosity, nobility of heart, kindness, full humanity, a welcoming attitude, and openness, as well as reciprocity. But this region is also home to recurring, state-sponsored armed violence, including genocide and the massive displacement of civilians.[30] So, one wonders, where is this *Ubuntu* in reality? Integral ecology is indeed a work in progress, and maybe it has just begun.

Bénézet Bujo has studied this concept of *ubushingantahe* in Burundi and observed that the individual person who possesses these qualities of *ubushingantahe* is known as *Mushingantahe*. He or she is a living embodiment of all noble qualities that are akin to the ethics of integral ecology from an African perspective: intensely humane, uniquely truthful, just, hardworking, responsible, exemplary, conciliatory, seeking peace in conflicts, and promoting the social, political, and economic prosperity of the whole society.[31]

I pick three of these qualities of *Mushingantahe* to link to integral ecology:

1. Responsible—A responsible person not only takes charge of human affairs, but he or she also takes good care of the environment.

2. Conciliatory—A conciliator tries to heal the wounds that human beings inflict on one another but also on creation. When humans cut

---

29. Magesa, *What Is Not Sacred?*, 13.

30. For a scholarly and highly critical analysis of the Great Lakes region's ethnic conflicts, including the genocide in Rwanda, see Mamdani, *When Victims Become Killers*. For a study of other conflicts in Africa, especially the Horn of Africa and southern Africa, see Nhema and Zeleza, *Roots of African Conflicts*; Adedeji, *Comprehending and Mastering African Conflicts*.

31. See Bujo, "Ecology and Ethical Responsibility," 287–88, 292.

down trees to construct roads, dams, etc., the environment is literally bleeding.

3. Advocatory—An advocate promotes the social, political, and economic prosperity of the whole society.

Caution must be taken, because these indigenous values have been systematically eroded by the new capitalistic ethics of the global village, an ethics marked by "domination of the earth, excessive materialism, and negation of the identity of the weak."[32] Largely responsible for the current ecological crisis and extreme wealth and poverty juxtaposed to each other, this ethics of consumerism and domination continues to reign, but a search is under way for an alternative ethical system. Magesa, a leading champion of African moral theology and the ethics of life, believes that a suitable alternative

> might be found in the original spirituality of humankind that can be traced to the African savannas, forests, and valleys, as far back as one hundred thousand years ago. Some archetypal values, in terms of the original human attempt to make sense of human life and the universe, must have developed there. Conceivably, they survive in the wisdom of the people of Africa.[33]

When one looks at the African context holistically—that is, socially, economically, politically, culturally, physically (geographically and biologically), and spiritually—one is confronted by a myriad of contradictions and an odd mixture of pessimism and optimism. Part of the task of an African ecotheology from an integral ecological perspective is to develop an objective and accurate understanding of this mysterious phenomenon called Africa. The African Union (AU) has been designing a grand plan titled *Agenda 2063*, a master plan for Africa's social, economic, and political transformation, as the continent prepares to take off and shake off the colonial boundaries and attain full integration.[34] This grand vision is called "a shared strategic framework for inclusive growth and sustainable development and a global strategy to optimize the use of Africa's resources for the benefit of all Africans," and the assumption is that Africa indeed has all the resources (material, cultural, intellectual, human, and even spiritual) to shape its destiny. Scientific studies have also shown that Africa can finance its own economic transformation if some innovative steps are taken that include an efficient tax system, cutting off illicit financial flows, and private equity.[35]

32. Magesa, *What Is Not Sacred?*, 17.
33. Magesa, *What Is Not Sacred?*, 17.
34. See African Union, *Agenda 2063*.
35. See Hamdok, *Innovative Financing*.

The most pressing question to anyone who observes the African continent closely is how the richest continent—in terms of natural resources, a youthful and energetic population, and favorable climate—can still be largely dependent on foreign aid and foreign direct investment and heavily burdened by debt. This same blatant contradiction can also be discerned in the religious sphere and intellectual spheres. How can a continent rich in diverse religious traditions, spiritualities, cosmogonies, indigenous knowledge systems, as well as Western-trained scholars, still be dependent on borrowed knowledge systems that inform policy and the day-to-day running of society? The theme of integral ecology carries a prophetic call for Africa to wake up from its borrowed dogmatic slumber. One of the major causes of the blatant contradictions the pope is discussing, is the colonial and missionary legacy that erased these very indigenous values of *Ubuntu* and *ubushingantahe* and replaced them with the so-called Western elite education[36] with its legal, positivistic outlook.

There is a new narrative of Afro-optimism that is even captured in the AU Anthem (in the first and third stanzas), which is loaded with *Ubuntu* ethics as well as ecotheology:

> Let us unite and celebrate together
> The victory won for our liberation
> Let us dedicate ourselves to rise together
> To defend our liberty and unity.
> Let us all unite and sing together
> To uphold the bonds that frame our destiny
> Let us dedicate ourselves to fight together
> For lasting peace and justice on earth.[37]

Since the theme of common good is central to integral ecology, a comment is in order about how this notion is faring with regard to the African nation-state. Generalizations can be tricky, but there seems to be a huge gap between what the nation-state claims it stands for and what it does. The general feeling is that the African nation-state has been captured by the ruling elite who, by and large, serve their interests. This perception has been captured by Jean-François Bayart, who coined the concept "politics of the belly"; he basically argues that the common good has been replaced by self-serving authoritarian rulers who are filling their bellies.[38] Emmanuel

---

36. Laurenti Magesa has made this point quite compellingly, using his own life story. See Magesa, *What Is Not Sacred?*, 14–22.

37. This African Union Anthem is found in the document *Agenda 2063*, inside front cover.

38. See Bayart, *State in Africa*.

Katongole articulates well this tragic state of disconnect between the nation-state and the aspirations of its citizens: "Given this disconnect between the political and the social, it is perhaps not surprising that the nation-state has failed to achieve legitimacy in the eyes of the majority of African citizens, since it does not connect and has never connected to their aspirations and everyday struggles."[39] Such a state can hardly be expected to serve the common good. Many suspect this nation-state was a creature of the colonial system, and so no one should be surprised if it fails to serve the citizens it claims it wants to serve. Similarly, it will also not protect the endangered environment. On the contrary, it will be its chief exploiter.

Integral ecology, viewed from an African perspective, should spark a new social imagination that Emmanuel Katongole has consistently and eloquently called for, in order to avoid the firefighting approach both to environmental and political issues facing Africa.[40] Katongole's line of thought—that failure of imagination is the issue but not lack of policy prescriptions—can help find some new imaginative approach in the integral ecology from an African perspective. Why do we continue to look for solutions from the nation-state or allow the nation-state to set the agenda for responses to climate change or environmental issues? An ecotheology of *Ubuntu* can form a new political framework for not only addressing environmental challenges but also poverty, governance, and violence. Katongole also calls "for storytellers who are able to offer people better stories than the ones they live by."[41] These stories do not come from the so-called experts but from anyone who has an interesting and transformative story. In the context of *Laudato Si'*, human beings will have to learn to listen to the story told by trees, because they also have a story to tell. And humans will have to learn the language of Mother Nature.

In this next final section, I narrate two related environmental initiatives in Africa linked to preserving ecosystems. I should say that it is actually one story told from the perspective of two countries—Uganda and Ethiopia. The choice of the two countries is to bring out some contrast but also to show how two solutions across countries can have some similarities.

---

39. Katongole, *Sacrifice of Africa*, 72.
40. See Katongole, *Sacrifice of Africa*, 9–63.
41. Katongole, *Sacrifice of Africa*, 61.

## "Gardens of Eden"—Religious and Cultural Approaches to Preserving Ecosystems and Biodiversity

We conclude our discussion of integral ecology of *Laudato Si'* with an African story of an environmental initiative in Africa, linking it to the creative development of some African ecotheological principles, themes, and practices. How do we address the African context and also speak to the world and the church? In this story (presented in two locations), I wish to propose an ethics of cosmic solidarity rooted in ecological praxis and performance. The choice of "gardens of Eden" is to allude to the story of Genesis's paradisal landscape that Adam and Eve disrupted by their disobeying God (Gen 2:4—3:19).

For over ten years, I have observed the Orthodox and Catholic Churches in Ethiopia, which are always surrounded by trees, such that they appear like small "gardens of Eden." Trees survive around churches, because there is little pressure to use them for either cooking or construction. They are largely for ornamentation and for providing shade to devout worshippers. Other people use the shade of the trees around the church to sell sacred items such as books, rosaries, crosses, and pictures of saints. Church compounds also house the graves of the most distinguished officials, kings, and queens of Ethiopia,[42] which adds to the sacred aura of the space but also helps to link the cosmic with the eschatological. Some Ethiopian churches also feature a museum on the compound to preserve national history.[43] There are thousands of churches, both Catholic and Orthodox, scattered across Ethiopia.[44] In Addis Ababa alone, there are well over 100. Among those that are wrapped in the "gardens of Eden" are the following: Entoto Maryam (on Entoto Mountain; Church of Mary), Wusha Mikael Church (Church of Michael), Holy Trinity Cathedral, Holy Saviour Church, St. Gabriel Church, St. Michael Church, St. Raphael Church, Kidane Mehret Church (Covenant of Mercy), St. George Cathedral, and St. Mary's Church.

---

42. For instance, Holy Trinity Cathedral is home to the graves of Emperor Haile Selassie and his wife, Empress Menen Asfaw; ministers killed by the Derg in 1974; patriots who died fighting the Italian occupation; and Sylvia Pankurst, a British citizen who protested Italy's occupation.

43. Churches which have a museum and are a great tourist attraction include St. George's Cathedral in Addis Ababa. Commissioned by Emperor Menelik to commemorate the defeat of Italians in 1896, and completed in 1911, its museum contains crowns, hand crosses, prayer sticks, holy scrolls, ceremonial umbrellas, and the coronation garb of Empress Zewditu and Emperor Haile Selassie.

44. For a detailed study of the remote churches of Ethiopia, see Friedlander and Friedlander, *Hidden Treasures of Ethiopia*. For a tourist guide to many of Ethiopia's churches, see Carillet et al., *Ethiopia and Eritrea*.

The other chapter in the story of Ethiopia's "gardens of Eden" are the numerous monasteries that date to the late sixteenth or early seventeenth century, especially those in Lake Tana, which possess an "artificial beauty . . . [and are] full of glorious treasures and paintings."[45] But the most glorious treasures around these monasteries are the lush, green vegetation of indigenous trees that the monks preserve with piety and devotion. These monasteries and their churches include Kebran Gabriel (Church of Gabriel); Narga Selassie; Daga Estefanos (Church of St. Stephen)—which contains the mummified remains of five former Ethiopian emperors of the thirteenth to sixteenth centuries—Tana Cherkos (where it is said the Ark of the Covenant was hidden for 800 years); Ura Kidane Meret; Debra Maryam; Azuwa Maryam; Beta Giorgis; and Mistsele Fasilidas.[46] These sound like fairytale places, but they are real!

The story of Ethiopia's "gardens of Eden" is not complete until one hears of the churches in the northern part of the country, where medieval Ethiopian church history can be discerned. Situated in Gondar, Debre Berhan Selassie Church is a marvel to behold. Other churches in this area were destroyed, unfortunately, by Sudanese dervishes in the 1880s[47]—violence destroys integral ecology. Other famous churches in northern Ethiopia include the Portuguese Cathedral, built by Susenyos, who was the Emperor of Ethiopia (reigned 1607–32); Debre Sina, built in 1608 also by Emperor Susenyos; Mendaba Medhane Alem, home to ancient biblical manuscripts; and Birgida Maryam, with its sixteenth-century paintings of Mary. If you think Gondar is a mystery, try Axum, the home of the legendary Queen of Sheba. Legend has it that the Ark of the Covenant resides here, in St. Mary of Zion Church museum, containing gold, precious stones, and the crowns of former rulers.[48] Dating to the fourth century are the monasteries of Abba Liqanos and Abba Pentalewon. Abba Pentalewon has a little church with manuscripts, metal crosses, censers, and sistra (an ancient musical instrument used both in Egypt and Ethiopia), and it is said that Abba Pentalewon, who built this monastery, prayed for forty years nonstop.[49] Legends like these are a part of integral ecology, helping to preserve culture and ancient beliefs.

The story of the "Garden of Eden in Ethiopia" also must mention the rock-hewn churches of Tigray (not to be confused with those of Lalibela),

---

45. Carillet et al., *Ethiopia and Eritrea*, 114.
46. Carillet et al., *Ethiopia and Eritrea*, 116.
47. Carillet et al., *Ethiopia and Eritrea*, 122.
48. Carillet et al., *Ethiopia and Eritrea*, 132–38.
49. Carillet et al., *Ethiopia and Eritrea*, 139.

which number 120!⁵⁰ But I will focus more on the Lalibela rock-hewn, churches which are considered the wonder of Africa; the sixteenth-century Portuguese writer, Francisco Alvares, said: "I am weary of writing more about these buildings, because it seems to me that I shall not be believed if I write more."⁵¹ Nearly 1,000 years old, these giant, breathtaking basilicas carved from rock must be seen to be believed. All scholars concur that Lalibela's eleven churches date to the twelfth or thirteenth century and coincide with the reign of King Lalibela, a Zagwe dynastic king who was a very devout Christian.⁵²

UNESCO World Heritage sites, these churches are a typical example of the cultural and human ecology that *Laudato Si'* speaks about. They provide aesthetic delight because of their amazing Christian and naturalistic art,⁵³ and they bring income to Ethiopia through tourism. Left behind by past generations, they need to be preserved for posterity. But also within the churches, there are bees that produce honey which "is believed to possess special healing properties";⁵⁴ nutritionists know that this is because it is made from nectar found in various flowers of phytotherapeutic plants. Around Lalibela are eight more churches dating to the sixth century that are built from brick rather than carved from rock⁵⁵ and have forest cover around them. One example is Arbatu Ensessa, thought to have been built by King Kaleb in AD 518, who ruled around 514–43 and was the last major Aksumite king of Ethiopia.

Other African countries can learn from Ethiopia's cherishing of sacred places about the need to preserve old churches. Whenever a new church is built, common practice is that the older church is first destroyed. Little do people know, however, that not only are they destroying cultural ecology and a huge source of income but also an important aspect of history of the country. In the name of modernity, many people are quick to erase history, considering it to be backward. This is also how valuable knowledge in the form of proverbs and folktales and uses for medicinal plants are lost. The main reason that Ethiopia has such a long tradition of history, myths, and legends is that this ancient African civilization was spared the colonial onslaught. It is proud of its history and makes no apologies about it.

50. Carillet et al., *Ethiopia and Eritrea*, 147–51.
51. Quoted in Carillet et al., *Ethiopia and Eritrea*, 156.
52. Carillet et al., *Ethiopia and Eritrea*, 157–61.
53. For the marvelous artwork in these churches, see Friedlander and Friedlander, *Hidden Treasures of Ethiopia*.
54. Carillet et al., *Ethiopia and Eritrea*, 160.
55. Carillet et al., *Ethiopia and Eritrea*, 163–65.

## "Garden of Eden"—The Tadeo Nyebirweki Rwakazooba Forest

*Ubuntu* philosophy, which entails self-reliance and positive appreciation of work, is what guided Tadeo Nyebirweki. Different from the substory of Ethiopia's "garden of Eden" churches is the lesser-known story of the Tadeo Nyebirweki Rwakazooba Forest (TNRF) found in Kabale, in southwestern Uganda, close to the Rwandan border. It is a forest of about five square kilometers of mainly eucalyptus and black wattle trees that were singlehandedly planted by Tadeo Nyebirweki, a committed Catholic with a strong devotion to St. Jude Thaddeus, after whom he was named. Nyebirweki was trained by the hardworking Missionaries of Africa (formerly known as the White Fathers) who were mainly from France, Belgium, and Canada;[56] he used to watch the missionaries working with their hands in the fields, especially helping to build churches in the rural parts of Kabale and planting trees around them.

Although Nyebirweki was a designer by profession and trained many youth in designing, he took on tree planting as a hobby but also as a means of supplementing his income, especially for educating his children. His slogan was "for every tree you cut, plant two." He did not plant this minimum, however; instead, he planted hundreds of thousands of trees for the next generation.

He invested the savings from his design and tailoring work by buying land, which he in turn used to plant trees. In a period of about fifty years, he managed to buy an entire mountain—one plot at a time. By the time he died in 2007, he had planted over 100,000 trees, including the whole mountain of Rwakazooba,[57] whose trees still stand. Nyebirweki's trees were also used for constructing traditional Kiga houses (made of mud, limestone mixed with cow dung, and wood) as well as for fencing and providing firewood and timber. Most importantly, Nyebirweki gave free firewood to women who struggled to find their own, to teachers at Kyasano Primary School, and to churches as building materials. He also left a will stipulating that his land would never be sold but rather used by his descendants and future generations to come. He was also radical in promoting gender equality; so that his daughters could plant trees, he allocated some plots that they could keep even after they were married, contrary to Kiga culture which forbids women from inheriting land. This story of one individual with a vision is a

---

56. For a discussion of the methods of the missionaries of Africa and how they planted the Christian faith across the continent, including Uganda, see Kittler, *White Fathers*.

57. "Rwakazooba" means "of the sun" in Rukiga, because the mountain faces east where the sun rises.

clear paradigm of integral ecology, *Ubuntu* ethics (sharing, solidarity, and generosity), and ecospirituality.

TNRF is like a living school of ecospirituality, instructing all those who pass by it to love, appreciate, and nurture Mother Nature. Its hundreds of thousands of trees prevent soil erosion and preserve mineral salts by reducing the force of rainwater so that rather than flooding, the water flows gently and slowly. The forest is also home to diverse plant species, many of which have medicinal value, including the following:

- eucalyptus (*Eucalyptus globulus*; *entusi* in Rukiga—the native language of Kiga tribe of southwestern Uganda)—the steam of boiled leaves is used to treat colds and the flu.
- stinging nettle (*Urica diocia*; *ecicuriganyi* in Rukiga and *samma* in Amharic)—it is used as a vegetable diuretic and for colds and the flu.
- neem leaf (*Azadirachta indica*)—used to make tea tonics, to help treat gastrointestinal disorders, as a natural insect repellant and immune system booster, it has antibacterial, antiviral, and antioxidant properties.
- bitter leaf (*Vernonia amygdalina*; *Omubirizi* in Rukiga, and it is used to treat malaria)
- passion flower (*passiflora*)—its leaves are used to help reduce anxiety and induce sleep.
- milk thistle (*Silybum marianum*)—it is used to help treat liver disease.
- dandelion (*Taraxacum officinale*)—its flowers help to strengthen the eyes; its leaves are used in diuretics, and its roots to help detoxify the liver.
- cleavers (*Galium aparine*; *Kaboha* in Rukiga)—it is used as a diuretic and lymphatic stimulant and to treat urinary tract infections.
- *Ocimum urticifoliu* (*Omwesyamuro* in Rukiga; *Damakese* in Amharic)—it is used to treat colds and the flu.
- holy basil (*Ocimum tenuiflorum*)—it is used to detoxify the liver and reduce fever.
- Abyssinian coral tree (*Erythrina abyssinica*; *Ekico* in Rukiga)—its leaves are used to treat common colds and malaria and to boost strength

- aloe vera (*Aloe barbadensis miller*; *Enkaka* in Rukiga)—it is used to clean blood, heal wounds, stimulate digestion, and treat skin infections.

- lemongrass (*Cymbopogon*; *Omuteeta* in Rukiga)—an antispasmodic, antirheumatic, anticonvulsant, and analgesic, it is used as a diuretic and to treat digestive disorders, diabetes, fever, cough, and upset stomach.

The medicinal value of these plants makes the TNRF a living pharmacy[58]—not just a pharmacy, but a cosmic hospital! And because the forest is free of human activity, numerous bird species also find their home and food there.

The forest is on the way to Rwanyena Catholic Parish, which is about thirteen kilometers from Tadeo Nyebirweki's home. In African cosmology, forests are considered sacred, and large trees and mountains like Rwakazooba are believed to host spirits. For this reason, cutting down large trees is seen as an abomination. As people walk through the forest, they can only contemplate the wonders of creation and silently praise the Creator—it is a sort of sacred pilgrimage, which culminates in the celebration of the Eucharist, uniting heaven and earth, at Rwanyena Parish. Inside the church is a drawing of the Samaritan woman carrying a massive jar of water, with Jesus seated by the well and the words *Yezu Muriisa Nganda* (Jesus who feeds nations).

Rwakazooba Mountain, where TNRF is located, in fact looks like Calvary, and the tall, enormous trees like crosses dotting the mountain, as if they are celebrating a cosmic resurrection of Mother Earth and awaiting cosmic resurrection. TNRF is like a gigantic cathedral and, in fact, Tadeo Nyebirweki used to refer to it as a sacred place. Each day, you could say that he had two prayer sessions contemplating creation—he always started his day at around 5:00 AM, working in the forest until 7:30 AM when he would go to Katuna (on the Rwandan border) for his design work, and then, from 6:00 PM to around 7:00 PM (during the rainy season), he would return to plant trees. A mountain like Rwakazooba best represents what

---

58. For studies on medicinal plants that have been confirmed to have healing properties from a purely scientific perspective, see Iwu, *Handbook of African Medicinal Plants*, and Dharani, *Field Guide to Common Trees*. And since the climatic conditions of Rwakazooba (with an altitude of about 2,500 meters above sea level) are similar to those of the Entoto Mountain in Addis Ababa and other parts of Ethiopia, some of the plants and trees found in the area are also similar; for a discussion of those, see Janeski, *Healing Ourselves Naturally in Ethiopia*; Demisswe and Nordal, *Aloes and Other Lilies*; Negash, *Selection of Ethiopia's Indigenous Trees*; Asfaw and Demissew, *Aromatic Plants of Ethiopia*; Leyew, *Wild Plant Nomenclature*; Shisanya, *Determinants of Sustainable Utilization*; Tadese, *Trees of Ethiopia*; Teketay, *Edible Wild Plants of Ethiopia*.

Pierre Teilhard de Chardin called the *Divine Milieu*, which celebrates God's presence felt throughout the created world.[59] His observation makes perfect sense: "Nothing, Lord Jesus, can subsist outside of your flesh. . . . All of us, inescapably, exist in you, the universal *milieu* in which and through which all things live and have their being."[60]

Rwakazooba Mountain is part of the great mountain range on top of which is the Church of Rwanyena. In Teilhardian mystical and eucharistic cosmology, this whole landscape is consecrated by the words of the priest during Mass:

> when, through the mouth of the priest, he says *Hoc est corpus meum* (this is my body), these words extend beyond the morsel of bread over which they are said: they give birth to the whole mystical body of Christ. The effect of the priestly act extends beyond the consecrated host to the cosmos itself. . . . The entire realm of matter is slowly but irresistibly affected by this great consecration.[61]

If Teilhard de Chardin is right—that matter is also transformed into the body of Christ—it should not be surprising that plants, rocks, soils, and animals carry the healing power that Christ has. So, then, the original words Jesus used at the Last Supper also transform the cosmos into the body of Christ—the very cosmos that was created through him and for him, according to Colossians 1:16.

The words of Teilhard de Chardin in his "Hymn to Matter" are also quite relevant to TNRF: "Blessed be you, harsh matter, barren soil, stubborn rock; you who yield only to violence, you who force us to work if we would eat."[62] Nyebirweki used to say: "*Kora nkomuhuuku obone kurya nk'omukama*—work like a slave so you can eat like a king." And he lived this adage to the letter and insisted his children do likewise. The soils of Rwakazooba were in fact not very fertile, but rather rocky and barren. But still Nyebirweki would buy from the sellers arguing that trees can grow there. Whenever he cleared the forest to plant trees, he would first harvest vegetables that would grow when the trees are still young. The main vegetable that grows at Rwakazooba is *Solanum nigrum* or *Eshwiga* in *Rukiga*, *Lisutsa* in Luhiya (a native Bantu language spoken in Western Kenya); in addition

---

59. See Teilhard de Chardin, *Hymn of the Universe*, 12–22, 28, 35–39.
60. Teilhard de Chardin, *Hymn of the Universe*, 29 (emphasis original).
61. See Teilhard de Chardin, *Hymn of the Universe*, 6.

to its high nutritional value, it also has medicinal properties and is used to treat malaria and stomach ailments as well as boost immunity.

The terrain of Rwakazooba has a natural mechanism for protecting itself against the destructive forces of modernity—its terrain is so rugged that it is impossible to construct a road and use a vehicle through the forest. Even though Katuna Town Council (a border town between Uganda and Rwanda) is just three kilometers from TNRF, and Kabale Municipality about twenty kilometers away, TNRF has remained free from urbanization. Although devoutly Christian, the community there has preserved its indigenous traditions and values, and TNRF can be best described as an ecospirituality and biodiversity sanctuary. Even without UNESCO's approval or recognition, TNRF will remain a famous cultural heritage site. For the world and the church, the lesson is to look out for such environmental protection from below, from grassroots individuals like Tadeo Nyebirweki who work unnoticed for our common home. They are the unsung champions and apostles of climate change scattered across the world, in rural and indigenous communities.

## Conclusion

*Laudato Si*'s integral ecology has an urgent message for the church and the world but also, in a special way, for Africa. It is the closest humanity has ever come to having a genuine Earth charter. The story of Lake Victoria's rising waters is a clarion call, a warning, of many environmental dangers that lie ahead. It is almost too late, since the numerous cities that have been built on wetlands and low-lying areas (not just in Africa but all over the world) cannot be moved in a short time. The two stories I have narrated spell out the dangers, but also the future promise, regarding our care for our common home. The first story of Lake Victoria clearly shows us that Mother Nature can hit back when offended by our human encroachment. And the second story of the "gardens of Eden" is an inspiring example of caring for the environment that shows African ecospirituality and cosmic *Ubuntu* as praxis of cosmic compassion. Participating in the bonds of life impels us to have a holistic view of all reality, since life in its physical, spiritual, and mystical dimensions is interconnected. When you plant a tree or cultivate a human relationship, you are participating in a cosmic dance that enhances life in its fullness.

# 6

## Lines of Approach and Action: An African Ecotheology of Justice, Praxis, and Social Transformation

TOUSSAINT MURHULA KAFARHIRE, SJ

Enforceable international *agreements are urgently needed*, since local authorities are not always capable of effective intervention. Relations between states must be *respectful of each other's sovereignty* but must also lay down mutually agreed *means of averting regional disasters* which would eventually affect everyone. *Global regulatory norms* are needed to impose obligations and prevent unacceptable actions, for example, when *powerful companies or countries dump contaminated waste or offshore polluting industries in other countries.*

—POPE FRANCIS, *LAUDATO SI'*[1]

### Environmental Vandalism in Africa

On November 6, 2006, the *Probo Koala*, a ship owned by the Dutch shipping conglomerate Trafigura, dumped 500 tons of toxic waste on the shores of Abidjan, Côte d'Ivoire. The resulting environmental crisis and number of human casualties caused an international outcry in subsequent years. On May 13, 2009, for instance, the BBC opened its *Newsnight* program

---

1. Francis, *Laudato Si'* (hereafter cited in text as *LS*), 173; emphases added.

by stating that the dumping was "the biggest toxic dumping scandal of the twenty-first century, the type of environmental vandalism that international treaties are supposed to prevent."[2] It declared, "Now *Newsnight* can reveal the truth about the waste that was illegally tipped on Ivory Coast's biggest city, Abidjan."[3] Who were the victims? According to a 2012 Amnesty International and Greenpeace Report, fifteen to seventeen people lost their lives, authorities reported, whereas "more than 100,000 people were treated, according to official reports, but it is likely that the number was higher as records are incomplete."[4] How could this be possible in the first place? How and why did local authorities allow such actions to happen?

The dumping of toxic waste on African shores not only illustrates another crack in the planet that we inhabit (*LS* 163) and in the conscience of humanity, it also reveals a pattern of international thinking and behavior that has demoted certain geographies and peoples as less deserving of protection and dignity. In the international behavior towards Africa, the Trafigura dumping case is only the tip of the iceberg. It exemplifies the manner in which the environment is often disregarded in the name of maximizing economic profit, and how "the poor" always represent the disproportionate victims of the ecological degradation (*LS* 49). As a matter of fact, the *Probo Koala* incident isn't the first in which Africa has been treated as a dumping site of hazardous wastes. Almost twenty years before, dealers in toxic waste lied that they had exported fertilizers to help poor farmers in the small fishing village of Koko, Nigeria.

It is important, therefore, to understand what makes possible such ecocide, as in the two aforementioned instances. Indeed, the United Nations Environmental Programme (UNEP) notes that "African nations have long been at the center of incidents involving hazardous waste dumping. From the leaking barrels of toxic waste in Koko, Nigeria, in 1988 and the *Probo Koala* scandal in Côte d'Ivoire in 2006, to the current piles of e-waste threating the health of West African communities, the continent continues to be disproportionately affected by the dumping of harmful chemical materials."[5] The leakage from the 2,000 drums, sacks, and containers happened to be hazardous wastes that caused upset stomachs, headaches, failing sight, and even death in the local community. The site in Koko village was rendered

---

2. "BBC Deletes Important Story," para. 3.
3. "BBC Deletes Important Story," para. 3.
4. Greenpeace and Amnesty International, *Toxic Truth*, 3.
5. United Nations Environment Programme (UNEP), "Bamako Convention," para. 1.

unsuitable for life, causing the evacuation of 500 people. To this day, villagers in Koko still remember the incident as the "drums of death."

Both incidents in Abidjan and in Koko are reminiscent of what the African peoples have endured at the hand of international profiteers. The West has often justified its condescending attitude and abusive practices in Africa using humanitarian discourse to legitimize its neo-colonial attitudes of intervention. As a matter of fact, even the multinational corporations conducting business on the continent have justified their presence along those lines. Despite some unsustainable environmental practices, they still allege that at least they are in Africa for the good of Africans, as they bring the much-needed capital to finance developmental projects and create jobs in poverty-stricken nations.[6] How is it that everyone comes to Africa for the sake of Africans, yet the conditions of those worst off have not improved at all? How is it that the rhetoric of knowledge transfer, provision of foreign aid, and exchange of expertise, and the extension of the benefits of development, have not yielded the promises of institutions like the World Bank or other multilateral development agencies? Were policies deliberately misrepresented to mislead Africa into the trap of dependency to the Western? As one African scholar rightly contends, the establishment of the colonial project and colonizing structures were meant to force Africa into the Western capitalist economy, reorganize its physical and symbolic spaces, and reformat the Africans' minds to make them comply with the existing international order.[7]

A few years into independence, Africans realized the various contradictions embodied in international development policies, and they started to question the West's development agenda in Africa. Also, they began to demand a new international economic order (NIEO), through the United Nations Conference on Trade and Development (UNCTAD). This was a set of proposals that sought to promote the developing countries' interests, improve the terms of trade, increase development assistance, reduce developed-country tariffs, and other similar expectations. These claims were, of course, resisted and dismissed by the West, who blamed Africa's misfortunes and development failures not on the structures and institutions in place but on the incompetence of African leadership. The West argued that it had no obligation to make more sacrifices to pay for the bad policies and poor choices of Africans.[8]

---

6. Blundin, "Corporate Social Responsibility."
7. Mudimbe, *Invention of Africa*, 2.
8. Murphy, "What the Third World Wants," 55–76.

The Western paradigm of development exported to Africa came with a wealth of cultural biases, racism, and historical prejudices that legitimize environmental vandalism in Africa. A paradigm is both the theoretical thinking and habits that permit existing patterns of behavior and social interactions with other human beings and the environment. It shapes the "forestructure" of understanding—that is, the antecedent and already-entrenched developed cognitive systems through which reading, interpretation, and meaning-making occur.[9] So, stemming from the spirit of modernity and embracing scientific rationality at the expense of religion, the development paradigm regarded all non-Western lifestyles as backward and extolled the virtue of the Western conquest, including colonization. This practice has evolved to equate today's politics of "short-term growth," maximization of profit, and privatization of interests; generating massive disparities between communities has indeed proved to be environmentally unsustainable (LS 178, 184).

It is crucial, therefore, to establish a good diagnostic of the environmental crisis in Africa as stemming from the Western system of conquest, legitimized by the church since the fifteenth century.[10] V. Y. Mudimbe rightly argues that "the more carefully one studies the history of missions in Africa, the more difficult it becomes not to identify it with cultural propaganda, patriotic motivations and commercial interest since the missions' program is indeed more complex than the simple transmission of the Christian faith."[11] Hence, as Michel Foucault tells us, a diagnosis of the present does not imply providing a comprehensive analysis of current practices in order to establish the conditions under which these practices became possible. The Martinican poet and statesman Aimé Césaire, one of the founding fathers of the Negritude movement, also contends in his *Discourse on Colonialism* that the main problem when dealing with the question of colonialism is to "be the dupe in good faith of a collective hypocrisy that cleverly misrepresents problems to better legitimize the hateful solutions provided for them."[12] In fact, what James Tully has said about the native Americans rings true for Africans because the colonial system sprang from the same mentality. Modern

---

9. Heelan, "Hermeneutical Realism and Scientific Observation," 1:79: Here, Patrick Heelan explores Martin Heidegger's concept of hermeneutics, or the philosophical practice of understanding and interpretation that comprises three parts. The *vorhabe* (fore-having) or set of praxes, embodiments, and skills that mediates the descriptive categories; the *vorsicht* (foresight) or common descriptive language; and the *vorgriff* (fore-conception) referring to a particular hypothesis about any subject matter at hand.

10. Lynch, *Wrestling with God*, 70–106.

11. Mudimbe, *Invention of Africa*, 45.

12. Césaire, *Discourse on Colonialism*, 32.

thinkers such as John Locke were derogatory of any form of governance different from the Western. Locke did not only downgrade the Amerindian forms of governance and property, but he also subjected their land and polity to the sovereignty of European concepts.[13]

The same colonial rationale that was operative in the dispossession of the native Americans is found in the legitimization of the dispossession of Africans and the destruction of their polity. Actually, the polluting of the African environment does not only involve degradation of physical space through exploitation of the minerals but also the minds of the people. In the former instance, Canadian philosopher Alain Denault and colleagues have documented how Western multinational companies deplete the African soil, pollute rivers, displace entire communities, and jeopardize the lives and health of the continent wherever important minerals are discovered. By digging minerals, they provoke the killing of miners by landslides, abandoning open pits when minerals are depleted, and sometimes provoking civil wars and, involuntarily (or maybe voluntarily), genocides in the pursuit of lucrative businesses.[14]

Lying in the name of development has caused a lot of damage to the environment. Both the colonial state and the missionary church coalesced to carry out the so-called humanitarian work of civilization and bring eternal salvation to the souls of pagans. While the former provided administrative agents and soldiers to guarantee a propitious business environment, the latter availed its missionaries to educate and format the native minds. Some have referred to this as the triple alliance, or the holy triumvirate, of state-church-and-multinational-companies. While papal decrees had previously allowed European conquerors to deprive natives of their lands by declaring all noncultivated land "vacant," the granting of land to both multinationals and the church by the colonial state through concordats paved the way for discrediting African traditional values and communal land ownership.[15] While African lands, rivers, forests, mines, oil, and other natural resources—as well as the human capital—were set for exploitation

---

13. Tully, *Approach to Political Philosophy*, 137–76.

14. Deneault et al., *Noir Canada*. Joye and Lewin, *Les Trusts au Congo*, 297, advance a similar argument and claim this is what happened in Congo-Kinshasa when the Union Minière du Haut Katanga (UMHK), a subsidiary of the Belgian "Société Générale," masterminded the Katanga secession in the early 1960s, resulting in a far-reaching, postindependence crisis. A similar situation was provoked in Congo-Brazzaville when Elf-Aquitaine and the group Bolloré rearmed former president Denis Sassou Ngouesso in 1997 to topple the then-democratically elected president Pascal Lissouba as Pierre Caminade (author of *Bolloré*) contends.

15. See Murhula, "Jesuits–Protestants Encounter," 194–214. See also Cline, "Church and the Movement," 48.

by Western powers under the colonial regime for the sake of capitalist profit, Pope Francis suggests precluding such damages through transparent policy processes, honest project evaluations, and the democratic participation of local communities (*LS* 167, 184) as we shall later see.

It is the iteration of these colonial practices—backed by a set of modern and liberal ideals—that lent force to the condescending relations that have characterized the Western development policies toward Africa. The resulting systemic abuses, epistemic violence, and institutionalized exploitation of both the African people (living either on the continent or in the diaspora) and the natural resources (that benefit the rest of the world but not the sons and daughters of the African continent) have left Africans with a feeling of being duped by the international institutions, as they powerlessly have a sense of neither owning their destiny nor belonging to their lands. The majority want to emigrate to the West where they are treated poorly as second-zone citizens and carry themselves with a sense of inferiority, almost as if they had lesser human worth. This is due both to a past of economic exploitation and a present of political marginalization and traumas. While this might be an oversimplification, it can also help interpret the generalized pattern of police profiling and racial killings of Blacks in the United States, and the racism in the rest of the world to which the now-worldwide Black Lives Matter movement set itself up against as a reaction. In Europe, two French journalists recently provoked a global outcry by proposing that Africans could be used as guinea pigs in development of a coronavirus vaccine.[16] At the root of this institutionalized mode of thinking are the history and the ideology of development that entail a form of epistemological violence which assumes Black lives to be cheaper and, therefore, open to social experiments for the advancement of science. Hence, dumping toxic waste in Africa appears almost the most natural course of action, given the perception that the continent is a place where nothing works or has ever worked.

Regarding the international medical experiment, Susan Reverby has indicated a pattern of US foreign policy behavior, revealing a certain way of thinking underlying the treatment of non-White, non-Western communities. Applying different standards of human dignity and rights to non-US human subjects abroad, the US Public Health Service (PHS) has actually treated non-White American citizens and other powerless, vulnerable

---

16. See "No African Guinea Pigs." To quote from this interview: "Earlier this week it was reported that Doctor Jean-Paul Mira, head of intensive care at Cochin Hospital in Paris said during the debate on the French TV channel LCI: 'If I was a bit provocative, I would say that we could go and do tests in Africa. They haven't got masks, no treatment, no intensive care system, we could go and test there.' For centuries, the world has used Africans as guinea pigs for their experiments" (para. 2).

populations as guinea pigs. Evidence includes the following: the infamous 1932–72 "Tuskegee experiment"; the 1953 incident in New York's Sing Sing Prison, where the PHS permitted prisoners to be inoculated with heat-killed and virulent organisms to study syphilis reinfection; the Guatemala case in which American scientists inoculated inmates and prostitutes with the syphilis virus without their informed consent first; and the sterilization of many Black women in the United States in the early 1970s without their knowledge.[17] It is this kind of environmental pollution, including thought and mindset pollution, that Pope Francis decries in his encyclical. He calls for a paradigm shift in thinking development; he also invites us to enter a frank conversation with politics and economics—one that will promote the common good, serve the human life and biodiversity, and include everyone (*LS* 163, 201).

## Lines of Approach and Action in *Laudato Si'*

There is increased evidence of illegal dumping of toxic waste in Africa with consequences affecting life now and in the future. Yet, the absence of sound institutional capabilities to resist the deleterious consequences of the human action on our common home compels us to develop new thinking and strategies to mitigate the environmental degradation. We are all stakeholders in the management of so-called "global commons" and we need a cosmopolitan approach, a global authority, and an agreement on systems of governance that would involve all of us in the discussion (*LS* 174). While it is not in the intention of the church to aspire to either replace politics or settle scientific questions, the concern is "to encourage an honest and open debate so that particular interests or ideologies will not prejudice the common good" (*LS* 188).

Chapter 5 of *Laudato Si'* outlines major paths of dialogue to help escape the spiral of self-destruction in which our current paradigm of development has induced us. While Pope Francis advocates inclusiveness in this global dialogue to save our common home, the timing during the planning process of ventures and projects is important to avert the environmental impacts (*LS* 190). These paths of dialogue are developed along five lines. First, instigating a new international normative framework to manage environmental issues; second, reclaiming the state regulatory power to control activities and operations of multinational companies within their boundaries; third, establishing transparent and participatory mechanisms in the

---

17. Reverby, "Ethical Failure and History Lessons," 1–18; Tilley, "History of Medicine," 743–53.

decision-making processes; fourth, utilizing political and economic institutions as ancillary tools for the fulfillment of human life; and fifth, bringing back ethics, spirituality, and God in the conversation, or reconciling religion and science. Allow me to expend on these points.

## 1. A Consensual Normative International Framework

An important assumption in international relations and foreign policy claims states to be neither good nor bad; they have a morality of their own which is inherent in the very nature of their identity. It is a mission to fulfill that consists of protecting their national security. For centuries, this assumption has guided the interaction of states in the international realm, making them defend jealously their equality and sovereignty in order to survive the anarchic context of international relations. In other words, left alone in a hostile environment with no global authority to protect them, regulate their self-interests, or impose an acceptable ethical conduct, states seek to maximize their relative power. As a result, the possibility of developing a real moral compass in the traditional sense is ruled out as each state has to stand for its self-interest.

The globalization phenomenon, however, has not only changed the nature of international relations but also transformed the traditional perception of self-serving sovereign entities. While

> relations between states must be respectful of each other's sovereignty, [they] must also lay down mutually agreed means of averting regional disasters which would eventually affect everyone. Global regulatory norms are needed to impose obligations and prevent unacceptable actions, for example, when powerful companies or countries *dump contaminated waste* or offshore polluting industries in other countries (*LS* 173).[18]

This is very important to note as Pope Francis introduces lines of approach and action. Indeed, the global "interdependence obliges us to think of *one world with a common plan* . . . as an interdependent world makes us more conscious of the negative effects of certain lifestyles and models of production and consumption which affect us all" (*LS* 164).[19]

It is obvious that the international system of sovereign states has become obsolete not only because "maintaining systems of governance inherited from the past is witnessing a weakening of the power of nation states"

---

18. Emphasis added.
19. Emphasis in original.

(*LS* 175), but also because borders are becoming meaningless, given the fact that economic and financial sectors are more and more transnational. Neither the pursuit of narrow nationalistic self-interest nor the clinging on to the sovereignty principle holds. As Pope Francis offers,

> a *global consensus is essential* for confronting the deeper problems, which cannot be resolved by unilateral actions on the part of individual countries. Such a consensus could lead, for example, to planning a sustainable and diversified agriculture, developing renewable and less polluting forms of energy, encouraging a more efficient use of energy, promoting a better management of marine and forest resources, and ensuring universal access to drinking water. (*LS* 164)

Since we hold the world in common, as a global common heritage, it is time to plan for a more sustainable development by moving away from the previous model of production and consumption that favors some but affects all. The time for superpowers' competition is over; it is necessary to achieve consensus in the management of the global commons.

In spite of scientific evidence showing that millions of lives are imperiled by continuing greenhouse gas emissions, powerful nations that happen to also be the biggest polluters refuse to abandon their old ways of acting in order to reduce their greenhouse gas emissions. Their leaders are not willing to give up on their pursuit of power politics. For example, former US President George W. Bush has said that "[w]e will not do anything that harms our economy, because first things first are the people who live in America."[20] At Rio de Janeiro's 1992 Earth Summit, when Bush senior, then-President George H. W. Bush, was asked by representatives of developing nations to put on the agenda the developed nations' (especially that of the United States) overconsumption of resources, he replied that "the American lifestyle is not up for negotiation."[21] The debate around the disproportionate impact on the planet by equal and sovereign states remains an open one. Rightly, the bishops of Bolivia have argued that "the countries which have benefited from a high degree of industrialization, at the cost of enormous emissions of greenhouse gases, have a greater responsibility for providing a solution to the problems they have caused" (*LS* 170).

However, "it is unacceptable for one people to bear certain costs of decisions made by another—decisions affecting industrialization or the birth rate, for example."[22] But how concretely shall we design such an internation-

---

20. Singer, *One World*, 1.
21. Singer, *One World*, 2.
22. Pogge, *World Poverty and Human Rights*, 105.

al normative framework unless it is commonly negotiated and democratically agreed upon in international summits? "Some strategies for lowering pollutant gas emissions call for the internationalization of environmental costs," (*LS* 170) and diplomacy should take on new importance to preclude serious problems affecting us all. In the same vein, "global regulatory norms are needed to impose obligations and prevent unacceptable actions, for example, when powerful companies or countries dump contaminated waste or offshore polluting industries in other countries" (*LS* 173). Besides, as the pope contends, this will require a strong leadership, honesty, and political will. Thinking boldly calls for the establishment of a global *political authority* in order to coordinate and "manage the global economy; to revive economies hit by the crisis; to avoid any deterioration of the present crisis and the greater imbalances that would result; to bring about integral and timely disarmament, food security and peace; to guarantee the protection of the environment and to regulate migration" (*LS* 175).

Actually, a number of conventions exist, among which are Stockholm (1972), Washington (1975), Vienna (1988), Basel (1989), Rio (1992), and the Rio+20 or 2012 Earth Summit. As it can be seen, international normative frameworks are not wanting. The real issue concerns the implementation mechanisms. Arguably, Rio 1992 was the first of its kind, prophetic in its perspective, but lacking in the implementing mechanism and the authoritative capability to enforce the principles. It was able to state the principles regarding forests and sketch an agenda with an action plan, but "its accords have been poorly implemented, due to the lack of suitable mechanisms for oversight, periodic review, and penalties in cases of non-compliance" (*LS* 167). Next, the Basel Convention on hazardous wastes was signed in 1989 and entered into force on May 5, 1992. It is mentioned as one among the positive international framework experiences (*LS* 168) which stipulate "that any transboundary movement of wastes (export, import, or transit) is permitted only when the movement itself and the disposal of the concerned hazardous or other wastes are environmentally sound."[23]

Other frameworks include "the binding Convention on international trade in endangered species of wild fauna and flora, which includes on-site visits for verifying effective compliance" (*LS* 168)[24] and "the Vienna Convention for the protection of the ozone layer and its implementation through the Montreal Protocol and amendments, the problem of the layer's thinning

23. United Nations Environment Programme (UNEP), *Basel Convention Technical Guidelines*, 6.

24. For more about this convention, the Convention on International Trade in Endangered Species of Wild Fauna and Flora (CITES), visit its website: https://www.cites.org/eng/disc/what.php.

seems to have entered a phase of resolution" (*LS* 168).[25] The 2012 Earth Summit issued a wide-ranging but ineffectual outcome document whereby "the strategy of buying and selling 'carbon credits' can lead to a new form of speculation which would not help reduce the emission of polluting gases worldwide" (*LS* 171). Nevertheless, most of the proclaimed principles in these international summits are still awaiting an efficient and flexible means of practical implementation (*LS* 167).

## 2. Citizen Participation and the Regulatory Power of the State

Globalization has blurred the traditional lines between centers and peripheries, developed and developing countries. The divide between winners and losers of development are no longer set along geographical lines, between a global North and the global South, because poverty and wealth are found within developed countries as well as in less economically endowed ones.[26]

(a) At the individual plane, leaders need to overcome "the myopia of power politics" to relate to the *leadership and true statecraft*, that manifest when, in difficult times, high principles are upheld in order to think of the long-term common good over against the short-term economic profits or political gains (*LS* 178, 181).

(b) At the civil society plane, both globally and locally, participation has been instrumental in raising awareness about issues affecting the planet and changing existing patterns of acting. The *participation of the civil society*, either at the individual level or as organized groups, is, therefore, crucial. It is the civil society that instills

> a greater sense of responsibility, a strong sense of community, a readiness to protect others, a spirit of creativity and a deep love for the land. They are also concerned about what they will eventually leave to their children and grandchildren

---

25. For the text of the Montreal Protocol and its amendments, visit https://ozone.unep.org/treaties/vienna-convention/articles/article-11-settlement-disputes and https://ozone.unep.org/treaties/montreal-protocol.

26. The debate whether globalization simply and unequivocally increases inequality between and within nations is no longer evident. While some scholars affirm that "For once, the proportionate gains of the poor exceed those of the rich," and that "[t]he patterns of global growth [show that globalization] has helped reduce inequality in the distribution of world income," (Griffin, "Global Prospects for Development and Human Security," 364) others contend that "the new geography of global income inequality [will] mean that national location—while still paramount—is declining in significance in the determination of one's income" (Firebaugh, *New Geography of Income Inequality*, 15).

... unless citizens control political power—national, regional and municipal—it will not be possible to control damage to the environment. (*LS* 179)

(c) At the national plane, it should be acknowledged that "a healthy, mature, and sovereign society must impose limits related to *foresight and security, regulatory norms* ... the elimination of corruption, effective responses to undesired side-effects of production processes, and appropriate intervention where potential or uncertain risks are involved" (*LS* 177). Indeed, "political and institutional frameworks do not exist simply to avoid bad practice but also to promote best practice, to stimulate creativity in seeking new solutions, and to encourage individual or group initiatives" (*LS* 177). The government's *policy planning* must integrate a far-sighted environmental agenda since the *responsibility to plan, coordinate, and regulate* economic activities within their borders pertains to individual states. As a result, the state must enact and enforce the *laws and regulatory frameworks* since, amid constantly developing technological innovations, a society cannot afford to forsake its authoritative capability as the source of the law.

### 3. Transparency and Participation in the Decision-Making Processes

The third path of action concerns transparency and participation in the decision-making processes. In discerning projects, some important questions must be asked, and others must have higher priority. For instance, "What will the project accomplish? Why? Where? When? How? For whom? And at what cost? Who will be responsible for those costs and how?" Unfortunately, in the prevalent neoliberal model, local communities are scarcely consulted or informed in a manner that is respectful of their cultural heritage, historical trajectories, and future impacts. The model also favors short-term gain and private interest, while it makes it easy to rubber-stamp authorizations and conceal information (*LS* 184). To address this problem, "assessment of the environmental impact of business ventures and projects demands transparent political processes involving a free exchange of views and information. It should come before, not come after the drawing up of a business proposition or the proposal of a particular policy, plan, or programme" (*LS* 182).

When evaluations are done in transparency, and when they are free of all economic or political pressure, economic returns can thus be forecast more realistically, taking into account potential negative externalities, that is, the scenarios for further investment to correct possible undesired side effects. Otherwise insufficiently studied, projects can end up profoundly affecting "the quality of life of an area due to very different factors such as unforeseen noise pollution, the shrinking of visual horizons, the loss of cultural values, or the effects of nuclear energy use" (*LS* 184). Honesty and truth are needed in scientific and political discussions. Concealing the actual environmental impact of a given project in exchange for favors is a form of corruption. The local population should have a special place at the table; they are concerned about their own future and that of their children, and can consider goals transcending immediate economic interest (*LS* 183). This is especially the case when a project may lead to a greater use of natural resources, higher levels of emission or discharge, an increase of refuse, or significant changes to the landscape, the habitats of protected species, or public spaces. It should be linked to a study of working conditions and possible effects on people's physical and mental health, on the local economy, and on public safety.

4. Political and Economic Institutions at the Service of Human Fulfillment

It should always be kept in mind that "environmental protection cannot be assured solely on the basis of financial calculations of costs and benefits. Once more, we need to denounce and reject a 'magical conception of the market,' which would suggest that problems can be solved simply by an increase in the profits of companies or individuals" (*LS* 190). Is it realistic to hope that those who are obsessed with maximizing profits will stop to reflect on the environmental damage which they will leave behind for future generations? The environment is one of those goods that cannot be adequately safeguarded or promoted by market forces.

> Where profits alone count, there can be no thinking about the rhythms of nature, its phases of decay and regeneration, or the complexity of ecosystems which may be gravely upset by human intervention. Moreover, biodiversity is considered at most a deposit of economic resources available for exploitation, with no serious thought for the real value of things, their significance for persons and cultures, or the concerns and needs of the poor. (*LS* 190)

Production is not always rational, and is usually tied to economic variables which assign to products a value that does not necessarily correspond to their real worth. This frequently leads to an overproduction of some commodities, with unnecessary impact on the environment and with negative results on regional economies. For instance, the financial crisis of 2007–08 provided an opportunity to develop a new economy, more attentive to ethical principles, and new ways of regulating speculative financial practices and virtual wealth. However, this opportunity was missed as governments went ahead to bailout those financial actors that were responsible for the failure in the first place, without feeling the need to reform the system. Politics and economics

> tend to blame each other when it comes to poverty and environmental degradation. It is to be hoped that they can acknowledge their own mistakes and find forms of interaction directed to the common good. While some are concerned only with financial gain, and others with holding on to or increasing their power, what we are left with are conflicts or spurious agreements where the last thing either party is concerned about is caring for the environment and protecting those who are most vulnerable. Here, too, we see how true it is that 'unity is greater than conflict.' (*LS* 198)

Hence, because both the economic institution of the market and political institution of the state institutions are, in reality, ancillary to human flourishing, there is urgent need for politics and economics to enter into a frank dialogue in the service of life and in the pursuit of the common good (*LS* 189).

## 5. Reconciliation of Dichotomies: Religion and Science

Finally, *Laudato Si'* argues that "religious classics can prove meaningful in every age; they have an enduring power to open new horizons. . . . Is it reasonable and enlightened to dismiss certain writings simply because they arose in the context of religious belief?" (*LS* 199). As a matter of fact, the suspicion between religion and science is very old and was initiated during the modern period by the church's rejection of the scientific revolution. In the last 500 years, the modern period seems to constitute the Vatican's worst nightmare not only because it inaugurated the demise of the church's monopoly of the ultimate truth, but also because it unleashed a paradigm shift in society.

The Catholic Church rejected the spirit of modernity, with its liberal ideals, as dangerously paving the way to liberalism, secularism, relativism, and atheism. In response, the church imprisoned one of the founding fathers of modern science, Galileo (1564–1642), who had, along with Kepler (1571–1630), invented the telescope that challenged an established dogma about heaven and earth.[27] Only 500 years later—in the "Closing Message" addressed to the scientist community after the Second Vatican Council—did the church state its reconciliation remarks, saying that "we too [the Church] are seekers after truth" and "your [scientific] truth is ours."[28]

*Laudato Si'* reminds us that there are multiple reasons, not only the scientific one, and we should hold all of them together. In other words, it is not the quantitative rationality of science that grasps the ultimate meaning about human existence. As the pope puts it,

> If we reason only within the confines of the latter, little room would be left for aesthetic sensibility, poetry, or even reason's ability to grasp the ultimate meaning and purpose of things.... The ethical principles capable of being apprehended by reason can always reappear in different guise and find expression in a variety of languages, including religious language. (*LS* 199)

Therefore, technical solutions need to be complemented by the compass of faith, morality, and human conscience.

## Development in Today's Context of Africa

### 1. The New COVID-19 Context

We celebrated the fifth anniversary of *Laudato Si'* in the new context of COVID-19. The context is changing all the time, and we have to adapt our thinking in these new social and physical environments. Like the economic crisis that marked the 1970s and led African nations to demand the establishment of a new international economic world order for them to thrive, and like the recent financial crisis in 2007–08 to which Pope Francis makes

---

27. What we call "modern science" emerged at a certain moment in history when Galileo and Kepler challenged the religious faithful's belief that the celestial heavens were the home of the divine powers who ruled life on Earth. They instead saw the Medicean planets of Jupiter, concluding that the heavens were just an extension of our terrestrial neighborhood. See Heelan, "Hermeneutic Consciousness" (notes received from the author).

28. Abbott and Gallagher, *Documents of Vatican Council II*, 730–31.

a reference (*LS* 189) as another missed opportunity to establish a more just international financial system, it was a new moral framework that needed international bailout instead of financial institutions that provoked the crisis in the first place.

Today's environmental crisis is yet another red flag signaling the need for humanity to change direction. Against the technocratic paradigm, Pope Francis proposes a new way of thinking about development: a paradigm shift, which occurs when a theory accepted by an epistemological community to explain a specific reality comes to lose its explanatory power. When the community that accepted a shared meaning encounters an anomaly that can no longer be explained by the dominant paradigm, it means the time has come to find a new one. More practically, the Vatican Dicastery for Promoting Integral Human Development calls it an ecological education, which involves rethinking and transforming educational curricula and institutions in order to bring the community, including parents, students, teachers, and leaders, up to date. All must work together to promote this new thinking in which the importance of spirituality, ethics, and God in human business is not overruled.

The current global health crisis caused by COVID-19 buttresses the above approach. Acting as an equalizer of humankind, COVID-19 is telling us we should acknowledge the limits of medical technology because it does not have ultimate answers to the challenges of life and death. While we will still depend on scientific and technological progress to meet our medical needs, the new thinking needed is telling us now that science and technology do not exhaust the meaning and measures of human progress. An integral ecological approach, therefore, can help transcend a materialist measurement and interpretation of health, wealth, growth, or development to include justice, human worth, cultural values, and collectively held meaning.[29]

## 2. The Market Ideology

Since science and technology are not the sole measure of human progress, neither should the market institution monopolize the role of promoting development. The market framework has, in fact, allowed this kind of thinking, as well as the possibility of environmental vandalism as experienced in

---

29. Most African taboos, for instance, were social norms to preserve the collective identity as well as the common areas such as forests, rivers, or the land that provided livelihood to the community. Violating taboos was punishable for the sake of the common good. See Chemhuru and Masaka, "Taboos as Sources."

the Probo Koala, or "drums of death," tragedies. The underlying ideology involves an overwhelming emphasis on privatization in the form of maximization of interests and externalization of the cost. To put it differently, the neoliberal credo in the market argues that individuals are responsible for their own failures and successes; they should be rewarded and punished accordingly; they are best able to provide for themselves, solve their problems, and decide what is best for them. Consequently, by trying to regulate the market, the state only contravenes individual freedom, given the belief that a free market is the best way to promote individuals' choices.[30]

But for centuries, abuses and injustices in the name of individual choices and freedoms have been happening through market institutions such as the slave trade, colonization, and multinational practices, resulting in violation of the community and degradation of the environment.[31] A passive acceptance of market standards can only legitimize existing disparities in the distribution of human worth, global wealth, and fundamental rights. When Pope Francis speaks of an "ecological debt" owed by the developed countries to the developing countries, he is reminding us not to fall into the trap of neoliberalism that blames the poor for being poor without understanding the processes and structures that organize such injustices and disparities.

A neologism in current political language portrays the negative impacts on the environment as mere "collateral damage" in the pursuit of development. In the neoliberal development slogan to support this view, the aphorism says "no pain, no gain!"[32] Africa's current conditions, in reality, result from history, practices, institutions, and structures that have set the continent to be the foil of the West. The poor local leadership alone, which, by the way, is a stepchild of the same system, is not responsible for our current condition. As Stephen Lewis rightly remarks, "[t]he problems of Africa are explained in part by colonialism and in part by the failings of the African leadership itself."[33]

Not bad decisions alone but also the Western poor conceptualization of development and neoliberal policies have stripped African states of their regulatory powers, aggressively promoting privatization of the "global commons," displacing African villages for the sake of natural resources exploitation, and externalizing the costs of production in the form of environmental pollution. The neoliberal paradigm that has rendered impossible

30. Hackworth, *Faith Based*.
31. Deneault et al., *Noir Canada*.
32. Harrison, "Authoritarian Neoliberalism and Capitalist Transformation," 274–88.
33. Lewis, *Race Against Time*, 8.

the thinking of alternative modes of production and produced social realities that we have come to take for granted can be resisted and replaced by another framework. The modernity conception of development can only produce dichotomies whereby non-Western geographies, peoples, and polities are construed as poor, traditional, if not backward, armpits of civilization. Its claim to universalization is responsible for the brutal domination and exploitation of other nations under the guise of spreading civilization.

It is unbelievable how international development policymakers still define the African problem today along the same civilizational (understood as cultural) terms. Take, for instance, French president Nicholas Sarkozy, who argued in Dakar as recently as 2007, in front of the Senegalese parliament, "that the African has not fully entered into history. . . . They have never really launched themselves into the future. . . . The African peasant only knew the eternal renewal of time, marked by the endless repetition of the same gestures and the same words. . . . In this realm of fancy . . . there is neither room for human endeavor nor the idea of progress."[34] In the same vein, Emmanuel Macron affirmed at the G20 Summit in Hamburg, Germany that the challenge of Africa is deeply civilizational. Africa in no way can claim progress with its failed states, the complex democratic transitions, and big families with as many as seven or eight children.[35] This is the kind of neoliberal mindset that needs to be debunked and resisted while it equates development with market consumerism.

3. The World and Future We Want

So, "what kind of world do we want to leave to those who come after us, to children who are now growing up?" (*LS* 167). As Ugandan theologian Emmanuel Katongole argues, "who we are and who we are capable of becoming depends very much on the stories we tell, the stories we listen to, and the stories we live."[36] Paying attention to the stories being written by generations of African scholars, we see a growing resistance to the epistemic violence and the injustice circulated through colonial tropes about Africa that facilitated profit-seekers to explore and exploit Africa's environment and peoples under the guise of bringing development. Yet, post-George Floyd's murder and the international conversation it sparked about global racial justice, we must shift the way we understand social justice from the "exclusive focus

---

34. Ba, "Africans Still Seething," paras. 7–8.
35. "Macron estime que l'Afrique a un problème démographique."
36. Katongole, *Sacrifice of Africa*, 2–3.

on strategies for fixing the structures of democracy and development"[37] to include the business of telling our stories, as Katongole concludes.

In line with the above, Laurenti Magesa tells of the African *Ubuntu* spirituality, noting that "a person becomes authentically such in a community with others."[38] He tells the story of the African worldview in which disease, pain, suffering, lack of offspring, and disharmony among people and between human beings and the rest of creation are the practical matters that demonstrate the lack of the fulfillment of human life. He shows how the African way of looking at reality already embodies the reconciliation between religion and science. "It would seem that African spirituality preserves this complexity of the process of creation by, in principle, not rejecting either the activity of the divine Word or the dynamics of natural selections in it while evolution does not remove divine agency in creation," he writes. He offers the African ecological-spiritual concern that the one "single integral community of the Earth . . . includes all its component members whether human or other than human,"[39] which is embodied in the African totemic system. And he also acknowledges that "care and respect of creation are the main principles that should guide human behavior in life."[40]

It is high time to denounce the injustices done to those whose cultures, spiritualities, and values were erased in the process of imposing a single Western approach to development. If an integral community should include both the ancestors and the not-yet-born, to whom we owe dignity and respect, Africans have always respected animals, plants, and the creation in whom they project the human spirit. Because the many manifestations of life and "the experience of metaphysical knowledge, of self-consciousness, and self-awareness, of moral conscience, of liberty, of aesthetic and religious experience" escapes the scientific method, the unity of the whole becomes the source of the ethical obligation of human beings towards nature.

## Conclusion

It is indeed impelling that we adopt a new approach and attitude toward the "other" who embodies not only my folks, those different in origins and beliefs, but also the environment and God. Narrowly defining the "other" from a biased cultural benchmark has led into the trap of Western parochialism, if not groupthink projections. The ongoing COVID-19 pandemic

37. Katongole, *Sacrifice of Africa*, 2.
38. Magesa, *What Is Not Sacred?*, 175.
39. Magesa, *What Is Not Sacred?*, 169.
40. Magesa, *What Is Not Sacred?*, 171–73.

crisis reminds us even more strongly about deep human interconnectedness and global interdependence. Hence, in constructing the kind of society we want, practicing the development we hope, we ought to include others who may not be physically in sight but spiritually connected to us and dependent on our actions, even the not-yet-born.

# 7

## Ecological Education and Spirituality: An African Ecological Ethics and Spirituality

KINIKONDA OKEMASISI

This chapter is divided into four sections. The first section discusses the issue of deforestation—one of the current global environmental crises affecting Africa. I will concentrate particularly on the situation in Kenya, beginning with recent ecological news reported in some parts of the country that provide evidence of the adverse effect of deforestation in Kenya and, by extension, Africa and in the world. The second section explores ecological education and spirituality from two perspectives, based on the themes of chapter 6 of *Laudato Si'*. The third part of the chapter will focus on African ecological ethics and spirituality. The last section of the chapter will examine the environmental initiative begun by the renowned late Kenyan woman, Wangari Maathai, an environmentalist and a Nobel laureate whose advocacy, environmental activism, and work largely contributed to a greater consciousness in Kenya of the crisis of climate change and the specific challenges facing Africa. I will show how her efforts brought changes in the approaches to meeting the challenges of the ecological crisis of our times through the planting of over 35 million trees in Kenya.

### Deforestation: An Ecological Crisis in Africa

Kenya has recently experienced unwavering raging floods in the Western part of the country that haven't been experienced in decades.[1] Justus Wanzala points out that "the Nzoia River that flows from Kenya's Western highlands into Lake Victoria burst its banks in the worst flooding displacing

---

1. Wanzala, "Floods on Record-High Lake Victoria."

over eight hundred thousand Kenyans living in Budalangi area located in Busia County."[2] According to Wanzala's report, the situation was made worse by flooded rivers channeling huge volumes of water into Lake Victoria, Africa's largest lake, causing the water to spill over onto its shores, destroying livestock and sweeping away crops.[3] Commenting on the floods in Budalangi area, George William Omonyi, a senior meteorologist at the Uganda National Meteorological Authority, attributed the high-ranging floods to human activities such as the clearing of the forest for farming on Lake Victoria's shores. William pointed out that human settlement, together with farming in protected forests along the rivers, has led to the loss of trees, causing the river to spill over, resulting in the massive destruction of property.

Another looming ecological crisis that has been reported by Reuters is that Kenya's freshwater Lake Baringo, which is teeming with fish, birds, crocodiles, and hippopotamuses, and which sustains tens of thousands of people, is threatening to merge with the alkaline Lake Bogoria.[4] "It will be an ecological disaster if the two lakes meet," commented Jackson Komen, senior warden for the government-run Kenya wildlife service (KWS) for Lake Baringo conservation area.[5] Lake Baringo has expanded by "60 percent to two hundred and seventy square kilometers (105 square miles) . . . [and] Lake Bogoria has swollen by a quarter to forty-three square kilometers."[6] Tor-Gunnar Vanegan, a scientist at the Nairobi-based World Agroforestry Centre, attributes the threatening merger of the two lakes to deforestation, which is causing erosion on nearby hills, leading the soil to wash into the lakes.[7]

The reported ecological happenings, and those threatening to happen in Kenya, provide a sad portrait of the environmental disasters threatening Africa and our earth. During her keynote speech at Forest Day 5 in Durban, South Africa, Helen Gichohi, the president of the African Wildlife Foundation, pointed out that Africa is experiencing a serious wave of deforestation, which has threatened the survival of both wildlife and human settlement.[8] Citing the example of Kenya, Gichohi affirmed that the country "has lost the

---

2. Wanzala, "Floods on Record-High Lake Victoria," para. 2.
3. Wanzala, "Floods on Record-High Lake Victoria," paras. 4–5.
4. "Photos."
5. "Photos," para. 3.
6. "Photos," para. 4.
7. "Photos," para. 5.
8. Cooney, "Forest Day 5 Experts."

majority of its forest cover to settlements and agriculture, leaving only 1.7 percent of its land" in actual forest.[9]

Africa is endowed with a myriad of natural resources, such as the Congo Basin, the second largest tropical rainforest next to the Amazon.[10] However, it is disheartening to learn that it "loses an estimated $195 billion annually of its natural capital through illicit financial flows, illegal mining, illegal logging, illegal trade in wildlife, unregulated fishing, environmental degradation and loss among others,"[11] such as deforestation.

Amsalu W. Yalew, an economist whose research focus is on the nexus between the environment and economic development, found that deforestation is a complex phenomenon to study in sub-Saharan Africa. He explains that, from 2000–10, Africa lost about 3.4 million hectares of forest.[12] The region's average annual rate of deforestation (0.8 percent) is still far higher than the world average (0.15 percent). Mwambazambi Kalemba, a professor at FATEB (Faculté de Théologie Évangélique de Banguis in the Central African Republic), estimates that 40 percent of the Congo's forests will be lost within the next forty years if nothing is done now.[13] In the same vein, Ruth Oniang'o and her colleagues found that trees are now being cut down across the planet at the rate of 4 billion a year.[14] They observe that, if trees continue to be cut without replacement, and the human population remains steady at 10 billion between 2050 and 2100, the ratio would become 1 to 24 in 2050, and 1 to 4 in 2100, meaning that much of the land that is now fertile will be arid, or become desert in the next few decades.[15]

Take the example of Kenya. The country has experienced unprecedented losses of forest cover through deforestation and environmental degradation in the last two decades. In its 2013 analysis of the underlying causes of forest cover change in Kenya's various forest types, the Ministry of Forestry and Wildlife affirms that, among other countries in East Africa, Kenya has experienced significant losses in forest cover.[16] Further, the regional coordinator of Youth 4 Africa, Paul Kaluki Mutuku, reports, "When Kenya gained independence in 1963, 10 percent of the country was covered in

---

9. Cooney, "Forest Day 5 Experts," para. 10.

10. Food and Agriculture Organization (FAO) of the United Nations and International Tropical Timber Association, *State of Forests*, 12.

11. United Nations Environment Programme, "Our Work in Africa," para. 3.

12. Yalew, "Perplex of Deforestation," 19–30.

13. Mwambazambi, "Glance on Environmental Protection in Africa," 19–26.

14. Oniang'o et al., "Action for Africa and the Earth," 515–33.

15. Oniang'o et al., "Action for Africa and the Earth," 515–33.

16. Ministry of Forestry and Wildlife, Kenya (MFW), *Analysis of Drivers*, 10–12.

forest. By 2009, this number had dropped to 6 percent as a result of charcoal and timber production, agricultural expansion, unregulated logging, and urbanisation."[17] He describes the shocking statistic that about 12 percent of the land area which was originally covered by closed-canopy forests has been reduced to a mere 1.7 percent of its original size. Poor governance of the forest sector has seen the excision by the government of 67,000 hectares of forest land, most of which is in water towers or critical water catchment areas such as the Mau Forest, Mount Elgon, and Mount Kenya.[18]

Segun Ogungbemi rightly observes that the drive to develop Africa to the status of developed nations and the introduction of technological innovation have helped precipitate desertification in formerly productive areas.[19] He further explains that Africa has exploited some of its essential minerals such as gold, copper, oil, diamonds, coal, and uranium, among many others, and this has consequently created an ecological imbalance. That is the reason why Mwambazambi Kalemba strongly asserts that it is fundamental to attack the environmental problems facing Africa and the whole world.[20] Unless Africa (including Kenya) takes speedy action to address aggressively its share of the environmental crisis, it risks leaving nothing but a desolate land to the next generation.

Given the statistics that have been discussed in this section, Africa—and, by extension, the entire world—there is a need to urgently address the deforestation crisis which is adding to the problem of climate change. In order to effectively do this, Africa, and indeed all nations on the planet, need to respond to Pope Francis's invitation in *Laudato Si'* to adopt a new lifestyle and manner in which we human beings relate to the environment.[21] In *LS* 202, Pope Francis calls us to have a change of attitude. He points out that, while many things have to change course, it is we human beings above all who need to change. The pope rightly observes that we lack an awareness of our common origin, of our mutual belonging, and of a future to be shared by everyone. He urges ecological conversion which will lead humanity to embrace new convictions and attitudes. This also challenges us to develop new forms of ecological education to bring about this ecological conversion that will guide us on the path of renewal. What Pope Francis is implying is that ecological education and spirituality can help to address the global environment crisis and aid all of us to lead healthy lives in a healthy

17. Mutuku, "Kenya has Lost Nearly Half of Its Forests," para. 5.
18. Ojunga et al., "Value of Forest Ecosystem Services," 93.
19. Ogungbemi, "African Perspective on the Environmental Crisis," 204.
20. Mwambazambi, "Glance on Environmental Protection in Africa," 19–26.
21. Francis, *Laudato Si'*, 203; hereafter cited in text as *LS*.

environment as God intended from the beginning. I will unpack the claims of Pope Francis on this important theme in the next section.

## Ecological Education and Spirituality: The Perspective of *Laudato Si'*

Given the pathetic deforestation crisis in Africa, it is obvious that the situation requires a complete change of attitude and behavior for the posterity of the African continent. In *LS* 205, Pope Francis is optimistic that all is not lost, because human beings, while capable of the worst, can make a new start, rise above themselves, and choose again what is good. The pope suggests that awareness of the gravity of the global environmental crisis can result in a new way of thinking that can lead to new habits and lifestyle changes that can promote a healthy relationship with the environment and all of creation. Francis asserts that ecological education can encourage ways of acting which can directly and significantly affect the world around us. He points out that these ecological ways and actions need not necessarily be monumental and conspicuous but, instead, can be manifested in simple efforts such as avoiding the use of plastic and paper, reducing water consumption, separating transport or carpooling, planting trees, turning off unnecessary lights, etc. (*LS* 211). In his view, these small but significant deeds reflect a generous and worthy creativity that brings out the best in human beings. He adds that, when done for the right reasons, reusing something instead of immediately discarding it can be an act of love which expresses our own dignity.

In *LS* 210, Francis suggests that environmental education, in its broad sense, can achieve ecological equilibrium and deeper ethical meaning that establishes harmony with ourselves, with others, with nature and other living creatures, and with God. This kind of education is open and can take place anywhere and in a variety of settings: at school, in families, in the media, in catechesis, and in our own cultures and traditions. The pope is of the view that ecological education is capable of producing "ecological citizenship," aided by ecological educators with an effective pedagogy to grow in solidarity, responsibility, and compassionate care.

Expounding on the ecological education Francis proposes, Michael Caduto opines that it begins with self-esteem, which ripples out to the larger world.[22] Caduto asserts that ecological education thrives in a warm, loving, and nurturing atmosphere. He explains that a child who is aware of the love and care of the family will most likely maintain positive relationships with

---

22. Caduto, "Ecological Education," 11–16.

other people and take the initiative to pick up litter, avoid stepping on plants or destroying animals' homes, conserve energy, and generally care for the earth and its creatures. He concludes that education understood this way is capable of bringing about the desired ecological transformation.[23]

Regrettably, Francis notes that the current education system which is expected to bring about this positive transformation and create ecological citizenship is, on the contrary, providing information that is incapable of fostering good habits. He also points out that, even when effective means of enforcement are present, the existence of laws and regulations are insufficient in the long run to curb bad conduct (*LS* 211). He is emphatic that, if laws are to bring the desired effect, the majority of society's members must be motivated individually to accept them and resolve to respond. Only by cultivating sound virtues will people be able to make a selfless ecological commitment. He asserts that selfless concerns for others and the rejection of every form of self-centeredness and self-absorption are essential if we truly wish to care for our brothers and sisters and for the natural environment.

Similar to Pope Francis, Raven LeFay asserts that the current Western education systems do not promote new thinking but rather encourage the passive acceptance of the political and consumeristic agenda.[24] He alleges that we are still taught not to think for ourselves, not to question the assumptions or political structures of Western culture.[25] LeFay points out that the core lessons being taught in our schools today are individualism, consumerism, careerism, and anthropocentrism, and have no bearing on what our ecological footprints might be or whether we have a future on Earth at all.[26] These core lessons do not promote ecological citizenship and should be discouraged; we should instead embrace an education that translates into new habits.

Pope Francis reminds us that our current progress and the accumulation of things and pleasures are not enough to give meaning and joy to the human heart. Making reference to the Earth Charter, which asks us to leave behind a period of self-destruction and make a new start, Francis observes that we have not yet developed the universal awareness needed to achieve this (*LS* 207). He points out that, unless we develop this awareness, other creatures will not be recognized for their true worth. However, he is hopeful about today's young people, who he says have a new ecological sensitivity and a generous spirit and are making admirable efforts to protect

23. Caduto, "Ecological Education," 11–16.
24. LeFay, "Ecological Critique of Education," 35–45.
25. LeFay, "Ecological Critique of Education," 35–45.
26. LeFay, "Ecological Critique of Education," 35–45.

the environment even though they have grown up in the milieu of extreme consumerism (*LS* 209).

The pope teaches that ecological education and spirituality can best be realized in the family (*LS* 213). He rightly explains that it is in the family where one grows in love and virtues such as the proper use of things, order, cleanliness, respect for the local ecosystems, and care for all creatures. He emphasizes that it is in the family where we receive integral education which enables us to grow harmoniously in personal maturity. In addition to the family, Francis also calls upon the political institutions and the church to help raise people's awareness of ecological education and spirituality. He states that we need institutions that are empowered to impose penalties for the damage inflicted on the environment and also that, in terms of the individual, we need the personal qualities of self-control and willingness to learn from one another.

Specifically addressing Christians on ecological conversion (*LS* 216), Pope Francis thus teaches that the gospel has the power to motivate us to a more passionate concern for protecting our world. Explaining that the gospel has the power to motivate us to a more passionate concern for protecting our world. He implies that Christians can spearhead the care of the environment through the influence of the gospel teachings. However, he observes that Christians have not always appropriated and developed the spiritual treasures bestowed on them by God upon the church to champion with love the care of the environment. Francis sadly points out that some Christians are passive and have chosen not to change their habits and have, thus, become inconsistent. He calls Christians to an ecological conversion to give witness to the gospel of Christ in the world around them, stating that living our vocation to be protectors of God's handiwork is essential to a life of virtue—it is not an optional or secondary aspect of our Christian experience.

Using the example of Saint Francis of Assisi, who embraced creation with a spirit of adoration, Pope Francis invites us to develop reverence for God's handiwork and embrace a healthy relationship with creation that will prompt us to a heartfelt repentance that recognizes sins, faults, failures, and leads to a desire to change (*LS* 218). In concluding this chapter, Pope Francis remarks that our efforts at ecological education will be inadequate and ineffective unless we collectively strive to promote a new way of thinking about human beings, life, society, and our relationship with nature (*LS* 215).

Though he does not explicitly mention them, in calling humanity and the church to a new way of thinking about our relationship with nature, Pope Francis precisely and adequately promotes many aspects of African ecological ethics and spirituality. This is why the encyclical's message resonates with many African cultures and can be easily applied to the ecological crisis facing our continent. The spirituality found among many African ethnic groups is centered on interrelationships between human beings and other creatures. As Godfrey Tangwa states, according to the traditional African metaphysical worldview, the dichotomy between "plants, animals, and inanimate things, between the sacred and the profane, matter and spirit, the communal and the individual, is a slim and flexible one."[27] Similarly, Mbih Jerome Tosam asserts that the African attitude towards nature is that of "live and let live, be and let be."[28] These two authors agree that the African attitude favors sustainable management of natural resources and that African environmental ethics extends the moral community beyond anthropocentric concerns to include nonhumans, animals, plants, the unborn, and the supernatural within the moral universe.[29]

## African Ecological Ethics and Spirituality

Ethics is defined by Philomena Ojomo as "a normative study of the principles of human conduct in relation to justice and injustice, good and evil, right and wrong, virtue and vice. It questions what ought to be done and the extent to which there is justification for a past action that had been done."[30] While environmental ethics is defined as a field in applied ethics that asks fundamental questions about humans and the environment, it examines the moral basis of environmental responsibility. Although philosophers throughout history have raised questions concerning the moral relationship between humans and the worth of the environment, it was only in the 1960s and 1970s that environmental ethics emerged as a distinct field of philosophical investigation.[31] It is an area of study that is developing in Africa today, and to which I hope to contribute by explicating some key principles and directions of an African ecological ethics in conversation with Pope Francis's teachings in chapter 6 of *Laudato Si'*. Many African theological ethicists and environmentalists have attempted a development for African spiritual and ecological ethics which provide us some important points of entry into this conversation.

Mike Ushe explains that "African spirituality originated from the people's environment and has been handed down from one generation to

27. Tangwa, "Some African Reflections," 387–95.
28. Tosam, "African Environmental Ethics," 172–92.
29. Tosam, "African Environmental Ethics," 172–92.
30. Ojomo, "Environmental Ethics," 101–13.
31. Tosam, "African Environmental Ethics," 172–92.

another and is lived and practiced by Africans today."[32] On the other hand, African environmental ethics shows how indigenous African societies employed different values and customs to make their environment physically and spiritually sustainable. There were taboos, values, and norms which prescribed the correct behavior towards nature.

While many African ethicists generally agree that African societies employed values and customs to relate to nature sustainably, the current massive exploitation of Africa's natural resources and the rate of deforestation caused by Africans themselves indicate a disconnect between theory and practice. This disconnect compels us to reexamine and question the African spirituality that has been handed down to and lived by the people of Africa as defined by Mike Ushe and which has been accepted by many African ethicists. The planet's ecological crisis calls for a new spirituality that is more responsive and in line with Pope Francis's message throughout the entirety of *Laudato Si'*.

I suggest that we embrace an "eco-heart," "eco-ear," and "eco-eye" spirituality and ethics. This is the type of spirituality that will lead us to empathize with our Mother Earth. It is likely to compel us to feel, hear, and see her devastating cry for our help. It will make us hear her groans of pain, pain that we have inflicted on her, and see the effect of our exploitative actions that have stripped her naked of her resources. Embracing an "eco-heart," "eco-ear," and "eco-eye" spirituality appeals directly to all of us, because it is a spirituality that builds on what we ordinarily possess with other factors held constant. It has no cost and does not require any training. All that is required is an examination of our conscience regarding our present and past actions and the decision to make a paradigm shift from being an exploiter to being a caretaker—to become a holistic ecological being with fully developed "ecological features and characteristics."[33] This is the spirituality and ethics that, if embraced, will resonate very well with Pope Francis's invitation to ecological conversion. This kind of spirituality will prompt us to return to our African worldviews of interconnectedness with nature and once more have reference for it.

This "eco-heart," "eco-ear," and "eco-eye" spirituality is the one I recommend to be lived by all Africans and the rest of humanity. It is the spirituality that I strongly advocate to be handed down to the next generation for the prosperity of the planet. Otherwise, we risk handing down an ecologically blind spirituality that will lead to the final damnation of the planet or a lame Western anthropocentric spirituality that, as alleged by

---

32. Ushe, "God, Divinities, and Ancestors," 155.
33. Terek and Dobrovic, "Ecologically Active Surfaces," 207.

many African ethicists, uses nature or other elements of creation at will. We need to make the "eco-heart," "eco-ear," and "eco-eye" spirituality our environmental "mantra" for the posterity of our Mother Earth.

Bénézet Bujo, for example, argues that Western spirituality is rooted in the Judeo-Christian tradition, which places humans at the center of the universe with a mandate to explore, dominate, and exploit nature, especially if it has a commercial value. Its anthropocentric nature maintains that "humans have a moral duty only towards one another; any duty they seem to have towards other species or entities is really only an indirect duty towards other beings."[34] Mbih Jerome Tosam explains that European colonization in Africa introduced the materialist and anthropocentric worldview, which encouraged the subjection and destruction of traditional African holistic and conservationist values and practices.[35] In the same manner, Philomena Ojomo sadly observes that the Western colonial encounter forced Africans to abandon some of their indigenous environmental values that linked them to the natural world,[36] which Mbiti says imbued them with the knowledge and values that made caring for the environment a priority.[37] Ojomo confirms that African spirituality and formation recognize and promote a relationship with nature, humanity, nonhuman animals, plants, and the unborn. African spirituality affirms the intimate link between water, land, and air. The use and management of these resources was not considered to be merely material, but rather, a process that was in harmony with all the forces of nature.[38]

It is notable from the foregoing explication that the understanding of spirituality as a relationship which potentiates the life of all human and nonhuman beings in the planet and the cosmos is a central affirmation of many African writers on this topic. However, blending this understanding with the suggested "eco-heart," "eco-ear," and "eco-eye" spirituality will, in my judgment, find striking resonance with Pope Francis's central affirmation of the spiritual foundation of the interconnection of all things in a new vision of this earth as our common home. Regrettably, as Segun Ogungbemi explains, the way in which natural resources such as land, water, and air are currently being used is contrary to the traditional African practice of environmental conservation.[39] In his view, the practice of totemism, the

---

34. Bujo, "Ecology and Ethical Responsibility," 281–97.
35. Tosam, "African Environmental Ethics," 172–92.
36. Ojomo, "Environmental Ethics," 102–12.
37. Mbiti, *New Testament Eschatology*.
38. Ojomo, "Environmental Ethics," 102–12.
39. Ogungbemi, "African Perspective on the Environmental Crisis," 205.

deification of some animal and plant species (and the taboos against killing or hunting such species), the restricted access to sacred sites, and the establishment of a relationship with some animal species are some of the abandoned environmentally friendly conservation practices. Aware that totemism is usually associated with sorcery and other malicious practices, Ogungbemi nonetheless maintains that it and similar practices encourage the conservation of some animal or plant species.

He believes that, if promoted, the practice of conserving parts of the community forest for spiritual and economic use—something that was common in some African communities—may not only help to preserve biodiversity but also protect the environment against the adverse effects of climate change.[40] In agreement with Ogungbemi, M. J. S. Masango opines that Africans need to unlearn what they have been made to believe about their spirituality, and that reeducation process will have to be premised on the understanding that Africa is not merely a lifeless object which can be dictated to or controlled remotely.[41] He is firm in his conviction that African spirituality is holistic and impacts the whole of life. It is not an individual affair but is rather expressed in all levels of society—socially, economically, politically—and, hence, contributes to the building of a nation.

Unfortunately, as Workineh Kelbessa notes, developing countries in Africa do not take seriously measures to respect and protect the indigenous knowledge and practices that encouraged natural conservation.[42] In particular, Kelbessa emphasizes that Africa's young people lack interest in learning such traditional African forms of wisdom. This contradicts Pope Francis's aforementioned commendation of the youth for their new ecological sensitivity and admirable efforts to protect the environment (LS 206). Could this imply that the youth have failed to see the indigenous wisdom as they witness the deforestation and exploitation of natural resources that is threatening their future? While Ogungbemi could be right that we need to revert to traditional practices such as totemism, my main concern is this: Do the animal and plant species—and the richly biodiverse local forests that are their home—which these practices would involve even exist now?

When I was growing up in the 1970s, we used to fetch water from beautiful flowing streams in cool forests full of biodiversity. We used to collect dry firewood here, chase after lovely butterflies of different sizes and colors, play with and scare one another with colorful chameleons, and pick and eat different types of berries, the names of which we knew only in our

---

40. Ogungbemi, "African Perspective on the Environmental Crisis," 205.
41. Masango, "African Spirituality that Shapes," 930–43.
42. Kelbessa, "Rehabilitation of Indigenous Environmental Ethics," 17–34.

mother indigenous tongues. However, now, because of deforestation, none of these plants, animals, or resources can be found in that locality. We cannot tell the young people today about the natural fruits and berries we used to enjoy, because we lack the equivalent word in English. We understood them so well by their local names, but the youth today cannot even fathom their existence. They do not know what they have missed. The forests of my childhood now look like a semidesert, because the trees have been cleared for agriculture and for charcoal. What was readily and freely available in nature in the 1970s and 1980s, the community now must buy at expensive prices. But the worst and most painful part of the story is that our young people do not know what we knew. Only on Google—if their parents are lucky enough to possess a smartphone—can they see a beautiful butterfly, a chameleon, or any number of other species. Only the wealthy can afford to take their children to the zoo or the animal orphanage to see what the people of my generation saw without any cost whatsoever.

We all need to take aggressive steps to restore the ecosystem and leave it beautiful for the next generation. Otherwise, this quotation cited by Raven LeFay in her article is probably right that "[o]ur massive tampering with the world's interdependent web of life—coupled with the environmental damage inflicted by deforestation, species loss, and climate change—could trigger widespread adverse effects, including the unpredictable collapses of critical biological systems whose interactions and dynamics we only imperfectly understand."[43]

It is clear that most African ethicists such as Segun Ogungbemi, Godfrey Tangwa, and Philomena Ojomo agree that Western civilization has promoted an anthropocentric worldview—bringing with it teleologism, utilitarianism, and deontology—which concerns itself only with the rights and duties of the present generation and is very short-sighted in matters concerning future generations. However, in my view, the current African worldviews as understood by many African ethicists are also not holistic, ecologically speaking, and are incomplete. There is a need to fill the lacuna in African spirituality, as defined previously by Mike Ushe, which is handed down from one generation to the next. To be more ecologically responsive, it needs to be modified by blending it with my suggested "eco-heart," "eco-ear," and "eco-eye" spirituality. This modification will strengthen the aspect of interconnectedness and resonate with Pope Francis's call to an ecological conversion and change of lifestyle. Unless we do this blending, I am afraid we shall continue blaming the youth and Western nations for own "ecological sins."

43. LeFay, "Ecological Critique of Education," 36.

Mbih Jerome Tosam reflects that, while Africa bears the least onus of responsibility for global warming and climate change, she suffers the greatest burden of adverse effects. The industrialized countries, which are largely responsible for the greatest amount of greenhouse emissions, are slow and reticent to implement the international agreements aimed at palliating the untoward effects of climate change.[44] He strongly argues for the urgent need to seek indigenous solutions to Africa's environmental crisis without compromising the much-needed development on the continent. He contends that we must rethink the way we relate to the environment, inviting all organizations and local populations—especially peasant farmers—to work together to restore it. His call to reexamine our relationship with nature is a true reflection of Pope Francis's invitation to care for our common home.

Francis has called upon all of us to make a paradigm shift in the way we behave towards nature. One good example of an African who yielded to care of the environment with passion, unconsciously embracing the spirit of the "eco-heart," "eco-ear," and "eco-eye," and who is deserving our due attention, is none other than the late Kenyan environmentalist Wangari Maathai. Through her nongovernmental organization, the Green Belt Movement, Maathai initiated and promoted the planting of trees, which largely changed the lives of Kenya's many peasant women. Her unwavering commitment to planting millions of trees attracted global attention, and it is important to explore her story as a representative model in this chapter.

## Nobel Laureate Wangari Maathai—The Tree Woman

Described as humble and caring, Wangari Maathai was the first African woman ever to receive the Nobel Peace Prize. Awarded the prize in 2004 because of her undying love for the environment, she spent her entire life planting trees and urging all Kenyans to plant at least one tree. Attracting global attention, the late Nobel Laureate spent decades helping an estimated 100,000 peasant women in rural Kenya to plant and sustain over 35 million trees. Through the Green Belt Movement, she made a significant contribution to reforestation in Kenya.[45] Her determination for the right course of action elevated her environmental conservationist manifesto to a global level. Besides receiving the Nobel Prize in June 1997, Maathai was selected by *Earth Times* as one of 100 people worldwide who had made a difference environmentally.[46] Some of her other international and environmental

---

44. Tosam, "African Environmental Ethics," 172–92.
45. Hayanga, "Wangari Maathai," 551–55.
46. Norwegian Nobel Institute, "Wangari Maathai."

awards include the 1991 Goldman Environmental Prize, the 1989 Woman of the World, the 1988 Windstar Award for the Environment, the 1986 Better World Society Award, and the 1984 Right Livelihood Award.[47]

In her Nobel Prize acceptance speech in the Oslo City Hall of Norway, Maathai recounted that, during her childhood, she witnessed forests being cleared and land converted to settlement. The community could no longer get fresh water. It was at that time that she understood that when the environment is destroyed, plundered, or mismanaged, the quality of life is undermined. This understanding prompted her to start the grassroots Green Belt Movement in 1977 to counteract the deforestation threatening the agricultural population's means of subsistence. In time, she also came to understand that sustainable development was not possible without democracy, peace, and concern for the environment. This led her to encourage women of her time to think "ecologically" during her tree-planting campaign. In her speech, she said that planting trees became a natural choice to help women of her time address some of the most basic needs that they had identified.

She was able to teach women about the links between their needs and the health and good management of the environment as well as about the scramble for scarce resources, inevitable poverty, and conflicts. She came up with a citizen education program, which enabled people to identify their problems as well as their causes and solutions. This program, she explained, helped citizens unlearn what "outsiders" had persuaded them to learn—that being poor also meant that they lacked the knowledge and skills to solve their local problems. Her dedication earned her the name "tree woman," and her green activism has become a model around the world.[48]

Wangari Maathai's environmental approach and efforts conspicuously reflect Pope Francis's message that small actions that aid the environment matter quite a bit.[49] In *LS* 211–12, Francis teaches that, through little daily actions, we can all contribute to conservation efforts. The late Wangari Maathai firmly believed that little actions play an important role in promoting environmental conservation. Her famous story of a hummingbird in a film by Bill Beneneson and Gene Rosow tells it all.[50]

---

47. Norwegian Nobel Institute, "Wangari Maathai," para. 2.
48. Hayanga, "Wangari Maathai," 551–55.
49. Hayanga, "Wangari Maathai," 551–55.
50. See "Wangari Maathai."

## A Hummingbird

> The story of the hummingbird is about this huge forest being consumed by a fire. All the animals in the forest come out and they are transfixed as they watch the forest burning and they feel very overwhelmed, very powerless, except this little hummingbird. It says, "I'm going to do something about the fire!" So, it flies to the nearest stream and takes a drop of water. It puts it on the fire, and goes up and down, up and down, up and down, as fast as it can. In the meantime, all the other animals, much bigger animals like the elephant with a big trunk that could bring much more water, they are standing there helpless. And they are saying to the hummingbird, "What do you think you can do? You are too little. This fire is too big. Your wings are too little and your beak is so small that you can only bring a small drop of water at a time." But as they continue to discourage it, it turns to them without wasting any time and it tells them, "I am doing the best I can."
>
> And that to me is what all of us should do. We should always be like a hummingbird. I may be insignificant, but I certainly don't want to be like the animals watching the planet going down the drain. I will be a hummingbird; I will do the best I can.

The hummingbird's commitment in this story is an open invitation and appeal to ecological responsibility. In environmental ecology, every little effort by every living creature counts. The story reflects what Pope Francis teaches in *LS* 211–12, that little efforts do indeed have a significant impact; in the Kiswahili language spoken in some parts of East Africa, the equivalent to this teaching would read *kidogo kidogo hujaza kibaba*. The Green Belt Movement is a good example of small actions that transformed the lives of thousands of women in Kenya and other parts of Africa and which, above all, earned the Wangari Maathai the most coveted Nobel Prize. In addition, Maathai's achievements are an inspiring blueprint for the contemporary African woman and strengthen the principle that promoting education and financial independence may serve to improve societal health, political freedom, and economic prosperity as a whole.

## Conclusion

This chapter has discussed Pope Francis's message to all of humanity about the urgent need to change our lifestyle in regard to the way we treat Mother

Earth and nature—God's creation. The pope has appealed to all races and nations, Christians and non-Christians alike, for an ecological conversion in order to have an integral relationship with nature and to stop our massive exploitation of her resources, which only results in our self-harm and destruction. Perhaps Francis's message would have been more touching if it had been accompanied by the statistics of how each nation has contributed to climate change. In my view, that information would have strongly impacted each individual nation in a unique way and would have probably compelled the nations with highest statistics to take urgent measures to individually and collectively save and restore Mother Earth. All the same, the pope has encouragingly reminded all of us that we have the capacity to change and respond to the call to develop a new way of thinking and undergo an ecological conversion.

In line with Francis's message, I have suggested in this chapter a new spirituality of "eco-heart," "eco-ear," and "eco-eye," which I believe has the potential to transform us into "ecological beings" with fully developed ecological features and a strong bond of interconnectedness with God, nature, and ourselves. I appeal to all of us to embrace this costless and universal spirituality, inspired by small actions like those of the late Wangari Maathai, to begin acting ecologically for the well-being of the planet and the posterity of future generations.

# 8

# Enacting *Laudato Si'* in Africa

EMMANUEL KATONGOLE

I am grateful to Stan Chu Ilo, the editor of the volume for inviting me to offer an afterword on a model of implementing *Laudato Si'* and to share something of the work underway in Uganda at Bethany Land Institute. I am very much honored, but I must begin by noting that Bethany Land Institute (BLI) is not a model that "implements" *Laudato Si'*. Implementation assumes a blueprint, a plan, or design, which then can be implemented or translated, perhaps with some modifications, depending on the local conditions or particular context. *Laudato Si'*, as I read it, is not such a blueprint; rather, it is a conversation, an invitation into dialogue (the word "dialogue" appears at least twenty-five times in the text of *Laudato Si'*) about what is going on and what it means to live and care for our common home. We at Bethany Land Institute see ourselves as engaged in this ongoing dialogue, in which we are constantly listening to and learning from the rich insights of *Laudato Si'*. That is why a better word for what we are about is "enactment," which simply means acting out, trying out, and experimenting with *Laudato Si'*.

It is also important to note that the conception of BLI predated *Laudato Si'*. At a retreat for our twenty-fifth priestly anniversary celebration in June 2012, I asked Fr. Cornelius, my classmate, if he knew a piece of land I could buy. I told him I wanted to plant a forest to replace the forest which had all been destroyed near the home where I grew up. Every time I would drive to my home village, I was shocked at the rate of deforestation and, overall, at the ecological devastation underway. On his part, Cornelius (an educationalist), was concerned about the kind of education that brainwashes young people into looking at the village as a place of backwardness and losers and so lets them pin their hope on finding employment in cities and towns—which has only contributed to the growing number of slums. Tony, our other classmate who later joined the conversation, drew our attention to the levels of poverty not only in the villages, but even more so, in the slums. The three of us together bought some land in Luweero (central Uganda) and started thinking about an initiative that would bring together these three *E*s: environment, education, and economics. At that time, we were thinking of planting a forest on this land and setting up a school and a farm (similar to St. Jude's Farm in Uganda) where we would teach young people. But we did not know exactly what this would look like, what kind of curriculum to teach, or what the glue holding these different activities together would be.

This all changed when *Laudato Si'* came out in 2015. I remember when I first read it at the beginning of September 2015—in a hotel room in Milan, where I had gone for a conference and could not sleep because of jet lag and so had picked up *Laudato Si'*—and how deeply moved I was by the text. I was touched by its simple and accessible language, its conversational style, its fresh and urgent message, its bold claims as well as its humble invitation to everyone (not just Christians) to listen and attend to the cry of the earth, our mother and our sister! In *Laudato Si'*, Pope Francis had not only put words to some of the restlessness that I and my classmates were already feeling, he had also provided both a vision and urgency for the Bethany Land Institute. In terms of its message, a number of insights stood out. First, Pope Francis was tracing the ecological crisis to the spiritual "wound"—our inability to see and acknowledge our deep connection with the land: "We have forgotten that we ourselves are dust of the earth."[1] Secondly, everything is interconnected. Accordingly, the cry of the earth and the cry of the poor belong together. Not only does "the deterioration of the environment and of society affect the most vulnerable people on the planet," (*LS* 48) a true ecological approach always becomes a social approach: "it must integrate questions of justice in debates on the environment, so as to hear *both the cry of the earth and the cry of the poor*" (*LS* 49).[2] Thirdly, responding to the cry of the earth, which is also the cry of the poor, requires an integrated approach: "Strategies for a solution demand an integrated approach to combating poverty, restoring dignity to the excluded, and at the same time protecting nature" (*LS* 139).

I was equally touched by the insight that responding to the twin cries of the poor and of the earth requires not simply a technical approach but a mindset change: "There needs to be a distinctive way of looking at things, a way of thinking, policies, an educational program, a lifestyle, and a

---

1. Francis, *Laudato Si'*, 2.
2. Original emphasis.

spirituality" (*LS* 111). The goal of the education program, according to *Laudato Si'*, is not merely to provide technical skills but to foster "ecological citizenship," (*LS* 211) which is to say a new sense of "belonging" and a restored relationship with God, neighbor, and earth (ecological conversion). The goal of the education program that *Laudato Si'* was calling for was not simply to provide "information" (*LS* 210) but "formation," that is, the cultivation of various "ecological virtues": care for creation, self-esteem, simplicity of life, sense of beauty, rhythm, gratitude, and service for the common good (*LS* 211–14). I remember sitting up in my hotel bed in Milan, scribbling copious notes in the margins of my copy of *Laudato Si'*, underlining and highlighting various sections and sentences, getting something like "a call," that this is what BLI should be: an education program to realize the kind of integral ecology that *Laudato Si'* was calling for. The following morning, I sent an e-mail to my priest colleagues in Uganda and encouraged them to get a copy of *Laudato Si'*. Over the years, as we have (re)read, discussed, and shared insights from this encyclical, we have become more passionate about the mission of BLI, and at the same time, we have shaped BLI's vision, mission, and programs to align more with the insights from *Laudato Si'*. The BLI mission is to train and equip leaders who are committed to address poverty, care for creation, and promote human dignity in the rural communities. The mission is realized by forming young people from the rural community into the spirituality, lifestyle, and practice of integral ecology. BLI trainees spend two and half years in the BLI formation program, which involves training in skills of sustainable agriculture, care for creation, leadership, economic entrepreneurship, and six months of community placement. At the end of their time at BLI, trainees graduate as "caretakers." Formed in the relevant spirituality, skills, and practice of integral ecology, BLI caretakers return to the community to set up their farms, which serve as an example and model of integral ecology. In this way, BLI caretakers become both leaders and change agents for sustainable livelihoods and creation care in rural communities.

We call BLI graduates "caretakers" for a number of reasons. The name is biblical and invokes the human vocation of ecological stewardship (Gen 2:15). As Pope Francis notes, "'Tilling' refers to cultivating, ploughing, or working, 'keeping' means *caring*, protecting, overseeing, and preserving" (*LS* 67). But the name "caretaker" also underscores a commitment to "heal" and foster integral ecology. Human life, Pope Francis says, "is grounded in three key and intertwined relationships: with God, with neighbor, and with the earth itself" (*LS* 66). If any one of those relationships is broken, the others suffer. These three fundamental relationships have been broken, and the key to advancing integral ecology is healing this threefold relationship: with

God, with neighbor, and with the earth. BLI caretakers get formed in, and are committed to, this spirituality of healing.

Thus, the name "caretaker" serves as a reminder that the Bethany Land Institute is not simply a "training" program; it is a "formation" program—and a "spirituality," which is fostered through the daily rhythm of manual work, learning, prayer, reflection, community, and rest. The stories from the village of Bethany—especially the stories of Martha, Mary, and Lazarus—provide a good example and model of the kind of lifestyle and spirituality we seek to foster at Bethany Land Institute. The stories offer a practical spirituality of productivity, hospitality, creation care, human dignity, and servant leadership necessary for the flourishing of rural communities.

At Bethany Land Institute, the formation of caretakers takes place in and through three key programs or learning centers:

(i) Mary's Farm: a sustainable farm where BLI trainees learn the principles and practice of integrated farming and care for the land;

(ii) Lazarus's Trees: a natural forest where the trainees learn the principles and practices of conservation and ecosustainability, and how to engage the community in ecological education and reforestation; and

(iii) Martha's Market: the "business school" of BLI which teaches the principles of leadership, economic innovation, financial management, etc., and also houses the caretaker credit and savings scheme.

Though the programs are distinct, they are interrelated, highlighting a key dimension of the interconnectedness which is at the heart of *Laudato Si'* and characterizes the notion and practice of integral ecology. At the same time, through these programs, we try to work out the material and practical implications of Pope Francis's insight in *Laudato Si'*, namely so that "social love is the key to integral human development" (*LS* 231). We try to arrive at this insight from different angles, which, however, are interrelated.

In conclusion, let me note that, in the process of setting up, establishing, and running BLI for integral ecology and rural transformation, we have encountered a number of challenges. But with each challenge have also come unexpected gifts. First, there is the issue of land. The land we first purchased and where our initial forest and demonstration farm were established has been embroiled in a series of land disputes and legal challenges (which are still unresolved). This has been a source of major heartache and ongoing frustration. However, in 2019, BLI entered into partnership with the Diocese of Kasana-Luweero, which leased 180 acres of land to BLI at Nandere Parish. Kasana-Luweero saw partnering with Bethany Land

Institute as a great evangelizing opportunity, which would help to spread the message of *Laudato Si'* throughout the diocese, and they were happy to offer the land at Luweero. This is where BLI's campus is being built and where our formation program will take place, even as we continue to till and cultivate the disputed land while the legal challenges are settled. But as we started working with the young people on the land, we soon realized how widespread and resistant the "technocratic paradigm" is. Not only did the young people expect quick results from their efforts, but it was also difficult to convince them not to use synthetic fertilizers and chemical pesticides on their crops. Related to this was the standard expectation that, since we are a "land institute," we were simply an agricultural "training" institute. Insisting on the "formation" dimension meant that we had to come up with our own unique curriculum. This required time, resources, and finding the right people to design the curriculum as well as lead the institute. We were fortunate to receive a grant that enabled us to spend extended time with a team of consultants reading *Laudato Si'* and designing a unique curriculum.

Building an institution requires a lot of resources, financial and otherwise. To be honest, I had greatly underestimated the resources that we would need to build, staff, and run a physical institute, and not just an NGO program. Fortunately, there are a number of people and organizations who believe in what we are doing and who have generously supported us. Finally, there is the issue of time. The initial vision for BLI was conceived in 2012, and we are only now getting around to formally launching the institute—hopefully in 2022. There are many times I have felt like, for every step we move forward, we take two steps back. We are learning and dealing with many things and realities that we could not have anticipated and quite often feel we do not know what we are doing. However, the unexpected gifts we receive along the way assure us that we are on the right path, and they renew our confidence in the invitation to live into the sublime communion of *Laudato Si'*'s integral ecology. If there is one key lesson I am learning in all of this, it is what Wendell Berry notes—namely, that "the real work of planet-saving will be small, humble, and humbling, [and] (insofar as it involves love) pleasing and rewarding."[3] I am also happily discovering that we are not alone in this effort. Thus, we continue to learn from and be inspired by the efforts underway by initiatives like Wangari Maathai's Green Belt Movement, St. Jude's Family Farm, Songhai Center, the Catholic Youth Network for Environmental Sustainability in Africa (CYNESA),[4] and others. We

---

3. Berry, "Out of Your Car," xxiii.

4. To learn more about these various initiatives, visit their websites: The Green Belt Movement, http://www.greenbeltmovement.org; St. Jude's Family Farm, https://www.innovations.harvard.edu/st-jude-family-project; Songhai Center, http://www.

need many more experiments like these and those which have been highlighted by the authors in this volume. It is through these experiments that the conversation and dialogue into which *Laudato Si'* invites us—of what it means to live in and care for our common home—is sustained.

For more on the Bethany Land Institute, visit www.bethanylandinstitute.org.

---

songhai.org; and the Catholic Youth Network for Environmental Sustainability in Africa, https://cynesafrica.webs.com.

# Bibliography

Abbott, Walter M., and Joseph Gallagher. *The Documents of Vatican Council II: 1962–1965.* New York: Guild, 1966.
Achebe, Chinua. *No Longer at Ease.* London: Heinemann, 1972.
———. *Things Fall Apart.* New York: Anchor, 1994.
Adebanwi, Wale, et al. "Religion and Indigenous Hermeneutics." *Journal of Africana Religions* 2.4 (2014) 457–64. doi:10.5325/jafrireli.2.4.0457.
Adedeji, Adebayo, ed. *Comprehending and Mastering African Conflicts: The Search for Sustainable Peace and Good Governance.* London: Zed, 1999.
African Development Bank. "Climate Change, Gender, and Development in Africa." *AfDB Chief Economist Complex* 1.1 (2011) 1–46. https://www.afdb.org/sites/default/files/documents/publications/climate_change_gender_and_development_in_africa.pdf.
"African Military Spending Up Nearly 20% Over the Last Decade." *defenceWeb,* April 28, 2020. https://www.defenceweb.co.za/daily-news/international-news/african-military-spending-up-nearly-20-over-the-last-decade.
African Union. *Agenda 2063: The Africa We Want: Framework Document.* Addis Ababa, Ethiopia: African Union Commission, 2015.
———. *Draft African Union Strategy on Climate Change.* AMCEN-15-REF-11. https://web.archive.org/web/20200814165752/https://www.un.org/en/africa/osaa/pdf/au/cap_draft_auclimatestrategy_2015.pdf.
African Union Commission (AUC), et al. *2017 Africa Sustainable Development Report: Tracking Progress on Agenda 2063 and the Sustainable Development Goals.* Addis Ababa, Ethiopia: AUC, UN Economic Commission for Africa (ECA), African Development Bank (AfDB), UN Development Programme (UNDP), 2017. https://www.africa.undp.org/content/rba/en/home/library/reports/africa-sustainable-development-report.html.
Ahmed, Hadra, and Jacey Fortin. "As Trash Avalanche Toll Rises in Ethiopia, Survivors Ask Why." *The New York Times,* March 20, 2017. https://www.nytimes.com/2017/03/20/world/africa/ethiopia-addis-ababa-garbage-landslide.html.
Alva, Reginald. "*Laudato Si'* Challenges Irrational Rationalization." *Asian Horizons* 9.4 (2015) 709–23.
Appiah-Kubi, Kofi. "Oh, Mother Earth." *Zygon* 19.1 (1984) 61–63.
Aquinas, Thomas. *Commentary on the Metaphysics.* Translated by John P. Rowan. Chicago: Regnery, 1961.
Arabome, Anne. "African Spirituality for a New Ecclesia in Africa." In *The Church We Want: Foundations, Theology, and Mission of the Church in Africa—Conversations on Ecclesiology,* edited by Agbonkhianmeghe E. Orobator, 145–53. Nairobi: Pauline Africa, 2015.

# BIBLIOGRAPHY

Arocho Esteves, Junno. "Clericalism, Wealth Prevent One from Knowing Christ, Pope Says." *Crux*, May 5, 2020. https://cruxnow.com/vatican/2020/05/clericalism-wealth-prevent-one-from-knowing-christ-pope-says.

Asfaw, Nigist, and Sebsebe Demissew. *Aromatic Plants of Ethiopia*. Addis Ababa, Ethiopia: Shama, 2009.

Ba, Diadie. "Africans Still Seething Over Sarkozy Speech." *Reuters*, September 5, 2007. https://uk.reuters.com/article/uk-africa-sarkozy/africans-still-seething-over-sarkozy-speech-idUKL0513034620070905.

Balasuriya, Tissa. *Planetary Theology*. Maryknoll, NY: Orbis, 1984.

Bassey, Nnimmo. *To Cook a Continent: Destructive Extraction and the Climate Crisis in Africa*. Cape Town: Pambazuka, 2012.

Bayart, Jean-François. *The State in Africa: The Politics of the Belly*. New York: Longman, 1993.

"BBC Deletes Important Story on Toxic Waste Dumping in the Ivory Coast after Legal Threats, 12 Dec 2009." https://wikileaks.org/wiki/BBC_deletes_important_story_on_toxic_waste_dumping_in_the_Ivory_Coast_after_legal_threats,_12_Dec_2009.

Beckerman, Wilfred. *Economic Development and the Environment: Conflict or Complementarity?* Washington, DC: World Bank Development Economics' Office of the Vice President, 1992.

Benedict XVI, Pope. *Africae Munus: On the Church in Africa in Service to Reconciliation, Justice, and Peace*. Vatican City: Libreria Editrice Vaticana, 2011. http://www.vatican.va/content/benedict-xvi/en/apost_exhortations/documents/hf_ben-xvi_exh_20111119_africae-munus.html.

———. *Caritas in Veritate: Charity in Truth*. Vatican City: Libreria Editrice Vaticana, 2009. https://www.vatican.va/content/benedict-xvi/en/encyclicals/documents/hf_ben-xvi_enc_20090629_caritas-in-veritate.html.

———. "The Listening Heart: Reflections on the Foundations of Law." Vatican City: Libreria Editrice Vaticana, 2011. http://www.vatican.va/content/benedict-xvi/en/speeches/2011/september/documents/hf_ben-xvi_spe_20110922_reichstag-berlin.html.

Béré, Paul. "Old Testament Sources of a Branded African Ecclesiology." In *The Church We Want: Foundations, Theology, and Mission of the Church in Africa—Conversations on Ecclesiology*, edited by Agbonkhianmeghe E. Orobator, 122–31. Nairobi: Pauline Africa, 2015.

Berry, Thomas. *The Great Work: Our Way into the Future*. New York: Bell Tower, 1999.

Berry, Wendell. "Out of Your Car, Off Your Horse: Twenty-seven Propositions about Global Thinking and the Sustainability of Cities." *The Atlantic*, February 1991. https://www.theatlantic.com/magazine/archive/1991/02/out-your-car-your-horse/309159.

Blundin, Christina. "Corporate Social Responsibility: Fallacies and Flaws." MBA thesis, Johnson and Wales University, 2012.

Bond, Patrick. *Looting Africa: The Economics of Exploitation*. New York: Zed, 2006.

Boulaga, F. Eboussi. *Christianity Without Fetishes: An African Critique and Recapture of Christianity*. Translated by Robert R. Barr. Maryknoll, NY: Orbis, 1984.

Brown-Hinds, Paulette. "Circle in African Tradition (1)." *Black Voices News*, August 5, 2015. https://blackvoicenews.com/2015/08/05/circle-in-african-tradition-1/.

Bryant, M. Darrol. "God, Humanity, and Mother Earth: African Wisdom and the Recovery of the Earth." In *God, Humanity, and Mother Nature*, edited by Gilbert E. M. Ogutu et al., 73–74. Nairobi: Masaki, 1992.

Bujo, Bénézet. "Ecology and Ethical Responsibility from an African Perspective." In *African Ethics: An Anthology of Comparative and Applied Ethics*, edited by Munyaradzi Felix Murove, 281–97. Scottsville, South Africa: University of KwaZulu-Natal Press, 2009.

———. *Foundations of an African Ethic: Beyond the Universal Claims of Western Morality*. Nairobi: Paulines Africa, 2003.

Burgis, Tom. *The Looting Machine*. London: Public Affairs, 2015.

Butler, Paula. *Colonial Extractions: Race and Canadian Mining in Contemporary Africa*. Toronto: University of Toronto Press, 2015.

Caduto, Michael J. "Ecological Education: A System Rooted in Diversity." *The Journal of Environmental Education* 29.4 (1998) 11–16.

Caminade, Pierre. *Bolloré: Monopoles, Services Compris, Tentacules Africains*. Paris: l'Harmattan, 2000.

Carillet, Jean-Bernard, et al. *Ethiopia and Eritrea*. London: Lonely Planet, 2009.

Carmody, Pádraig. *The New Scramble for Africa*. Malden, MA: Polity, 2016.

Cartwright, Jon. "Cape Town 'Day Zero' Water Crisis Due to Migrating Moisture Corridor." *Physics World*, January 22, 2019. https://physicsworld.com/a/cape-town-day-zero-water-crisis-due-to-migrating-moisture-corridor/.

Casey, J. P. "Tanzania Fines Acacia $2.4M over Environmental Damage." *Mining Technology*, May 20, 2019. https://www.mining-technology.com/mining-safety/tanzania-fines-acacia-2-4m-over-environmental-damage.

Césaire, Aimé. *Discourse on Colonialism*. Translated by Joan Pinkham. New York: Monthly Review, 2000.

Chemhuru, Munamato, and Dennis Masaka. "Taboos as Sources of Shona People's Environmental Ethics." *Journal of Sustainable Development in Africa* 12.7 (2010) 121–33. http://www.jsd-africa.com/Jsda/V12No7_Winter2010_A/PDF/Taboos%20as%20Sources%20of%20Shona%20Peoples%20Environmental%20Ethics.pdf.

"Chemical Fire Sends Toxic Gas over Cape Town Community." *AP News*, December 17, 1995. https://apnews.com/article/f3eecfbf1e33493db6eda13952a0cb56.

Chibuko, Patrick C. "Forestation—Deforestation—Reforestation: Implications for Ecology and Liturgy in Dialogue." *AFER* 52.2–3 (2010) 189–212.

Chirongoma, Sophie. "Karanga-Shona Rural Women's Agency in Dressing Mother Earth: A Contribution towards an Indigenous Eco-Feminist Theology." *Journal of Theology for Southern Africa* 142 (2012) 120–44.

Chryssavgis, John, ed. *On Earth as in Heaven: Ecological Vision and Initiatives of Ecumenical Patriarch Bartholomew*. New York: Fordham University Press, 2012.

Cline, Catherine Ann. "The Church and the Movement for Congo Reform." *Church History* 32.1 (1963) 46–56.

Colwell, Mary. "The Empty Sky." *The Tablet*, May 18, 2019.

Conradie, Ernst. "Approaches to Religion and the Environment in Africa." In *The Routledge Companion to Christianity in Africa*, edited by Elias Kifon Bongmba, 438–54. London: Routledge, 2016.

———. *Christianity and Ecological Theology: Resources for Further Research*. Matieland, South Africa: Sun, 2006.

Cooney, Daniel. "Forest Day 5 Experts: New Wave of Deforestation Threatens Africa's Climate Resilience." *Forest News*, December 5, 2011. https://forestsnews.cifor.org/5756/experts-new-wave-of-deforestation-threatens-africas-climate-resilience?fnl.

Cornish, Sandie. "*Laudato Si*': Making the Connections." *Asian Horizons* 9.4 (2015) 609–20.

Dang, Tam, et al. "Physician Beware: Severe Cyanide Toxicity from Amygdalin Tablets Ingestion." *Case Reports in Emergency Medicine* (2017) 1–3.

Das, Pamela, and Richard Horton. "Pollution, Health, and the Planet: Time for Decisive Action." *The Lancet* 391.10119 (2018) 407–8. http://www.thelancet.com/journals/lancet/article/PIIS0140-6736(17)32588-6/fulltext.

Demisswe, Sebsebe, and Inger Nordal. *Aloes and Other Lilies of Ethiopia and Eritrea*. Addis Ababa, Ethiopia: Shama, 2010.

Deneault, Alain, et al. *Noir Canada: Pillage, Corruption et Criminalité en Afrique*. Montréal: Ecosociété, 2008.

Dharani, Najma. *Field Guide to Common Trees and Shrubs of East Africa*. Cape Town: Struik Nature, 2011.

Donders, Joseph. *Non-Bourgeois Theology: An African Experience of God*. Maryknoll, NY: Orbis, 1985.

Dunne, Daisy. "Q&A: Are the 2019–20 Locust Swarms Linked to Climate Change?" *CarbonBrief: Clear on Climate*, March 10, 2020. https://www.carbonbrief.org/qa-are-the-2019-20-locust-swarms-linked-to-climate-change.

Duraiappah, Anantha K. "Poverty and Environmental Degradation: A Review and Analysis of the Nexus." *World Development* 26.12 (1998) 2169–79.

Easterly, William. *The White Man's Burden: Why the West's Efforts to Aid the Rest Have Done So Much Ill and So Little Good*. New York: Penguin, 2006.

Engler, Yves. *Canada in Africa: Three Hundred Years of Aid and Exploitation*. Vancouver: Fernwood, 2015.

———. "Trudeau's Oil Views Spur African Famine." *Canadian Dimension*, March 29, 2017. https://web.archive.org/web/20210116081931/https://canadiandimension.com/articles/view/trudeaus-oil-views-spur-african-famine.

Esteves, Junno Arocho. "Clericalism, Wealth Prevent One from Knowing Christ, Pope Says." *National Catholic Reporter*, May 5, 2020. https://www.ncronline.org/news/vatican/francis-chronicles/clericalism-wealth-prevent-one-knowing-christ-pope-says.

Feinstein, Andrew. *The Shadow World: Inside the Global Arms Trade*. New York: Farrar, Straus & Giroux, 2011.

Firebaugh, Glenn. *The New Geography of Income Inequality*. Cambridge, MA: Harvard University Press, 2003.

Food and Agriculture Organization (FAO) of the United Nations and International Tropical Timber Association. *The State of Forests in the Amazon Basin, Congo Basin, and Southeast Asia: A Report Prepared for the Summit of the Three Rainforest Basins, Brazzaville, Republic of Congo (31 May–3 June, 2011)*. Rome: FAO, 2011. http://www.fao.org/3/i2247e/i2247e00.pdf.

Forouzanfar, Mohammad H., et al. "Global, Regional, and National Comparative Risk Assessment of 79 Behavioural, Environmental and Occupational, and Metabolic Risks or Clusters of Risks, 1990–2015: A Systematic Analysis for the Global

Burden of Disease Study 2015." *The Lancet* 388.10053 (2016) 1659–724. https://www.thelancet.com/journals/lancet/article/PIIS0140-6736(16)31679-8/fulltext.

Francis, Pope. *Evangelii Gaudium: The Joy of the Gospel*. Washington, DC: US Conference of Catholic Bishops, 2013.

———. *Gaudete et Exsultate: On the Call to Holiness in Today's World*. Vatican City: Libreria Editrice Vaticana, 2018. https://www.vatican.va/content/francesco/en/apost_exhortations/documents/papa-francesco_esortazione-ap_20180319_gaudete-et-exsultate.html.

———. "Inaugural Homily." Given in Vatican City at St. Peter's Square, March 19, 2013. https://www.vatican.va/content/francesco/en/homilies/2013/documents/papa-francesco_20130319_omelia-inizio-pontificato.html.

———. *Laudato Si': On Care for our Common Home*. Vatican City: Libreria Editrice Vaticana, 2015. http://www.vatican.va/content/francesco/en/encyclicals/documents/papa-francesco_20150524_enciclica-laudato-si.html.

———. "Meeting with the Muslim Community." Address given at the Central Mosque of Koudoukou, Bangui, Central African Republic, November 30, 2015. http://www.vatican.va/content/francesco/en/speeches/2015/november/documents/papa-francesco_20151130_repubblica-centrafricana-musulmani.html.

———. *Querida Amazonia*. Vatican City: Libreria Editrice Vaticana, 2020. http://www.vatican.va/content/francesco/en/apost_exhortations/documents/papa-francesco_esortazione-ap_20200202_querida-amazonia.html.

Fredriksson, Per G., and Eric Neumayer. "Corruption and Climate Change Policies: Do the Bad Old Days Matter?" *Environmental and Resource Economics* 63.2 (2016) 451–69.

Friedlander, Maria-José, and Bob Friedlander. *Hidden Treasures of Ethiopia: A Guide to the Remote Churches of an Ancient Land*. London: Taurus, 2015.

Gajanan, Mahita. "'You Have Stolen My Dreams and My Childhood': Greta Thurnberg Gives Powerful Speech at UN Climate Summit." *TIME*, September 23, 2019. https://time.com/5684216/greta-thunberg-un-climate-action-summit-climate-speech.

Gallardon, Miguel E., and Mackenzi Kingdon. "Applying Latina/o Psychology to Address Social Issues." In *Social Issues in Living Color: Challenges and Solutions from the Perspective of Ethnic Minority Psychology*, edited by Arthur W. Blume, 1:93–128. 3 vols. Santa Barbara, CA: Praeger, 2017.

Gebara, Ivone. *Longing for Running Water: Ecofeminism and Liberation*. Minneapolis: Fortress, 1999.

Gitau, Samson K. "Environmental Crisis: A Challenge to the Church in Africa." *AFER* 53.2 (2011) 308–32.

Gore, Al. *An Inconvenient Truth: A Global Warning*. Australia: Universal Sony Pictures, 2006. DVD.

Greenpeace, and Amnesty International. *The Toxic Truth about a Company Called Trafigura, a Ship Called Probo Koala, and the Dumping of Toxic Waste in Cote d'Ivoire*. https://www.amnestyusa.org/wp-content/uploads/2017/04/afr310022012eng.pdf.

Griffin, Keith. "Global Prospects for Development and Human Security." *Canadian Journal of Development Studies* 16.13 (2011) 359–70.

Guardini, Romano. *The End of the Modern World*. Rev. ed. Wilmington, DE: ISI, 1998.

Guruswamy, Lakshman D., and Mariah Zebrowski Leach. *International Environmental Law in a Nutshell*. St. Paul, MN: Thomson/West, 2012.

Hackworth, Jason. *Faith Based: Religious Neoliberalism and the Politics of Welfare in the United States*. Geographies of Justice and Social Transformation. Athens: University of Georgia Press, 2012.

Hairsine, Kate. "Panama Papers: Africa's Elite Are Plundering Their Countries." *Deutsche Welle*, October 18, 2017. https://p.dw.com/p/2m38i.

Hamdok, Abdalla, ed. *Innovative Financing for the Economic Transformation of Africa*. Addis Ababa, Ethiopia: UN Economic Commission for Africa, 2015.

Harrison, Graham. "Authoritarian Neoliberalism and Capitalist Transformation in Africa: All Pain, No Gain." *Globalizations* 16.3 (2019) 274–88.

Hayanga, Awori J. "Wangari Mathai: An African Woman's Environmental and Geopolitical Landscape." *International Journal of Environmental Studies* 63.5 (2006) 551–55.

Healey, Joseph. *Towards an African Narrative Theology*. Nairobi: Paulines, 1996.

Heelan, Patrick A. "Hermeneutical Realism and Scientific Observation." In *PSA 1982: Proceedings of the Biennial Meeting of the Philosophy of Science Association*, edited by Peter D. Asquith and Thomas Nickles, 1:77–87. 2 vols. Chicago: The University of Chicago Press, 1982.

———. "Hermeneutic Consciousness, Perception, and Natural Science." Washington, DC: Georgetown University, 2010. http://www.ishs.hu/comment-the-abstracts-of-the-2010-conference/item/116-hermeneutic-consciousness-perception-and-natural-science.

Human Rights Watch. *The Price of Oil: Corporate Responsibility and Human Rights Violations in Nigeria's Oil Producing Communities*. New York: Human Rights Watch, 1999.

Idowu, E. Bọlaji. *African Traditional Religion: A Definition*. London: SCM, 1973.

Ilo, Stan Chu. *The Church and Development in Africa: Aid and Development from the Perspective of Catholic Social Ethic*. Eugene, OR: Pickwick, 2014.

———. "Fragile Earth, Fragile Africa: An African Eco-Theology for Human and Cosmic Flourishing." In *Fragile World: Ecology for the Church*, edited by William T. Cavanaugh, 129–50. Eugene, OR: Cascade, 2018.

———. *A Poor and Merciful Church: The Illuminative Ecclesiology of Pope Francis*. Maryknoll, NY: Orbis, 2018.

Iwu, Maurice M. *Handbook of African Medicinal Plants*. London: CRC, 2014.

Janeski, John S. *Healing Ourselves Naturally in Ethiopia: A Guide to the Use of Herbs, Food, and Products Found Locally*. Addis Ababa, Ethiopia: Knowledge Gate, 2015.

John Paul II, Pope. *Ecclesia in Africa: On the Church in Africa and its Evangelizing Mission towards the Year 2000*. Vatican City: Libreria Editrice Vaticana, 1995. http://www.vatican.va/content/john-paul-ii/en/apost_exhortations/documents/hf_jp-ii_exh_14091995_ecclesia-in-africa.html.

Jones, Nick Ashton. *The ERA Handbook to the Niger Delta: The Human Ecosystems of the Niger Delta*. London: Environmental Rights Action, 1998.

Jones, Shirley. "Dune Mining for St Lucia?" *The Witness*, January 2, 2009. https://www.news24.com/witness/archive/dune-mining-for-st-lucia-20150430.

Joy, Bill. "Why the Future Doesn't Need Us." *Wired*, April 1, 2000. https://www.wired.com/2000/04/joy-2/.

Joye, Pierre, and Rosine Lewin. *Les Trusts au Congo*. Bruxelles: Société Populaires d'éditions, 1961.

Kamoga, Jonathan. "More Displacements in Uganda as Lake Victoria Swells." *The East African*, May 2, 2020. https://www.theeastafrican.co.ke/tea/news/east-africa/more-displacements-in-uganda-as-lake-victoria-swells-1440646.

Kanyandago, Peter. "Let Us First Feed the Children (Mark 7:27): The Church's Response to the Inequitable Extraction of Resources and Related Violence." In *Reconciliation, Justice, and Peace: The Second African Synod*, edited by A. E. Orobator, 171–80. Maryknoll, NY: Orbis, 2011.

Katongole, Emmanuel. *The Journey of Reconciliation: Groaning for a New Creation in Africa*. Maryknoll, NY: Orbis, 2017.

———. *The Sacrifice of Africa: A Political Theology for Africa*. Grand Rapids: Eerdmans, 2011.

Kaza, Silpa, et al. *What a Waste 2.0: A Global Snapshot of Solid Waste Management*. Washington, DC: World Bank, 2018.

Kelbessa, Workineh. "The Rehabilitation of Indigenous Environmental Ethics in Africa." *Diogenes* 52.3 (2005) 17–34.

Kittler, Glenn D. *The White Fathers*. Garden City, NY: Image, 1961.

Klein, Naomi. *This Changes Everything: Capitalism vs. the Climate*. New York: Simon & Schuster, 2014.

Knox, Peter. "*Laudato Si'* and *Veritatis Gaudium*: Teaching Care of Our Common Home in a Catholic University." Paper presented at the 2019 Academic Conference of AMECEA Universities and Colleges: Catholic University Education Today, Hekima University College, Nairobi, November 21, 2019.

———. "Theology, Ecology, and Africa: No Longer Strange Bedfellows." In *Reconciliation, Justice, and Peace: The Second African Synod*, edited by A. E. Orobator, 159–70. Maryknoll, NY: Orbis, 2011.

Kolinjivadi, Vijay. "Inside Addis Ababa's Landfill Disaster." *New Internationalist*, August 17, 2017. https://newint.org/web-exclusive/2017/08/17/inside-addis-ababa-landfill-disastes.

Landrigan, Philip J., et al. "The *Lancet* Commission on Pollution and Health." *The Lancet Commissions* 391.10119 (2018) 462–512. https://www.thelancet.com/journals/lancet/article/PIIS0140-6736(17)32345-0/fulltext.

"*Laudato Si'* Anniversary Year Plan 2020–2021." https://www.humandevelopment.va/en/news/2020/laudato-si-special-anniversary-year-plan.html.

Leeson, Craig, dir. *A Plastic Ocean*. Malibu, CA: Plastic Oceans Ltd., 2016. DVD.

LeFay, Raven. "An Ecological Critique of Education." *International Journal of Children's Spirituality* 11.1 (2006) 35–45.

Le Grange, Lesley. "Ubuntu/Botho as Ecophilosophy and Ecosophy." *Journal of Human Ecology* 49.3 (2015) 301–8.

Leswing, Kif. "Apple CEO Tim Cook's Total Pay Dropped Last Year, but He Still Took Home over $125 Million." *CNBC*, January 3, 2020. https://www.cnbc.com/2020/01/03/apple-ceo-tim-cook-2019-compensation-dropped-from-2018.html.

Lewis, Stephen. *Race Against Time: Searching for Hope in AIDS-Ravaged Africa*. Toronto: House of Anansi, 2005.

Leyew, Zelealem. *Wild Plant Nomenclature and Traditional Botanical Knowledge Among Three Ethnolinguistic Groups in Northwestern Ethiopia*. Addis Ababa, Ethiopia: OSREA, 2011.

Lynch, Cecelia. *Wrestling with God: Ethical Precarity in Christianity and International Relations*. Cambridge: Cambridge University Press, 2020.

Maathai, Wangari. *Replenishing the Earth: Spiritual Values for Healing Ourselves and the World*. New York: Doubleday, 2010.

———. *Unbowed: A Memoir*. New York: Anchor, 2007.

———. "We Are Called to Help the Earth to Heal." In *Moral Ground: Ethical Action for a Planet in Peril*, edited by Kathleen D. Moore and Michael P. Nelson, 271–74. San Antonio, TX: Trinity University Press, 2010.

"Macron estime que l'Afrique a un problème démographique." *BBC News Afrique*, July 11, 2017. https://www.bbc.com/afrique/monde-40572207.

Mafundikwa, Ish. "Drought Ignites Human-Wildlife Conflict in Zimbabwe." Agence France Presse, January 10, 2020. https://news.yahoo.com/drought-ignites-human-wildlife-conflict-zimbabwe-022746631.html.

Magesa, Laurenti. *What Is Not Sacred? African Spirituality*. Nairobi: Paulines Africa, 2014.

Mamdani, Mahmood. *Citizen and Subject: Contemporary Africa and the Legacy of Late Colonialism*. Princeton: Princeton University Press, 1996.

———. *When Victims Become Killers: Colonialism, Nativism, and the Genocide in Rwanda*. Princeton: Princeton University Press, 2001.

Martindale, Greg. "Opinion: Trophy Hunting in the Greater Kruger versus Broader Conservation Policies." *Africa Geographic*, April 2, 2019. https://africageographic.com/stories/opinion-trophy-hunting-in-the-greater-kruger-versus-broader-conservation-priorities/.

Masango, M. J. S. "African Spirituality that Shapes the Concept of Ubuntu." *Verbum et Ecclesia Journal* 27.3 (2006) 930–43.

Maseno, Loreen. "Towards an African Inculturated Sophiology: The Case of African Wisdom Traditions from Myths for Ecological Concerns." In *Religion and Ecology in the Public Sphere*, edited by Celine Deane-Drummond and Heinrich Bedford-Strohm, 125–38. New York: T. & T. Clark International, 2011.

May, Barbara, and Monica Söö. *The Great Cosmic Mother: Rediscovering the Religion of the Earth*. San Francisco: Harper & Row, 1987.

Mazrui, Ali. *The African Condition*. Cambridge: Cambridge University Press, 1990.

Mbiti, John S. *African Religions and Philosophy*. Nairobi: Heinemann Kenya, 1969.

———. *Introduction to African Religion*. New York: Praeger, 1975.

———. *New Testament Eschatology in an African Background*. Oxford: Oxford University Press, 1971.

McCall, Daniel F. "Mother Earth: The Great Goddess of West Africa." In *Mother Worship: Themes and Variations*, edited by James J. Preston, 304–24. Chapel Hill: The University of North Carolina Press, 1982.

McDonagh, Sean. *On Care for Our Common Home, Laudato Si': The Encyclical of Pope Francis on the Environment*. Maryknoll, NY: Orbis, 2016.

Meadows, Donella H., et al. *The Limits to Growth*. New York: Universe, 1972.

———. *Limits to Growth: The Thirty-Year Update*. Burlington, VT: Chelsea Green, 2004.

Mendoca, Valerian. "A Metaphysics of Intersubjectivity for an Integral Ecology: The Relevance of Teilhard and Whitehead for the Vision of *Laudato Si*.'" *Asian Horizons* 9.4 (2015) 748–62.
Mesey, Christel. "Greta Thunberg's Speech to the World." *Geneva Business News*, December 21, 2018. https://www.gbnews.ch/greta-thunbergs-speech-to-the-world/.
Ministry of Forestry and Wildlife, Kenya (MFW). *Analysis of Drivers and Underlying Causes of Forest Cover Change in the Various Forest Types of Kenya*. Nairobi: MFW, 2013. http://www.kenyaforestservice.org/documents/redd/Analysis%20%20of%20Drivers%20of%20Deforestation%20&forest%20Degradation%20in%20Kenya.pdf.
Moffat, David, and Olof Linden. "Perception and Reality: Assessing Priorities for Sustainable Development in the Niger River Delta." *Ambio* 24:7/8 (1995) 527–38.
Mudimbe, V. Y. *The Invention of Africa: Gnosis, Philosophy, and the Order of Knowledge*. Bloomington: Indiana University Press, 1988.
Murhula, Touissant Kafarhire. "Jesuits–Protestants Encounter in Colonial Congo in the Late Nineteenth Century: Perceptions, Prejudices, and Competitions for African Souls." In *Encounters between Jesuits and Protestants in Africa*, edited by Robert A. Maryks and Festo Mkenda, 194–214. Boston: Brill, 2018.
Murphy, Craig N. "What the Third World Wants: An Interpretation of the Development and Meaning of the New International Economic Order Ideology." *International Studies Quarterly* 27.1 (1983) 55–76.
Mutuku, Kaluki Paul. "Kenya Has Lost Nearly Half of Its Forests—Time for the Young to Act." *The Africa Report*, August 12, 2019. https://www.theafricareport.com/16150/kenya-has-lost-nearly-half-its-forests-time-for-the-young-to-act/?fbclid=IwARot_KKgLGzWd3JinHV5aoRtZ9OIMNm3zicrVaalgu7VS9aHgZllSIbpyws.
Mwambazambi, Kalemba. "A Glance on Environmental Protection in Africa: Theological Perspective." *Ethiopian Journal of Environmental Studies and Management* 3.2 (2009) 19–26.
Negash, Legesse. *A Selection of Ethiopia's Indigenous Trees: Biology, Uses, and Propagation Techniques*. Addis Ababa, Ethiopia: Addis Ababa University Press, 2010.
Nhema, Alfred, and Paul Tiyambe Zeleza, eds. *The Roots of African Conflicts: The Causes and Costs*. Oxford: James Currey, 2008.
Niang, I., et al. "Africa." In *Climate Change 2014: Impacts, Adaptation, and Vulnerability. Part B: Regional Aspects. Contribution of Working Group II to the Fifth Assessment Report of the Intergovernmental Panel on Climate Change*, edited by V. R. Barros et al., 1203–5. Cambridge: Cambridge University Press, 2014.
Nicas, Jack. "Apple's Plan to Buy $75 Billion of Its Stock Fuels Spending Debate." *The New York Times*, April 30, 2019. https://www.nytimes.com/2019/04/30/technology/apple-stock-buyback-quarterly-results.html.
"Nigerian Leafy Vegetables." http://www.9jafoodie.com/2013/06/nigerian-leafy-vegetables.
"No African Guinea Pigs for Coronavirus Vaccine: DRC Minister of Human Rights, Andre Lite." *Africa Faith and Justice Network*, April 4, 2020. https://afjn.org/africans-not-guinea-pigs-for-coronavirus-vaccine.
Norwegian Nobel Institute. "Wangari Maathai: Biographical Facts." https://www.nobelprize.org/prizes/peace/2004/maathai/lecture.

Ogungbemi, Segun. "An African Perspective on the Environmental Crisis." In *Environmental Ethics: Readings in Theory and Application*, edited by Louis P. Pojman and Paul Pojman, 203–9. Belmont, CA: Thomson/Wadsworth, 2007.

Ojomo, Philomena A. "Environmental Ethics: An African Understanding." *Journal of Pan African Studies* 4.3 (2011) 101–13.

Ojunga, Samson, et al. "The Value of Forest Ecosystem Services of Mau Complex, Cherangany and Mt. Elgon, Kenya." *East African Agricultural and Forestry Journal* 84.1 (2021) 91–100.

Olupona, Jacob K. *African Religions: A Very Short Introduction*. Oxford: University of Oxford Press, 2014.

———. "The Spirituality of Matter: Religion and Environment in Yoruba Tradition, Nigeria." *Dialogue and Alliance* 9.2 (1995) 69–80.

O'Malley, John W. *The First Jesuits*. Cambridge, MA: Harvard University Press, 1994.

Oniang'o, Ruth C., et al. "Action for Africa and the Earth [Eulogy]." *World Nutrition* 2.10 (2011) 515–33. https://worldnutritionjournal.org/index.php/wn/article/view/451/397.

Onwurah, Emeka. "The Mother Earth in Igbo Religion." *Journal of Dharma* 18.1 (1993) 42–49.

Paul VI, Pope. *Gaudium et Spes: Pastoral Constitution on the Church in the Modern World*. London: Catholic Truth Society, 1966.

Pettersson, Oloff. *Mother Earth: An Analysis of the Mother Earth Concepts According to Albrecht Dieterich*. Lund, Sweden: CWK Gleerup, 1967.

"Photos: Kenyans Fear 'Ecological Disaster' if Two Swollen Lakes Merge." *Reuters*, September 4, 2020. https://gulfnews.com/photos/news/photos-kenyans-fear-ecological-disaster-if-two-swollen-lakes-merge-1.1599218481097?slide=7.

Pogge, Thomas. *World Poverty and Human Rights*. Cambridge: Polity, 2002.

"The Price of Oil: The Impact of Oil Pollution on Niger Delta Communities." *Amnesty International*, November 3, 2015. https://www.amnesty.org/en/latest/news/2015/11/human-face-oil-pollution-niger-delta/.

Priyanka, Mahadappa, and Sahadeb Dey. "Ruminal Impaction Due to Plastic Materials: An Increasing Threat to Ruminants and Its Impact on Human Health in Developing Countries." *Veterinary World* 11.9 (2018) 1307–15. https://www.ncbi.nlm.nih.gov/pmc/articles/PMC6200578/pdf/VetWorld-11-1307.pdf.

Project Learning Tree. "Words to Live by—A Tribute to Wangari Maathai." https://www.plt.org/educator-tips/words-to-live-by-tribute-wangari-maathai.

Prunier, Gérard. *Africa's World War: Congo, the Rwandan Genocide, and the Making of a Continental Catastrophe*. Oxford: Oxford University Press, 2009.

Radford Ruether, Rosemary. "Religious Ecofeminism: Healing the Ecological Crisis." In *The Oxford Handbook of Religion and Ecology*, edited by Roger S. Gottlieb, 362–75. Oxford: Oxford University Press, 2006.

Ramose, Mogobe B. "The Philosophy of Ubuntu and Ubuntu as Philosophy." In *The African Philosophy Reader*, edited by P. H. Coetzee and A. P. J. Roux, 270–80. Cape Town: Oxford University Press, 2002.

Reid, Barbara E. "Foot Washing: Reflections on the Fourth Gospel and the Exemplary Leadership of Pope Francis." In *New World Pope: Pope Francis and the Future of the Church*, edited by Michael L. Budde, 9–23. Eugene, OR: Cascade, 2017.

Reverby, Susan M. "Ethical Failure and History Lessons: The U.S. Public Health Service Research Studies in Tuskegee and Guatemala." *Public Health Reviews* 34.13 (2012) 1–18.

Reyntjens, Filip. *The Great African War: Congo and Regional Geopolitics, 1996–2006.* New York: Cambridge University Press, 2009.

Rizzo, Dominic. "Computers 4 Africa: Where Our Technology Is Going and How It's Being Used." *The Urge to Help*, August 12, 2019. https://theurgetohelp.com/articles/computers-4-africa-where-our-technology-is-going-and-how-its-being-used/.

"Robots 'to Replace up to 20 Million Factory Jobs' by 2030." *BBC News*, June 26, 2019. https://www.bbc.com/news/business-48760799.

Rockström, Johan, et al. "Planetary Boundaries: Exploring the Safe Operating Space for Humanity." *Ecology and Society* 14.2 (2009) art. 32. http://www.ecologyandsociety.org/vol14/iss2/art32/.

Rodney, Walter. *How Europe Underdeveloped Africa*. Rev. ed. Washington, DC: Howard University Press, 1981.

Rohr, Richard, and Mike Morrell. *The Divine Dance*. London: SPCK, 2016.

Rushe, Dominic, and Mona Chalabi. "'Heads We Win, Tails You Lose': How America's Rich Have Turned Pandemic into Profit." *The Guardian*, April 26, 2020. https://www.theguardian.com/world/2020/apr/26/heads-we-win-tails-you-lose-how-americas-rich-have-turned-pandemic-into-profit.

Sakupapa, Teddy C. "Ecumenical Ecclesiology in the African Context: Towards a View of the Church as Ubuntu." *Scriptura* 117.1 (2018) 1–15.

Scanland, James P. *Dostoevsky: The Thinker*. Ithaca, NY: Cornell University Press, 2002.

Shisanya, Chris A. *Determinants of Sustainable Utilization of Plant Resources in the Former Kakamega District, Kenya*. Addis Ababa, Ethiopia: OSREA, 2011.

Shorter, Aylward. "Secularism in Africa: Introducing the Problem." *African Christian Studies* 13.1 (1997) 1–5.

Sindima, Harvey. "Community of Life: Ecological Theology in African Perspective." In *Liberating Life: Contemporary Approaches in Ecological Theology*, edited by Birch Charles et al., 137–47. New York: Orbis, 1990.

Singer, Peter. *One World: The Ethics of Globalization*. New Haven: Yale University Press, 2002.

Singh, Jasdip, et al. *Defining an Environmental Strategy for the Niger Delta*. Washington, DC: World Bank, 1995.

Solomon, Leera, et al. "Environmental Pollution in the Niger Delta and Consequential Challenges to Sustainable Development of the Region: The Role of an Individual." *Researcher* 9.8 (2017) 10–15.

"A Statement of the Pan-African Catholic Congress on Theology, Society, and Pastoral Life." In *Faith in Action, Volume 1: Reform, Mission and Pastoral Renewal in African Catholicism Since Vatican II*, edited by Stan Chu Ilo et al., 1:9–12. 3 vols. Lagos, Nigeria: Paulines, 2020.

Steffen, Will, et al. "Planetary Boundaries: Guiding Human Development on a Changing Planet." *Science* 347.6223 (2015). https://science.sciencemag.org/content/347/6223/1259855.full.

Steyn, Phia. "Oil, Ethnic Minority Groups, and Environmental Struggles against Multinational Oil Companies and the Federal Government in the Nigerian Delta Since the 1990s." In *A History of Environmentalism: Local Struggles, Global*

*Histories*, edited by Marco Armeiro and Lise Sedre, 57–82. New York: Bloomsbury Academic, 2014.

Stockholm International Peace Research Institute. "Global Military Expenditure Sees Largest Annual Increase in a Decade—Says SIPRI—Reaching $1917 Billion in 2019." https://www.sipri.org/media/press-release/2020/global-military-expenditure-sees-largest-annual-increase-decade-says-sipri-reaching-1917-billion.

Stone, Madeleine. "A Plague of Locusts Has Descended on East Africa: Climate Change May Be to Blame." *National Geographic*, February 16, 2020. https://www.nationalgeographic.co.uk/environment-and-conservation/2020/02/plague-of-locusts-has-descended-east-africa-climate-change-may.

Sui, Celine. "China's Racism Is Wrecking Its Success in Africa." *Foreign Policy*, April 15, 2020. https://foreignpolicy.com/2020/04/15/chinas-racism-is-wrecking-its-success-in-africa.

Tadese, Kebede. *Trees of Ethiopia*. Addis Ababa, Ethiopia: Washera, 2012.

Tangwa, Godfrey. "Some African Reflections on Biomedical and Environmental Ethics." In *A Companion to African Philosophy*, edited by Kwasi Wiredu, 387–95. Oxford: Blackwell, 2004.

Taylor, Alan. "Bhopal: The World's Worst Industrial Disaster, 30 Years Later." *The Atlantic*, December 2, 2014. https://www.theatlantic.com/photo/2014/12/bhopal-the-worlds-worst-industrial-disaster-30-years-later/100864/.

Teilhard de Chardin, Pierre. *Hymn of the Universe*. New York: Harper & Row, 1965.

Teketay, Demel. *Edible Wild Plants of Ethiopia*. Addis Ababa, Ethiopia: Addis Ababa University Press, 2010.

Tenywa, Gerald. "Climate Change: Where Is the Money?" *New Vision*, February 1, 2016. https://www.newvision.co.ug/news/1416069/climate-change-money.

Terek, Jozef, and Ján Dobrovic. "Ecologically Active Surfaces, Methodological Approach to the Study of Ecological Functions." *Ekológia* 34.3 (2015) 207–15.

Thiessen, Gesa E., ed. *Theological Aesthetics: SCM Reader*. London: SCM, 2004.

Thunberg, Greta. *No One Is Too Small to Make a Difference*. New York: Penguin Random House, 2019.

Tilley, Helen. "History of Medicine: Medicine, Empires, and Ethics in Colonial Africa." *AMA Journal of Ethics* 17.7 (2017) 743–53.

Tornielli, Andrea, and Giacomo Galeazzi. *This Economy Kills: Pope Francis on Capitalism and Social Justice*. Collegeville, MN: Liturgical, 2015.

Tosam, Mbih Jerome. "African Environmental Ethics and Sustainable Development." *Open Journal of Philosophy* 9.2 (2019) 172–92.

Tully, James. *An Approach to Political Philosophy: Locke in Contexts*. Cambridge: Cambridge University Press, 1993.

Tutu, Desmond. *God Has a Dream: A Vision of Hope for Our Time*. London: Rider, 2005.

———. *No Future Without Forgiveness*. New York: Doubleday, 1999.

UNICEF. "Children Adjust to Life Outside Nigeria's Almajiri System." September 17, 2020. https://www.unicef.org/nigeria/stories/children-adjust-life-outside-nigerias-almajiri-system.

United Nations Climate Change. "The People's Seat: Transcript of the Speech by Sir David Attenborough." December 3, 2018. https://unfccc.int/sites/default/files/resource/The%20People%27s%20Address%202.11.18_FINAL.pdf.

United Nations Environment Programme (UNEP). "Bamako Convention: Preventing Africa from Becoming a Dumping Ground for Toxic Wastes." January 30, 2018. https://www.unenvironment.org/news-and-stories/press-release/bamako-convention-preventing-africa-becoming-dumping-ground-toxic.

———. *Basel Convention Technical Guidelines: General Technical Guidelines for the Environmentally Sound Management of Wastes Consisting of, Containing or Contamined* [sic] *with Persistent Organic Pollutants (POPs)*. Basel Convention Series, SBC Nr 2005/1. Châtelaine, Switzerland: Secretariat of the Basel Convention, 2005. http://archive.basel.int/pub/techguid/pop_guid_final.pdf.

———. *Measuring Progress: Towards Achieving the Environmental Dimension of the SDGs*. Nairobi: UNEP, 2019. https://www.unenvironment.org/resources/report/measuring-progress-towards-achieving-environmental-dimension-sdgs.

———. "Montreal Protocol on Substances That Deplete the Ozone Layer." https://ozone.unep.org/treaties/montreal-protocol.

———. "Nature's Dangerous Decline 'Unprecedented' Species Extinction Rates 'Accelerating.'" May 6, 2019. https://www.unep.org/news-and-stories/press-release/natures-dangerous-decline-unprecedented-species-extinction-rates.

———. "Our Work in Africa." https://www.unenvironment.org/regions/africa/our-work-africa.

———. "Vienna Convention for the Protection of the Ozone Layer." https://ozone.unep.org/treaties/vienna-convention.

United Nations Environment Programme (UNEP), and International Waste Management Association (IWMA). *Global Waste Management Outlook*. Nairobi: UNEP, 2015. https://www.unenvironment.org/resources/report/global-waste-management-outlook.

United Nations Office for Disarmament Affairs (UNODA). *The Biological Weapons Convention*. Geneva: UNODA, 1972. https://www.un.org/disarmament/biological-weapons/.

URN. "Court Orders MPs to Return Shs 10 bn to Public Coffers." *The Observer*, April 29, 2020. https://observer.ug/news/headlines/64540-court-orders-mps-to-return-shs-10bn-to-public-coffers.

Ushe, Mike. "God, Divinities, and Ancestors in African Traditional Religious Thought." *Igwebuike* 3.4 (2017) 154–79.

van Lohuizen, Kadir. "Drowning in Garbage." *The Washington Post*, November 21, 2017. https://www.washingtonpost.com/graphics/2017/world/global-waste/.

"Wangari Maathai—'I Will Be a Hummingbird.'" https://thekidshouldseethis.com/post/wangari-maathai-i-will-be-a-hummingbird.

Wanzala, Justus. "Floods on Record-High Lake Victoria Expose Need for Water Cooperation." *Reuters*, August 19, 2020. https://www.reuters.com/article/kenya-floods-environment-idUKL8N2EE3DL.

Webster, Timothy. "China's Human Rights Footprint in Africa." *Columbia Journal of Transnational Law* 51 (2012) 626–63.

White, Lynn, Jr. "The Historical Roots of Our Ecologic Crisis." *Science* 155.3767 (1967) 1203–7.

Woldeyes, Yirga Gelaw, and Tekletsadik Belachew. "Decolonising the Environment through African Epistemologies." *Gestión y Ambiente* 24.1 (2021) 61–81. https://doi.org/10.15446/ga.v24nsupl1.91881

"WWF Reaction to Stiegler's Gorge Hydropower Dam Construction Launch." *WWF News*, July 26, 2019. https://wwf.panda.org/wwf_news/?350611/WWF-reaction-to-Stieglers-Gorge-hydropower-dam-construction-launch.

Yalew, Amsalu W. "The Perplex of Deforestation in Sub-Saharan Africa." *Journal of Tropical Forestry and Environment* 5.1 (2015) 19–30.

# Index

abundant life, 6, 8, 44, 46, 54, 57, 58
abuse,
   Africans, of, 111, 122
   children, of, 1
   ecological, 15–16, 18–19, 37, 46, 51, 61–62, 86
   physical, 1
   power, of, 51, 68
   sexual, 1, 41
   women, of, 15, 19, 41
Abyei, 74
Acacia Mining, 77
Achebe, Chinua, 76
Adam and Eve, 58, 98
Africa,
   East, 12, 128, 140
      Kiswahili language, 140
   gifts of, 5
   religious traditions, xii–xiii, 96
   scholars, 2, 61, 108, 123
   Southern, 74
   sub-Saharan, 22, 26, 39, 128
   traditions, 9, 18, 54, 68, 77, 80, 110, 133, 135–36
   West, 2, 107
African Synods,
   First (1994), 3, 36, 36n33
   Second (2009), 30, 35
African Union (AU), 22, 39, 80, 95
   *Agenda 2063*, 95, 96n37
   Anthem, 96, 96n37
African Wildlife Foundation, 127
Afro-optimism, 96
agriculture, 5, 10–12, 14, 21–23, 28–30, 60, 84–85, 127–29, 137, 139, 143–46
   sustainable, 114, 144–45

*almajiri*, 1–2
Alvares, Francisco, 100
Amazon rainforest, 128
Amnesty International, 107
animism, 17, 68, 88
Anthony of Egypt, 44
Anthropocene, 7
anthropocentrism, xv, 51, 55, 67, 86, 131, 133–35, 137
anthropology, xi, 46, 67, 84n9
Aquinas, Saint Thomas, 45
Arabome, Anne, 7, 88
Aristotle, 45
artificial intelligence (AI), 67, 69, 72
Atekyereza, Peter, 84, 84n9
atheism, 120
Attenborough, David, x

Banro Mining Corporation, 65, 78
Bantu, 92–93, 104
   Luhiya language, 104
Bartholomew, Patriarch, 16, 44, 63
Basil the Great, Saint, 45
Bassey, Nnimmo, 75
Bayart, Jean-François, 96
BBC, 1, 106
beauty, xiv, 8, 21–22, 31, 38, 41–49, 54, 58, 61–63, 144
   creation, of, 11, 16, 34n28, 43–44, 61–62
Belachew, Tekletsadik, 6
Belgium, 101
Benedict, Pope, xii, 30, 35, 90
Beneneson, Bill, 139
Benin, 11, 17n16
   Songhai Farm, 11, 146, 146n4
Béré, Paul, 89
Berry, Wendell, 146

## INDEX

Bible, 44–46, 52, 89, 92, 99, 144
   Bethany, Martha, Mary, Lazarus, 145
   Colossians, 104
   2 Corinthians, 80
   Genesis, 8, 38, 46, 50, 52, 55, 68, 78–79, 98, 144
   gospel, 77, 88, 132
   Revelation, 81
   Romans, 80
biodiversity, x–xi, 36, 76, 98, 105, 112, 118, 136
   loss, 7, 22, 29, 65
biology, 30, 34, 37, 72, 86, 95, 137
BLI. *See* Bethany Land Institute.
blood diamonds, 67, 74
Bolivia, 114
Bond, Patrick, 73
Botswana, 29
Buhari, Muhammadu, 10
Bujo, Bénézet, 94, 135
Burundi, 83, 94
Bush, George H. W., 114
Bush, George W., 114

Caduto, Michael, 130–31
Canada, 101, 110
canon law, 92
capitalism, 68–71, 73–75, 78, 81, 92, 95, 108, 110–11
careerism, 131
Catholic Youth Network for Environmental Sustainability in Africa (CYNESA), 36n36, 146, 146n4
Catholicism, x, 45, 89, 98, 101, 103, 120, 146
   educators, xiv
   social teaching (CST), xv, 5, 13, 16, 52, 55–56, 85, 91
   Vatican, 119
      Dicastery for Promoting Integral Human Development, 3, 121
      Second Vatican Council, 85, 120
Central African Republic, 64, 72, 74, 128
   FATEB (Faculté de Théologie Évangélique de Banguis), 128
Central America, 51
Césaire, Aimé, 109

Chad, Lake, 11
chemistry, 27, 85–87, 94
China, 3, 16, 34, 39–40, 46, 70, 74
Christology, 55–57
civil society, xiii, 116
clericalism, 76, 81
climate change, 27–28
   adaptation, 2, 138
   anthropogenic, 12, 28
   causes, 14, 40, 129, 141
   challenges of, x, 6, 28, 38, 78, 82
   champions of, 105
   crisis, 51, 74, 82, 86, 126
   critics, x, 16, 27–28
   education, xiv
   effects, xi, 10, 22, 28, 40–41, 137
      Africa, on, 4–7, 34, 60, 126
      life, on, 33n26, 37
      water, on, 21, 28–29, 83
      wildlife, on, 21–23, 29–30
      women, on, 12–13
   global warming, and, x–xi, 6, 9–10, 16, 138
   integral ecology, and, 51
   Laudato Si', considered in, 27–28, 82, 85
   mitigation of, 69, 75–76, 86–87, 97, 136
colonialism, 6–7, 36, 68, 71, 73–76, 78–80, 95–97, 100, 108–11, 122–23, 135
   neo-colonialism, 6, 75, 108
coltan (columbite-tantalite), 64, 70, 74
common good, xii, 68, 71, 86, 91–92, 96–97, 112, 116, 119, 121n29, 144
   fostering of, 57–59, 76–77, 91–92, 94, 112
Conference of the Parties 26 (COP26), 6
Congo Basin, 30, 128
Conradie, Ernst, 52
conservation, 30, 36, 127, 135–36, 138–39, 145
consumerism, xiv, 25, 33, 66, 68–71, 76, 78–81, 88, 95, 123, 131–32
Cook, Tim, 70

COP26. *See* Conference of the Parties 26.
Cornish, Sandie, 91
corruption, 36, 36n35, 73–76, 78–79, 117–18
cosmic,
  compassion, 105
  emergence, 59
  flourishing, 2–3, 5, 8, 11, 38, 44, 46, 48, 52–54, 57–58
  harmony, 7, 54, 58
  *koinonia*, 54
  liturgy, 44, 54
  participation, 58
  resurrection, 103
  solidarity. *See* solidarity, cosmic.
  stories, 57, 59
  sustainability, 7, 55
  wholeness, 53, 76–77
cosmogonies, 8, 38, 52–55, 96
cosmologies, 79
  African, 17–18, 53, 92–93, 103
  eucharistic, 104
  Teilhardian mystical, 104
cosmos, xii–xiii, 51, 56, 58, 62–63, 66, 81, 85, 104, 135
Côte d'Ivoire, 106–7
  Abidjan, 106–8
COVID-19, 1–4, 9, 34, 41–42, 51, 70, 82, 82n1, 120–21, 124
  children, and, 2
  coronavirus, 42, 82n1, 84, 111
  garbage and, 25
  money and, 78
creation, xii–xiii, xv–xvi, 6–8, 17–18, 42–59, 61–63, 80, 86, 93–94, 124, 141
  African theology of, 3–4, 8, 38, 57
  care for, 9, 130, 132, 144–45
  dependence on, 31
  gift of, 7, 103
  moaning of, 13
  trinitrarian theology of, 61
  use of, 135
cross (of Jesus), 55–59, 62, 98–99, 103
cry,
  Africa, of, 8, 38, 59–61
  Creation, of, 59–61, 67
  earth, of, xvi, 7, 21, 32, 59, 69, 78, 91, 143
  people, of, 69
  poor, of, xvi, 7, 32, 41, 59, 91, 143
  women, of, 7
cyanide, 27, 32, 65

dams, 31, 83, 95
  Owen Falls Dam (Uganda), 83
  Stiegler's Gorge Dam (Tanzania), 31n22
debt,
  ecological. *See* ecology, debt.
  financial, 34, 39, 72, 96
decision-making, participatory, 8–9, 11, 37–38, 111–13, 116–18
decolonization, 6–7, 9, 75, 79
deforestation, xvi, 11, 33n26
  African, 14, 30, 65, 68, 76–77, 84, 126–42
dehumanization, 66, 72, 77, 79, 87, 90, 107, 111
Democratic Republic of Congo (DRC), 64, 70, 72, 74, 78, 110n14, 128
  South Kivu, 64–65
Denault, Alain, 110
deontology, 137
desertification, 5, 11, 30, 33n26, 75, 128–29, 137
development, sustainable, 9, 21–22, 55, 92, 95, 108, 139
  agriculture. *See* agriculture, sustainable.
  natural resources, 133
  technological, 77
  waste management, 41
dialogue, 11, 13, 15–16, 44–45, 50, 56, 61, 112, 119, 142, 147
domination, 62, 66, 68–69, 86, 123
  nature, of, 17, 19, 43, 46, 50–51, 70, 95, 135
Dostoevsky, Fyodor, 41
dualism, 56–58, 90

Earth,
  Mother, xiii–xvi, 7, 13, 16–20, 103, 134–35, 141, 143
  Sister, 15, 143

# INDEX

Earth Charter, 105, 131
*Earth Times*, 138
Easterly, William, 71
Eastern Orthodox, 44, 98
ecclesiology, African, 53
Ecocide, 6, 107
ecoethics, 2–4 6–8, 38, 42–44, 52,
    56n28, 61–62, 126, 130, 133–38
ecofeminism, 13, 15, 17, 19–20
ecology, xi, 3c 47
    African, 4, 6, 9, 12–15, 52–53, 61,
        93, 97–98, 124
    citizenship, 144
    conversion, 2, 7, 28, 37, 41, 92, 129,
        132, 134, 141, 144
    crisis, xiv, 2, 6–11, 14–16, 41–43,
        64–81, 86, 95, 106, 126–30,
        133–34, 138, 143
    human roots, 64–81, 84
    cultural, 52, 86, 88–90, 100
    debt, 33, 75, 122
    economic, 87
    education, xiv–xv, 9, 91–92, 121,
        126, 129–33, 143–46
    environmental, xi–xiii, 87, 140
    ethics. *See* ecoethics.
    feminism. *See* ecofeminism.
    gospel, xv
    gratitude, xv
    human, xi–xiii, 13, 86, 90, 100
    integral, x–xv, 9, 16, 38, 41–43, 48,
        50–51, 55, 82–105, 144–46
        African basis for, 8, 44, 51, 54,
            61, 82, 92–97
    performance, 98
    praxis, 3, 9, 83, 98, 105
    social, 80, 87–88
    spirituality. *See* ecospirituality.
    systems. *See* ecosystems.
    theology. *See* ecotheology.
    violence, xiv
    virtues, xv
    wisdom. *See* ecowisdom.
ecospirituality, 35–37, 44, 62, 102,
    105, 129–38
    African, 2–3, 9, 11, 13, 52, 54, 83,
        105

"eco-heart," "eco-ear," and "eco-eye"
    134–35, 137–38, 141
    integral, 9, 83
    vulnerability and care, 38
ecosystems, x–xi, 5, 7, 11, 84, 86–87,
    97–98, 118, 132, 137
    degradation of, x, 14, 30
ecotheology, 3, 7, 9, 35, 38, 42–44,
    52–58, 62–65, 78–83, 92–98, 106
ecowisdom, xi–xii, 5–8, 38, 51–52, 62,
    68, 74, 80, 95, 136
Egypt, 9, 44, 83, 99
electricity, production and distribution, 26, 60, 83
environment,
    activism, xiv, 2, 36–37, 40, 69, 126,
        133, 138–39
    crisis. *See* ecology, crisis.
    degradation, xi–xii, 7, 13–14, 34,
        41, 60, 65–66, 70–72, 76–80,
        110–12, 122, 128, 143
        as collateral damage, 67, 122
        poverty, and, 14, 75, 107, 119
    disaster, 40, 127
    justice, x, 9, 59
    protection, xii–xvi, 6–7, 66, 87, 97,
        105–7, 115, 118–19, 131–32,
        136, 143–44
    areas, of, 11, 31, 36, 84, 117, 127
    species, of, 63, 118
    stewardship, xiii, xv, 46–47, 55, 59,
        66–68, 71, 78–80, 86, 144
    vandalism, 106–7, 109, 121–22
epistemology, 6–7, 9, 20, 66, 87, 111,
    121, 123, 86
Epistemicide, 6–7
    Western, 6
erosion, 5, 11, 14, 65, 102, 127
eschatology, 47, 56, 98
ethicists, 133–35, 137
Ethiopia, 9, 39–41, 83, 97–101, 98n44,
    103n58
    Addis Ababa, 39, 79, 98, 98n43,
        103n58
    Pope Francis Botanical Garden,
        79
    Axum, 99
    emperors, 98–99

INDEX   167

Entoto Mountain, 98, 103n58
Gondar, 99
Lalibela, 99–100
Qoshe, 39–41, 60
Tana, Lake, 99
Tigray, 99
Ethnocide, 7
Eurocentrism, 6
Europe, 26n12, 32, 71, 110–11, 135

fishing, 24n8, 29, 31–32, 36, 83, 85, 107, 128
Floyd, George, 41, 123
food,
    animal, 103
    chain, 24n8
    hunger, and, 1, 42, 66
    malnutrition, and, 59, 70
    migration, and, 22–23
    processed, 40
    production, 11, 14, 19, 21
    security, xi, 5, 12, 75, 115
    starvation, and, 28, 41
    waste, 27, 33
fossil fuels, 2, 27–29, 37, 40, 40n5, 60, 72, 77, 110
Foucault, Michel, 109
France, 101, 111, 111n16, 123
Francis of Assisi, Saint, x, xvi, 13, 15–16, 18, 61, 132
Fulani, 10

Galileo, 120, 120n27
garbage, 8, 14–15, 24n7, 25–28, 37–41, 62, 67–68
    COVID-19, and. See COVID-19, garbage and.
    e-waste, 25, 26n12, 27n15, 40, 107
    hazardous, 24, 26–27, 26n13, 40, 107, 115
    landfills, 27, 27n14–15, 39–41, 46, 60, 106–8, 111–13, 115
        Kiteezi (Uganda), 40
        Olusosun (Nigeria), 40–41, 60
        Qoshe (Ethiopia), 39–41, 60
    plastic xvi, 24n8, 27, 29
    radioactive, 26n13
Garden of Eden, 58, 61, 99–101
genocide, 76, 80, 94, 110

Ghana, 18, 18n18, 27n15, 52
    Akan people, 18–19, 18n18
Gichohi, Helen, 127
global North and South, 116
global warming. See climate change.
globalization, xi, xiii, 73, 81, 113, 116
Gnosticism, 43
Gore, Al, 16
gospel,
    biblical. See Bible, gospel.
    creation, of, 38, 42–43, 45, 50, 55, 57
    ecological, xv
    exploitation, 68
    imperialist, 79
grassroots movements, 80, 105, 139
Great Lakes (Africa), 94, 94n30
greed, xiii, 16, 59, 68, 70–71, 73, 77, 79
Green Belt movement, 11, 138–40, 146, 146n4
Green-washing, 28, 34
greenhouse gases (GHG), 14, 28, 40, 60, 114, 138
Greenpeace, 107
Guatemala, 112
Guinea Coast, 18n18

Haile Selassie, 98n42–43
Hausa language, 1
Healey, Joseph, 83
Heelan, Patrick, 109n9
Heidegger, Martin, 109n9
hermeneutics, 7, 43, 46, 48, 109n9
    indigenous, 6, 52
    womanist, 7
HIV/AIDS, 14, 25
Holy Spirit, 48, 56, 90
Horn of Africa, 12, 94n30
human,
    flourishing, 2, 5, 8, 44, 56, 48, 53–54, 58, 61, 92
    trafficking, 36, 67, 74
hummingbird story, 139–40

Idai, Cyclone, 7, 12
Ignatius of Loyola, Saint, 87, 87n13
    spirituality, 87, 87n13
Ilo, Stan Chu, 8, 142

168  INDEX

Iloabani, Anayo, 10–11
immanence, divine, xii, 45–47
Important Birding Areas (IBAs), 36
incarnation, 42, 62
India, 26, 27n16
 Bhopal, 27n16
indigeneity,
 African, 134–38
 American, 109–10
 hermeneutics. *See* hermeneutics, indigenous.
 knowledge, 6, 52, 76, 96
 languages, 6, 137
 peoples, xi, 17, 60n31, 88–89, 105
 traditional religions, 88–89
 trees, 99
 values, 89, 95–96, 105
individualism, xii, 69, 77, 79–80, 92, 131
industrialization, xi, 11, 114, 138
inequality, 2, 7, 32–34, 51, 66, 68, 70–71, 77, 91, 95, 116n26
International Union for the Conservation of Nature (IUCN), 30, 30n19, 36
 Red Lists of Threatened Species, 30n19
IPCC regional report for Africa, 5
Iraq, 72
Islam, 1, 10
Italy, 98n42–43
 Milan, 143–44

John XXIII, Pope Saint, 13
John Paul II, Pope Saint, 36
Joy, Bill, 69
Jude Thaddeus, Saint, 101

Kagera, River, 83–84
Kalahari Desert, 29
Kalemba, Mwambazambi, 128–29
Karfahire, Toussaint, 9
Katongole, Emmanuel, 10, 83, 96–97, 123–24, 142
Kelbessa, Workineh, 136
*kenosis*, 58
Kenya, x, 9, 11, 21, 29, 83, 104, 126–29, 138, 140
 Baringo, Lake, 127
 Bogoria, Lake, 127
 Budalangi, Busia County, 127
 Hwange National Park, 21
 independence, 128
 Mau Forest, 129
 Ministry of Forestry and Wildlife, 128
 Mount Elgon, 129
 Mount Kenya, 129
 Nairobi, 21, 127
  Nairobi National Park, 21
 Western highlands, 126
 Wildlife Service (KWS), 127
 World Agroforestry Centre, 127
Kepler, Johannes, 120, 120n27
Knox, Peter, 7–8, 15
Kolinjivadi, Vijay, 39
Komen, Jackson, 127

Latin America, 23, 71
Leeson, Craig, 24n8
LeFay, Raven, 131, 137
Leton, Chief (Ogoni), 60
Lewis, Stephen, 122
liberalism, 111, 120
 neoliberalism, 71, 117, 122–23
Liberia, 64
Linguicide, 6
Locke, John, 110
Luhiya language, 104

Maathai, Wangari Muta, x, xiv, 17, 126, 138–41, 146
 Nobel Prize, and, x, 17, 126, 138–40
Macron, Emmanuel, 123
Magesa, Laurenti, xii, 35, 88, 93, 95, 96n36, 124
malaria, 25, 41, 65, 75, 102, 105
Mali, 64, 72, 74
Marwa, Mwita, 77–79
Masango, M. J. S., 136
Maseno, Loreen, 52
materialism, 76, 95, 121, 135
Maximus the Confessor, Saint, 44
Mayanja, Evelyn, 8–9
Mayans, 51
Mazrui, Ali, 61
Mbiti, John, 35, 53, 135
McDonagh, Sean, 48, 60

medical care, 65, 72, 111, 121
medicines, 28, 30, 65, 81, 100, 102–5
Mendonca, Valerian, 87
Menen Asfaw, 98n42
Mexico, 51, 71, 109
migration,
   animal, 5, 22, 29, 36
   economic, 28
   human, 28, 33, 71, 111, 115
minerals, 21–22, 31, 36, 64–65, 70, 72, 74, 76, 102, 110, 129
mining, 17, 27, 30, 31n21, 34, 65, 70, 73, 110, 110n14, 128
   companies, 65, 73, 77–79
   gold, 27, 64–65, 70, 77
Mira, Jean-Paul, 111n16
missionaries, 68, 88, 96, 101, 109–10
Missionaries of Africa (White Fathers), 101
modernism, 39, 56
modernity, 9, 39, 55, 67, 70, 73, 100, 105, 123
   spirit of, 109, 120
   Western, 6, 51
Mozambique, 12
Mubangizi, Odomaro, 8–9, 79, 82
Mudimbe, V. Y., 109
multinational companies (MNCs), 14, 68, 88, 108, 110, 112, 114, 122
*Mushingantahe*, 94
mutuality, xii–xv, 46, 48–49, 52–54, 93, 129
Mutuku, Paul Kaluki, 128
mythology, African, 18, 52, 55, 100

Namib Desert, 29
nation-states, 96–97, 113–16
natural law, 52, 54, 56n28
Negritude movement, 109
new international economic order (NIEO), 108, 120
NGO, 146
Niger Delta, 14–15, 29, 60, 60n31
Nigeria, 1–2, 10–11, 14–15, 17, 19, 27, 40, 60, 107
   Achi, 10
   Enugu, 10
   Igbo people, 19
   Kaduna, 1–2
   Kano, 1
   Koko, 107–8
   Lagos, 40–41
   Ogoni people, 60, 60n31
   Olusosun, 40–41, 60
   Yoruba people, 17–19, 17n16
Nile River, 9, 83–84
North America, 26n12
Norway, 139
Oslo, 139
Nyebirweki, Tadeo, 101
Nzoia River, 83, 126–27

oceans, xvi, 5, 24–25, 24n8, 28–29, 31–32
Ogungbemi, Segun, 129, 135–37
Ojomo, Philomena, 133, 135, 137
Okemasisi, Kinikonda, 9
Olupona, Jacob, 6, 52
Omonyi, George William, 127
Oniang'o, Ruth, 128
ontology, 58, 93
otherness, xii, 32, 43, 47, 50, 82n2, 124
overpopulation, 15
ozone layer, 27, 33, 33n26, 115

*Pacem in Terris*, encyclical, 13
paganism, 17, 68, 88, 110, 117
Pan-African Catholic Congress (2020), 3
Pan-African Catholic Theology and Pastoral Network, 3
panentheism, 42
Pankhurst, Sylvia, 98n42
pantheism, 42
Paul, Saint, 56
Paul VI, Pope Saint, 89, 89n16
*perichoresis*, 48
physics, xi, 85–86
Plato, 90
pneumatology, 55–56
pollution, x–xi, 7, 14–15, 22–33, 37–41, 60, 65–66, 77, 106–7, 110–18, 122
poor, 67, 118
   African, 8, 12, 14–15, 65, 108, 143
   countries, 32, 34, 88, 123
   cry of. *See* cry, of the poor.

poor (*continued*)
  environmental degradation and, xi, 13–14, 55, 60, 75, 107
  exploitation of, 71
  inequality and, 33, 51, 62, 66, 71, 77–78, 91, 95, 116
  malams, 1
  mistreatment of, xi, 8–9, 33, 37, 39, 49, 60, 76, 80, 122, 107
  option for, 91
  poorest of the, 27–28, 33, 39, 91
  solidarity with. *See* solidarity, poor, with the.
Portugal, 74, 99–100
poverty, 87, 97, 119, 139
  causes of, 14
  effects of, 18, 25, 27, 33, 39, 50, 67, 71, 91, 139
  mitigation of, 39, 54, 67, 71, 87, 143, 144
privatization, 29, 109, 122
profit, 26, 28, 31, 36, 66–69, 88, 107–11, 116, 118, 123
prophetic role, x–xi, xiii, xv, 4, 8, 70, 76, 96, 115

racism, 51, 73–74, 80–81, 109, 111
Ramose, Mogobe, 93
reason, x
reciprocity, xiii, xv, 7, 48, 52, 93–94
recycling 26–27, 40
relationality, 42, 46–56, 58, 61
  cosmology, 53
  creation (God's), 13, 44, 53, 61, 135
  earth and life, 19
  humans and animals, 133, 136
  humans and architecture, 89
  humans and God, xii, 20, 24, 49–50, 54, 79, 87, 135
  humans and nature, xii–xiv, 4–7, 13, 16n12, 48–56, 62, 65–67, 73, 130–35, 138, 141–43
  humans, between, 43, 49, 51, 53–54, 62, 69, 73, 93–94, 105, 125, 130–31
  humans, God, and nature, 49–50, 144–45
  international, 106, 111, 113–16
  interrelatedness, 4, 8, 38, 50, 52–53, 86–87, 89, 94, 133, 145
  poor, the, and nature, xi, 13
  poor, with, 76
  self, with, xiv
  states, between, 106
  trinitarian, 48
  Ubuntu, and, 54, 58, 93
relativism, 67, 120
religion and science, 45, 113, 119–20, 124
Reverby, Susan, 111
Rizzo, Dominic, 26n11
Rodney, Walter, 75
Rohr, Richard, 47
Rosow, Gene, 139
Ruether, Rosemary Radford, 17
Russia, 74
Rwanda, 9, 83, 94, 94n30, 101, 103, 105

Sahara Desert, 11, 22, 26, 39, 74, 128
Sahel, 11, 29
Sakupapa, Teddy, 53
Sarkozy, Nicholas, 123
secularism, 80, 120
Seifu, Girma, 39
Senegal, 123
  Dakar, 123
Sierra Leone, 64
Sindima, Harvey, 78–79
slavery, 6, 59, 73, 75, 122
social justice, xii, 59, 78, 80, 123–24
social media, 32, 72
solidarity, xv, 8, 34, 48–50, 57, 62, 79, 91, 93, 102, 130
  African traditional, xiii
  cosmic, 98
  creation as invitation to, 50–51
  ethoethics, and, 38
  global, 4, 28
  humans and nature, between, xii, 8, 13, 61, 65
  intergenerational, 31
  poor, with the, 41, 61
South Africa, 27, 27n16, 29, 31n21, 31n23, 35, 61, 94, 127
  Cape Town, 27n16, 29
  Durban, 127

Kruger National Park, 31n21
National Parks, 31n23
South Sudan, 30, 64, 74
stewardship, xiii, 46–47, 55, 59, 67–68, 71, 80, 86, 144
Sudan, 9, 99
  Darfur, 64, 72
Symposium of the Episcopal Conferences of Africa and Madagascar (SECAM), 3, 89n16
syphilis, 112
Syria, 72

taboos, 35–37, 121n29, 134, 136
Tadeo Nyebirweki Rwakazooba Forest (TNRF), 9, 101–5
Tangwa, Godfrey, 133, 137
Tanzania, 9, 29, 31n22, 53, 77, 83
  Jita people, 53
  Selous Game Reserve, 31n22
technocratic paradigm, 65–66, 121, 146
technology, 6, 8, 13, 23, 26, 28, 34, 64–81, 117
  advancement, 68–69, 129
  development, 73–74, 76, 81
  devices, 70, 74, 86
    computers, 25–26, 26n11, 72, 74
    phones, 25, 64, 70, 74, 76, 137
  engineering
    biomedical, 90
    genetic, 67, 69, 90
  medical, 121
  nanotechnology, 65, 69
  nuclear, 34
  production, 64–65
  progress, 33n26, 56–81, 121, 129
technocratic paradigm, 65–66, 121, 146
technologism, 51
technotheology, 80
Teilhard de Chardin, Pierre, 87, 104
teleologism, 137
Tempels, Placide, 92
theologians, 3, 15, 41, 61, 79, 83, 85–86, 88, 123
theology,
  aesthetics, 42–45, 48, 50, 56, 61
  grammar 57

Thunberg, Greta, xiv–xv, 2, 69
Tindimugaya, Callist, 83–84, 84n6–7
TNRF. *See* Tadeo Nyebirweki Rwakazooba Forest,
Togo, 17n16, 52
  Basari, 52
Tosam, Mbih Jerome, 133, 135, 138
Trafigura Group, 106–7
transcendence, 44–45, 49–50, 67
trees,
  black wattle, 101
  eucalyptus, 101–2
  planting, 68, 79, 101–3, 105, 130, 142–43
  Kenya, 126, 138–39
Trinity, xiii, 8, 38, 42–45, 47–48, 56, 61, 98
tuberculosis, 25, 65
Tully, James, 109
Tutu, Desmond, 93

Ubuntu, xiii, 44, 60–62, 82–83, 82n2, 92–94, 96–97, 101–2, 105, 124
  ethics, 8–9, 53–54, 57–58, 61–62, 83, 93–94, 102
  theology of creation. *See* creation, theology of, African.
*ubushingantahe* (*obufura, ubupfura*), 92, 94, 96
Uganda, 10–11, 53, 68, 78, 83–84, 89n16, 97, 101–2, 105, 123, 142–44
  Albert, Lake, 84
  Bethany Land Institute (BLI), 10–11, 142–47
  Buganda, 68
  Entebbe, 84
  Gandu people, 53
  Jinja, 84
  Kabale, 9, 101, 105
  Kampala, 40, 84, 84n9
    Makerere University, 84n9
  Kasana-Luweero Diocese, 145
    Nandere Parish, 145
  Katuna, 103, 105
  Kiga people, 101
  Kiteezi, 40
  Kyoga, Lake, 84
  language, 94

Uganda (*continued*)
  Luweero, 143
  National Meteorological Authority, 127
  Rukiga language, 102–4, 101n57
  Rwakazooba Mountain, 9, 101, 103–5, 103n58
  Rwanyena Catholic Parish, 103–4
  St. Jude's Farm, 143, 146, 146n4
  South Western, 9
UN. *See* United Nations.
unemployment, 14, 28, 32, 40, 67, 70, 72, 88, 108, 142
Union Minière du Haut Katanga (UMHK), 110n14
United Nations (UN), xi, 1, 2, 22, 34, 71, 73–75, 80, 86, 107–8
  conventions and climate agreements, 106, 112, 115, 119, 138
    Basel Convention, 115
    Convention on International Trade in Endangered Species of Wild Fauna and Flora (CITES), 115n24
    Paris Agreement, 69, 75
    Rio de Janeiro Earth Summits, 114–16
    Vienna Convention and Montreal Protocol, 115–16, 116n25
  Environment Programme (UNEP), 22, 107
  Sustainable Development Goals (SDG), 22
  UNESCO, 31n21–22, 100, 105
  UNICEF, 2
  Universal Declaration of Creation Rights (UDCR), 86
  United Nations Conference on Trade and Development (UNCTAD), 108
United States, 16n12, 23, 70–71, 74, 111–12, 114
  Black Lives Matter movement, 111
  natives, 109–10
  New York, 72
    Sing Sing Prison, 112
  non-whites, 111–12
  Public Health Service (PHS), 111–12
  Tuskegee Experiment, 112
universe, 4, 8, 38, 42, 45, 48–49, 55, 62, 86–87, 95, 135
urbanization, xi, 5, 11, 39, 41, 90, 105
Ushe, Mike, 133–34, 137
utilitarianism, 30, 137

Vanegan, Tor-Gunnar, 127
Victoria, Lake, flooding, 8, 82–85, 84n9, 105, 126–27
vital force, 53–54, 58, 92–93, 92n22
von Balthasar, Hans Urs, 41
vulnerability, 5, 19, 42, 62–63, 70
  care, and, 8, 38, 62
  ethics of, 62

Wanzala, Justus, 126–27
war, 5, 25, 34, 41–42, 64, 72, 74–75, 78, 110
  Cold, 74
Watson, Robert, xi
weather, 11–12, 22, 28, 60
  rainfall, 5, 19, 29, 84
    drought, 12, 14, 21–22, 28–29, 75
    flooding, 5, 11–12, 14, 22, 28, 58, 75, 83–85, 102, 126–27
Western Sahara, 74
White, Lynn Jr., 17
Whitehead, Alfred North, 87
Woldeyes, Yirga Gelaw, 6
World Bank, 39, 108
worldview,
  African, 18, 52, 76–77, 88–89, 92–93, 124, 133–34, 137
  Western, 77, 80, 92, 135, 137

Yalew, Amsalu W., 128
Yemen, 72
Youth 4 Africa, 128

Zambia, 53
  Chewa people, 53
Zimbabwe, 11, 21, 53
  Shona people, 53

www.ingramcontent.com/pod-product-compliance
Lightning Source LLC
Chambersburg PA
CBHW020849160426
43192CB00007B/845